Ghassan Kanaf

T0278001

Selected Political Writings

"Ghassan Kanafani is a giant for many reasons, foremost among them his unwavering commitment to class analysis and critique, and his mastery of these two transformative (but undervalued) political frameworks. Kanafani's revolutionary writings are as elucidating as they are incendiary, transcending the reductive identitarianism that often hinders revolutionary literature, transcending perfunctory symbolism and inaccessible jargon, and cutting through the noise of 'blind language'. No other author has been as profoundly formative for me as Kanafani, and I am certain this holds true for countless others – writers or otherwise, Palestinians and beyond. English speakers are fortunate to access a fraction of his formidable erudition through this collection."
—Mohammed El-Kurd, poet, writer and journalist, author of *Rifqa*

"More than fifty years after his assassination, Ghassan Kanafani continues to educate, mobilise and advocate for Palestine. This collection of political works emphasises that he is as relevant today as he was in the 1960s and 1970s."
—Ghassan Abu Sittah, award-winning surgeon, humanitarian and educator

"A timely collection of one of Palestine's foremost intellectuals and leaders. I cannot think of a better collection to guide anyone seeking a moral role for the left today in the struggle for the liberation of Palestine. Kanafani's fusion of humanism, universalism and commitment to Palestine will eternally serve as a model in our own struggle for a free Palestine."
—Ilan Pappé, historian and author of *The Ethnic Cleansing of Palestine*

"Masterfully translated, *Ghassan Kanafani: Selected Political Writings* offers a powerful clutch of previously untranslated writings by Palestine's most well-known militant intellectual on topics that remain relevant today, ranging from the first proposal of a Palestinian state in the Occupied Territories, to Marxism and Arab nationalism to revolutionary anti-colonial organising. This volume definitively evinces Kanafani as squarely among the most brilliant, dynamically analytic and intellectually agile anti-colonialist and revolutionary intellectuals of the twentieth century."
—Stephen Sheehi, co-author of *Psychoanalysis Under Occupation: Practicing Resistance in Palestine*

"In the current historical moments, as the Zionist settler colonial project finds no means to deter the Palestinian from resistance except through the total eradication of the Palestinian material and political being, arises the importance of reading the theoretical and political works of Ghassan Kanafani. This book is a necessity for revolutionary subjectivities aspiring for liberation."
—Lena Meari, Institute of Women's Studies, Birzeit University

Photograph of Ghassan Kanafani (1936–1972).
Courtesy of Anni Kanafani.

Ghassan Kanafani

Selected Political Writings

Edited by
Louis Brehony and Tahrir Hamdi

With translations editor Ourooba Shetewi

Translations by As'ad AbuKhalil, Louis Brehony, Hiyem Cheurfa,
Lena Haddadin, Barbara Harlow, Asma Hussein, Ameen Nemer,
Ourooba Shetewi, Amira Silmi and Nejd Yaziji

PLUTO PRESS

First published 2024 by Pluto Press
New Wing, Somerset House, Strand, London WC2R 1LA
and Pluto Press, Inc.
1930 Village Center Circle, 3-834, Las Vegas, NV 89134

www.plutobooks.com

British Library Cataloguing in Publication Data
A catalogue record for this book is available from the British Library

ISBN 978 0 7453 4937 4   Paperback

This book is printed on paper suitable for recycling and made from fully
managed and sustained forest sources. Logging, pulping and manufacturing
processes are expected to conform to the environmental standards of the country of origin.

Typeset by Stanford DTP Services, Northampton, England

Simultaneously printed in the United Kingdom and United States of America

Contents

CONTENTS

Figures

Acknowledgements

Following in the spirit of Ghassan Kanafani and those who inspired and were inspired by him, the editors wish to underline the collective nature of this book. We must thank, first, the scores of friends, comrades and colleagues who have worked tirelessly on translation, peer reviewing, proofreading, introduction-writing and reviewing of the texts – including those that made it into the final volume and those that did not. Many of the contributors brought high-quality materials into completion while working under conditions of extreme stress, including being present during the Zionist genocide in Gaza from October 2023, losing family members and friends, as well as draconian border regimes, sanctioned access to the internet and electricity, and outrageous attacks on the right to teach, speak and work on research related to Palestine in the West. All contributed to this text out of solidarity and commitment to the cause.

Translator names appear at the beginning of each chapter, but we would like to single out Ourooba Shetewi, who took on the role of a translations editor, and Ameer Nemer and Amira Silmi, whose work laid the basis for our "Early Kanafani" appendix. We thank all of the introduction writers for bearing with the demands and unpredictability of the process, and for offering insightful writings towards what we see as a developing field of Kanafani studies.

This book has been produced in accordance with the wishes of the Ghassan Kanafani Cultural Association and we are grateful to all who facilitated our multitude of requests. In particular, we thank Anni and Leila Kanafani for their warm welcome in Beirut, for their support and for their rigorous feedback on our work.

Those facilitating access to the huge archives generated by Ghassan and his comrades include the libraries and records of the American University of Beirut, American University of Cairo, Ghassan Kanafani Cultural Foundation, Institute of Palestine Studies, International Centre of Palestine Studies, Palestinian

Museum, Palestinian Poster Project and Rimal books. We owe gratitude to Wisam al-Fuqawi, Ayman Dwaik and all of the editorial team at *al-Hadaf*. Others who have supported the project at various stages include Marwan Abd el-'Al, Jaldia Abubakra, Ahmed al-Aydi, Omar Ayoub, Al Azzam, Greg Burris, Ramadan Ghaben, Issam Hijjawi, Fayez Kanafani, Hadeel Karkar, Charlotte Kates, Maha Salah and Bob Shepherd. Without the hospitality and patience of Fadi Zaraket in South Lebanon, this project would have proved impossible.

We must note the enthusiasm and professionalism of David Shulman and all at Pluto Press.

Finally, we thank our partners and loved ones, the Hamdi and Hirbawi, and Anbar and Brehony families, and especially Dirar and Reem.

While underscoring the idea that this book is a work of interpretation, we willingly take full responsibility for any mistakes, errors or omissions.

Introduction

The Revolutionary Journey of Ghassan Kanafani

Louis Brehony and Tahrir Hamdi

Lemon, blossom and Damask rose
You, my land, are the light of my eyes
Now a bullet, shrapnel
from the day we learned the path to freedom
Once a wish, now a song
Ghassan, Ghassan
Ghassan taught us the love of the cause

Ghazi Mikdashi[1]

Resistance is the essence – these words embody the literary, artistic, theoretical and political life of Ghassan Kanafani. With his Palestine ablaze in popular defiance more than 50 years since his assassination, Ghassan has returned: his name sung by *thob*-wearing women, celebrating precious victories of released Palestinian political prisoners; his image on the walls of refugee camps and the T-shirts and banners of student activists; his name gracing solidarity encampments; onstage in reworkings of his plays and as a backdrop to politically conscious dance troupes; and in a new scramble to read his stories, articles and studies. Generation after generation, Ghassan teaches the love of the Palestinian cause.

Resistance, in its plethora of meanings and images, is what motivated Ghassan Kanafani to write. In his literary and political writings, the reader encounters the very essence of resistance, a resistance in action, thought and in language itself. Undoubtedly, Kanafani's Palestinian experience represents the very basis of his writings, whether literary, theoretical or political. Catastrophic suf-

---

1 Lyrics to the song "*Ghassan 'alimna hubb il qadiyya*" ["Ghassan Taught Us the Love of the Cause"], recorded by Ghazi Mikdashi and Firqat al-Koral al-Sha'bi.

fering, displacement and dispossession have the effect of placing humanity under the spectre of the immediacy of death. This was indeed Kanafani's reality, which gave birth to his resistant and revolutionary mind.

The literary world knows his novels and short stories, with *Men in the Sun, Returning to Haifa* and the collection *Land of Sad Oranges* among his popular writings. These chronicles were fuelled by Kanafani's own displacement from the city of Akka in the 1948 Nakba, and a life among fellow refugees in Syria and Lebanon. The catastrophe, the ethnic cleansing of Palestine, pushed him to write, and he would admit that he could not pinpoint whether his literary or political development came first. He did, though, meet and work with his mentor and leader "al-Hakim"[2] George Habash years before he published his own writing.[3] Kanafani's dozens of stories, including novels, short tales and theatrical scripts were, in fact, dwarfed by his contribution of hundreds of political articles, studies, analyses and manifestos; these were linked to the publications of organisations to which he belonged, the Popular Front for the Liberation of Palestine (PFLP) and its precursor, the Arab Nationalist Movement (ANM). This book seeks to shine a light on these largely unknown political texts.

Linked to his activism, which reached an apex with his leading role in the PFLP and his editorship of its newspaper *al-Hadaf* (*The Target*) from July 1969 until his assassination by Israeli Mossad agents on 8 July 1972, Kanafani cut an extraordinarily engaged and prolific figure. Yet, as his daughter Leila Kanafani reminds us, "Ghassan was not a one man show".[4] Much in his writing and cultural activities – he was also a skilled visual artist and one-time poet – was generated through collective input, discussion and democratic centralism. The atmosphere he built around *al-Hadaf* was avant-garde, vivacious and internationalist. Inviting dissident Iraqi theatre director Kasim Hawal to write and organise with the newspaper in Beirut in 1969, Kanafani told him: "Come with us, starve with us when we are hungry and be filled with us when we

---

2   "The wise" or "the doctor": George Habash was also a trained physician.
3   See "On Childhood, Literature, Marxism, the Front and *Al-Hadaf*", Chapter 1.
4   Discussion with the editors, Beirut, July 2023.

are full."[5] The works in this book should be read with the awareness that Kanafani was inextricable from his comrades in struggle
and that some materials were written collaboratively.

It would likewise be impossible to separate Kanafani's "political"
literature from his multi-pronged artistry. According to his friend
and comrade Fadle al-Nakib, Kanafani "walked the path of total
resistance", combining all the skills and artforms at his disposal.[6]
Still – in Arabic, let alone in any other language – the contemporary world has seen only the tip of Kanafani's iceberg. Supposedly
progressive areas of study, such as post-colonial theory, draw
on anti-colonial and revolutionary thinkers, whose writings are
readily available. But to this day, there has been no genuine effort
or even recognition of Kanafani's work as a revolutionary intellectual of anti-imperialist liberation from Zionism, colonialism,
global capitalism and Arab reaction. This book proposes to break
this unjust silence on Ghassan Kanafani. Kanafani was Palestine's
greatest Marxist thinker. His ideas – forged in the firepit of war,
crisis and armed resistance – are flammable materials, rich in the
lessons of the revolutionary sparks which ignited his era.

As the political and theoretical writings in this volume show,
Kanafani was a revolutionary intellectual whose deep, critical
consciousness put him ahead of his time. His development from
a budding artist, thinker and *adib* (literary figure) as a youth in
the mid-1950s, to a vastly experienced journal editor and polem-
icist still evolving at the time of his martyrdom, was very much
a journey, a revolutionary *becoming*. His public beginnings
came with his writing of the Palestinian story, through Nasse-
rite Arabism, to Marxism–Leninism and its total liberation of the
social consciousness. Throughout, Palestine was always the focus
of Kanafani's concern, the compass, or "cornerstone",[7] that would
unite Arabs and other peoples fighting Zionism, imperialism and
capitalism.

5   Ahmad Badir, "Kasim Hawal: Hakatha ʿasht maʾ Ghassan Kanafani wa- ʿarifto"
["How I Lived With and Knew Ghassan Kanafani"], *al-Hadaf* online, 8 August
2001, https://hadfnews.ps/post/43604.
6   Ghassan Kanafani, *al-Dirasat al-Siyasiyya: al-Majallad al-Khamis* [*Political
Works: Volume 5*] (Cyprus: Rimal, 2015), 2.
7   See "Resistance is the Essence", Chapter 4.

Kanafani saw the dangers of turning the Palestinian cause into a religious, nativist or ethnic one; he would warn against petty divisions between armed Palestinian factions, while underlining their class basis; he would underscore that the Palestinian *Nakba* is not an Arab–Israeli or Palestinian–Israeli *conflict*, but rather, he insisted, a confrontation between imperialism and an anti-imperialist liberation movement against brutal settler colonialism; and he would admonish Arab ruling classes seeking to liberalise or co-opt the struggle. At the root of his scientific socialist analysis was his identification of the poor, oppressed and disinherited masses – not the occupiers, financiers or compromising bourgeoisies – as the life blood and deciding factor in the fights to come. Our contention, by presenting his revolutionary words in today's contexts, is that Kanafani was an outstanding and sometimes prophetic visionary, whose works are as relevant today as they have ever been.

GHASSAN KANAFANI: A BIOGRAPHY

Soon after the 1948 Nakba, Damascus had become a hotbed of political radicalism. Inspired by Gamal Abdel Nasser's 1952 revolution in Egypt and by the Palestinians' violent displacement from their homeland, the city witnessed a coming together of young writers and intellectuals. Becoming organised, they converged around the Arab socialist printing press, where Ghassan Kanafani had begun as an apprentice. When he joined the editorial board of the ANM newspaper *al-Ra'i* (*The Viewpoint*) in 1955, he was barely 19 years old. The young Kanafani was recruited to the ANM by George Habash, one of the organisation's 1951 founders, and threw his talents into writing for the cause. During this period, Kanafani balanced studies, art, writing and editing with teaching in Kuwait, from where he would send most of his wages back to Syria to support his proletarianised family.

The Kanafanis had left Akka on 9 April 1948, the day of the infamous Deir Yassin massacre, leaving behind their relative prosperity in a disjointed trip through Saida, southern Lebanon, towards the Syrian capital. Kanafani would both lament and weaponise the by-products of his childhood schooling at the missionary Les Frères school, Yafa, where a focus on French and English had meant an imperfect early grasp of formal Arabic. In Damascus, Kanafani would develop rapidly and his private notebooks show a young man on a mission to contribute; his teaching career in UNRWA[8] schools began while he was still a student. Embedded in the pan-Arab scene, Kanafani joined the Life and Literature group founded by *al-Ra'i* editor Hani al-Hindi in 1957, further combining his political and literary activities. Kanafani wrote a short story and political commentary for the paper every month, gave speeches at demonstrations and in the Palestinian refugee camps, and had theatrical pieces performed on the radio.

Al-Nakib remembered attending a meeting in summer 1959 at al-Farouq Café, Damascus, with ANM leader al-Hakam Druza bringing Kanafani, Ahmed Khalifa and Bilal al-Hassan to discuss the cultural strategy of the movement. Directed by the ANM, the group resolved excitedly to write a collection of short stories for distribution in the camps. Though the book was never published, Kanafani stood out for his insistence in commenting on the work of his comrades, provoking surprise and awe at his drive to be both writer and critic. It was also an indication of the level of collective thought behind the stories and novels that bore his name. A year later, Kanafani would be called upon to move to Beirut and edit the cultural section of the Movement's weekly magazine, *al-Hurriyya* (*Freedom*). Lacking papers upon his arrival, Kanafani spent months in hiding, writing his most famous novel *Men in the Sun* in 1962, compelled by the grim realities faced by displaced Palestinians in the Arab Gulf.

By 1963, Kanafani had risen to the rank of editor-in-chief of the new daily newspaper *al-Muharrir* (*The Liberator*), as well as its bi-monthly *Filastin* (*Palestine*) supplement. Over a four-year period, Kanafani's daily writing would typically include a main news story, an editorial, a column in the paper, plus a short story, novel section or study for the cultural section. Kanafani would also travel throughout the Arab world and internationally as a reporter and political representative. On his visits to China, Kanafani wrote up long reports and interviews for *al-Muharrir* (1965) and took

---

8 UNRWA: United Nations Relief and Works Agency for Palestine Refugees in the Near East.

part in the Afro-Asian Writers Conference (1966). His work as editor of *al-Anwar* (*The Lights*; July 1967–March 1970) and as editor in chief of *al-Hadaf* (from July 1969 until his death) multiplied his written output and sharpened his viewpoint into the critical, Marxist methodology we will discuss below.

The titles of Kanafani's seven novels, three plays and many short stories are well-known and repeatedly republished in Arabic, collectively forming one component of his oeuvre. Kanafani published hundreds of political articles and theorisations, under his own name as well as under the pseudonyms Abu al-Ezz, Ginkaf, Fares Fares, G., Abu Fayez, Rabie Matar and others still to be uncovered. Kanafani's prolificacy was underlined in a June 1971 interview in which he reflected upon his role as a novelist in the Palestinian resistance movement:

> Literature has a very important role to play in society, especially when it speaks directly to the people and is not abstract. When a writer, then, is committed to a certain cause, it is very difficult for him to be satisfied writing only novels...

> We are, today, committed to the highest form of struggle, armed struggle, and for us events are always developing rapidly. We lose comrades every day. Day after day, in fact, comrades are killed and then they are forgotten because others are killed. This makes it difficult to continue writing. It is unfair, under these circumstances, to ask the novelist to keep writing, because as soon as he begins to write he discovers that his writing belongs to the past even if he is attempting to write about the future. It is as if he is suspended and his generation, his comrades, are passing him by – advancing faster than he is. Therefore, there are times when a novelist can't write.

> On the other hand, there are times that the novelist can't stop writing. The novelist lives, therefore, with this kind of contradiction, a kind of suffering.[9]

---

9 Interview with James Zogby, "Kanafani the Novelist", *Middle East International* 47 (May 1975): 27.

Many have been amazed at the prolific work of revolutionary Palestinian cartoonist Naji al-Ali, a protégé of Kanafani, who published around 40,000 drawings (more than four per day) before his life was cut short in 1987. The same drive flourished in Ghassan Kanafani. According to Anni Kanafani, her husband "was always busy, working as if death was just around the corner".[10] These descriptions are comparable to Edward Said's characterisation of "late style", an ironic, resistant approach, which "does not admit the definitive cadences of death; instead, death appears in a refracted mode, as irony".[11] This mortal realisation energised the potent energy and life of Kanafani's writings. After his assassination, Bassam al-Sherif told his comrades: "We must stick together. This is the path of the revolution – you must expect to lose a dear friend at any time."[12]

Kanafani had dabbled with poetry as a teenager, but his first love had been drawing. On top of his already burgeoning output, Kanafani would produce masses of paintings, pamphlet sleeves, graphics and iconic posters, combining imagery of Palestinian revolution with concrete demands and slogans. Among his 1969 works, for example, were: the novel *Returning to Haifa*; the play script *The Hat and the Prophet*; a critical editorial series in *al-Hadaf* of the post-1967 "settlement" promoted by Israel and its backers; a selection of literary reviews for *al-Anwar*, under the pseudonym Fares Fares; writing towards the epochal PFLP *Strategy for Liberation*; and an iconic, yellow poster proclaiming that: "The path of armed struggle is the path to a liberated Palestine". This is before the fact of Kanafani's additional responsibilities as PFLP central committee member and spokesperson. When foreign correspondents came to Beirut, journalist Talal Salman would take them straight to Kanafani.[13] With the backdrop of huge prints of Guevara, Marx, Lenin, Hô, Habash and Palestinian *fida'iyya* Therese Halasa, behind the desk of the PFLP's Beirut office – a hive of organisation and international media – Kanafani's image was iconic, and his message clear to all who would listen.

10 Anni Kanafani, Preface to Ghassan Kanafani, *On Zionist Literature*, trans. Mahmoud Najib (Oxford: Ebb, 2022), xiii.
11 Edward Said, *On Late Style* (New York: Pantheon, 2022), 27.
12 Badir, "Kasim Hawal".
13 Editors' interview with Marwan Abd el-'Al, 17 July 2023.

In these intensely productive *al-Hadaf* years, where avant-garde Marxist literature joined hands with the *fida'i* struggle, Kanafani's leadership role in the PFLP became more pronounced. By the organisation's third congress, held in al-Beddawi camp, Lebanon in March 1972, Kanafani's forceful arguments on the need for a long-term war of liberation galvanised the attendees. He was elected to write the resulting document, *Tasks of the New Stage*, which concluded that, in the face of the liquidationist strategies of imperialism, Zionism and Arab bourgeois opportunism: "The subject of building a Marxist–Leninist Party is now a central issue for the Palestinian revolution."[14]

The PFLP had a rocky relationship with the PLO and Kanafani was a key critic, while calling for a principled national unity. At the same time, he combined with Majed Abu Sharar and Kamal Nasser to form the PLO Information Office. Within a decade, all three had been assassinated by Zionist paramilitaries. Kanafani was killed just before 10:30am on 8 July 1972, blown apart with his 17-year-old niece Lamis Najm, after Mossad agents detonated their car bomb in Hazmieh. Though it had been a barely concealed secret, the Zionist state did not admit to killing Kanafani until 2005, as an Ariel Sharon-led regime sought to crush another intifada.[15] Kanafani's martyrdom came as Golda Meir had formed a sub-government committee dedicated to wiping out Palestinian leaders. Its members included war criminals Moshe Dayyan, Yig'al Alon, Yesrael Galilee, Zfika Zamir, Aharon Yarif and Rehavam Ze'evi. Ze'evi was killed in a Palestinian operation on 17 October 2001 in response to the murder of PFLP leader Abu Ali Mustafa.

In the wake of 8 July, the Zionist *Haaretz* newspaper celebrated the killing of the "PFLP No. 3",[16] while *Maariv* painted his killing as part of a continuing "war on terrorism".[17] Patrice Lumumba, Mehdi Ben Barka, Che Guevara, Kwame Nkrumah: the wider

---

14 *Foundational Texts of the PFLP* (Utrecht: Foreign Languages Press, forthcoming).

15 Eitan Haber, *Yedioth Ahronoth*, 3 October 2005.

16 The article claimed that Kanafani was a "planner" of the Lydd airport attack carried out by Japanese Red Army militants on 30 May 1972. *Haaretz*, 9 July 1972.

17 "The Killing of Kanafani", *Journal of Palestine Studies* 2, no. 1 (1972): 149, https://doi.org/10.2307/2535986.

war on revolutionary anti-colonial movements was international. Amilcar Cabral and Walter Rodney would join the list and, by the end of the 1980s, Lebanese communist Mahdi Amel and Palestinian artist Naji al-Ali would fall to the hit-lists of reaction and imperialist racism. The Lebanese *Daily Star* announced: "There will never be another Ghassan Kanafani." Al-Hakim admitted in a letter to Anni Kanafani, "we have taken a really painful hit".[18]

Ghassan Kanafani was killed for his committed approach to revolutionary culture and for his leading role in the PFLP. As'ad AbuKhalil writes: "Presumably, Israel wanted to kill Kanafani and silence his voice. Yet the plan did not work as intended."[19] Decades on from his killing, "Kanafani's presence is ubiquitous". His image means identification with the forces and methods of "total resistance" and a commitment to revolutionary critique. Palestinian political prisoners organise study days to understand his works; his significance is restated at commemorations in the camps; his books are read widely, and film adaptations of his novels re-released; and Kanafani remains the central intellectual figure in Palestinian leftist imaginations, despite his attempted co-option by forces linked to the Palestinian Authority. "As regards peace," Kanafani once said, "it cannot be established on the basis of injustice".[20]

"WORDS WERE BULLETS": GHASSAN KANAFANI'S PALESTINIAN MARXISM

History is not produced by a magic wand but is transformed by the masses who understand it and are determined to change it.
"The Resistance and its Challenges", 1970

On a late Saturday evening in summer 1970, Fadle al-Nakib was Ghassan Kanafani's guest in Beirut, with the two planning

---

18   George Habash, *Safhat Min Masirti al-Nidaliya* [*Pages of My Path of Struggle*] (Lebanon: Centre for Arab Unity Studies, 2019), 219.

19   As'ad AbuKhalil, "The Second Life of Ghassan Kanafani", *The Electronic Intifada*, 12 July 2017, https://electronicintifada.net/content/second-life-ghassan-kanafani/21051.

20   Clara Halter, "The Liberation of the Occupied Territories is Only the First Step", *New Middle East*, September 1970.

a trip to the mountains the next day. Driving, Kanafani apologised profusely that he'd forgotten something important in the *al-Hadaf* offices and rushed back to collect it. He returned to the car carrying a pamphlet he had read and re-read, and which was required material in the *fida'i* training camps: Lenin's *State and Revolution*.[21]

For Kanafani, art and politics were inseparable. In 1968, he contrasted the "Resistance Literature in Occupied Palestine" to the "poetry of exile", with the former characterised not by "a note of lamentation or despair, but reflect[ing] an admirable hope and a constant revolutionary fervour".[22] This philosophical reasoning has proven its validity, not only in what Kanafani called resistance literature, but also in the real-life experiences of the oppressed, the defiantly resistant Palestinian masses. That Palestinians continue to constitute a fighting people is witnessed to this day in Palestine under occupation (Jenin refugee camp) and constant, genocidal siege (Gaza). Thus, the consummate negativity of Zionist colonial settler brutality does indeed delineate the mirror-image of its opposite – fierce Palestinian resistance – a concept that Kanafani theorised in his characterisation of resistance literature. His own literature was built in this image and evolved with a collective shift towards Marxism.

Kanafani was a lifelong socialist, but the parameters and conceptualisation of his socialism changed with the dramatic transformation of the Palestinian movement in the 1960s. From the outset of his political life, he presented a sharp awareness that extreme forms of occupation, siege, oppression and suffering

---

21 Kanafani, *al-Dirasat al-Siyasiyya*, 47. Al-Nakib is mistaken, however, in stating that Kanafani's purpose of revisiting Lenin was towards the study, "*Al-Markssiyyah fi al-Majal al-Nazari, al-Majal al-Tatbiqi: Munaqasha*" ("Marxism in Theory and Practice: A Discussion"), contained in the same volume. The notebook carried the clear signs of Ghassan Kanafani's earlier position and, as confirmed by Anni and Leila Kanafani, had actually been written in the mid-late 1950s, not in 1970. It is possible that the study he was working on at the point of this meeting with al-Nakib was *The Underlying Synthesis of the Revolution*, published the following year and which focused on the relevance of Marxism–Leninism as demonstrated in the Vietnamese struggle.
22 Ghassan Kanafany [sic.], "Resistance Literature in Occupied Palestine", *Lotus Journal* 1, nos 1–2 (1968): 70.

could only produce their opposite in the oppressed – a fierce resistance to a barbaric settler colonialism. In his notebooks in the late 1950s, Kanafani saw socialism as "the right of all people to live their lives enjoying all of their basic human rights".[23] Like Habash, Wadi' Haddad and other ANM comrades, Kanafani's concept of revolution in this early period was tied primarily to the wave of anti-colonial resistance heralded by Nasserism.

Founded in February 1958, while Kanafani worked in Kuwait, the Egypt–Syria United Arab Republic (UAR) represented an opportunity to "change the history of the region" and "destabilise" the strategic and colonial interests of outside forces.[24] Kanafani developed an understanding of imperialism, Arab reaction and opportunism from this basis, during a time in which the Palestinian resistance movement was slowly rebuilding itself. Initially, at least, the ANM saw their role as supporting agents to the Cairo-led challenge, seeing regional developments through the lens of this confrontation while pushing for principled Arab unity. The Ba'athist takeover in Iraq, for instance, was violently opposed to the communists and Kurds, on whom Kanafani saw the Ba'athists "waging a war of extermination" in 1963,[25] but also to the anti-imperialist unity represented by the UAR.

Included in Kanafani's early critique were pro-Soviet communists, and particularly those "official" Arab communist parties presenting class-based critiques of Nasserism. In the pages of the Egyptian-funded *al-Muharrir* newspaper, Kanafani and other writers saw the kind of charismatic leadership represented by Nasser as providing a necessary figurehead to the Arab socialist movement, inspiring the people to struggle. This line was maintained through the dark days of the June 1967 *hazima* (defeat),[26] but the full scale

---

23 "*Al-Manhaj al-Tatbiqi lil-Ishtirakiyya al-Arabiyya*" ["Methodology for Implementing Arab Socialism"], in Adnan Kanafani (ed.), *Ghassan Kanafani: Ma'rij al-Ibda'* [*Ghassan Kanafani: The Rise to Ingenuity*] (Jordan: Dar Mu'assasat Filastin lil-Thaqafa, 2009), 181. Translation by Amira Silmi.
24 "Al-Qadiyya al-'Arabiyya Fi 'Ahd Jim 'Ayn Mim" ["The Arab Cause in the Era of the UAR"], in Kanafani, *al-Dirasat al-Siyasiyya*, 145–46. Translation by Ameen Nemer.
25 *Al-Muharrir*, 22 November 1963.
26 Kanafani and his comrades generally did not use the word *naksa*, or setback, to describe the events of June 1967.

of the conquest by Zionist forces was soon revealed more broadly. In the months after this catastrophic setback, Kanafani reflected that only "the fighting people" could genuinely decide the fate of Palestine and the whole region.[27] Working-class and oppressed peoples would lead any genuine liberation movement.

Kanafani later attacked Nasserism for its compliance with the US Rogers Plan in summer 1970, standing against the politics of "surrender" and "attempt[s] to drive a wedge between the resistance and the masses".[28] For Kanafani and his comrades, true socialism had come to mean embracing Marxism–Leninism. This evolution can be traced, in part, through the group's position on the Soviet Union, coming to recognise its role as a "major supporter of the Arab masses in their fight against imperialism" in the period of rising liberation struggle.[29] It is crucial to add that Kanafani's earlier ideas were just that, with incomplete essays such as "Marxism in Theory and Practice" and "A Methodology for Implementing Arab Socialism" forming sketchpads composed more than a decade before his killing, and which he would choose not to publish. Like Che Guevara, Kanafani had been critical of the Soviet model, but helped to develop the PFLP so that the Soviet Union represented a positive counterbalance to US-led imperialist interventionism; the organisation also received Soviet weaponry, training and scholarships.

Kanafani and other PFLP figures would describe the June 1967 defeat in transformative terms, as the final impetus towards a higher mode of thinking. The founding statement of the PFLP on 11 December referenced the *hazima* as heralding a "new phase… in which the revolutionary masses must take on leadership responsibility" in the fight against imperialism and Zionism.[30] Habash explained that, though this did not negate the role of progressive

---

27 See "Resistance is the Essence", Chapter 4.
28 George Hajjar, *Kanafani: Symbol of Palestine* (Lebanon: Karoun, 1974), 122–23. On 23 July 1970, Nasser accepted the proposals of US Secretary of State William Rogers for a ceasefire between Egypt and Israel, in what was dubbed the "Second Rogers' Plan". The basis of Rogers' proposals was seeking Arab recognition of the rights to a "secure" Israel, with no commitment to ending the occupations of 1967 or of 1948.
29 See "Excerpts from PFLP: Strategy for the Liberation of Palestine", Chapter 7.
30 *Foundational Texts of the PFLP.*

Arab forces in the fight for regional liberation, the experience of
Vietnam showed that "the confrontation must have as its basis the
organised and armed masses".[31] The realisation that this meant a
deeper adoption of Marxism as "the ideology of the working class"[32]
was also based on an understanding of the role of regional bourgeoisies – and petit bourgeoisies, as Kanafani and his comrades
came to view Egypt's leaders – in acting to liquidate the revolutionary trend. Third World Marxism, wrote Rodney, answered the
"failure of bourgeois thought to deliver the goods".[33]

This ideological and organisational shift did not occur over-
night. As early as 1964, Habash had led discussions in the ANM
towards establishing the Palestinian branch as an alternative to
the organisation's Leadership Committee for Palestinian Work,
spurred on by the Nasser government's insistence that the cause
should remain under its leadership.[34] The "third stage" in this relationship after 1967, writes Matar, meant breaking with Nasserism
and forging a new path.[35] The fight for "Arab Hanois", taken up
vociferously by Kanafani, found roots in this earlier stage. On his
watch, *Filastin* magazine had published features on the Vietnamese "art of guerrilla warfare" in 1965,[36] arguing with reference to
the communists' victories so far – and against the grain of Nasserism – that this strategy was the only path to liberation.

Visiting socialist China in August 1964, Claudia Jones in her
poem "Yenan – Cradle of the Revolution", hailed:

Yenan – Cradle of the Revolution;
Of their dreams, their fight;
Their organisation, their heroism.[37]

31 Habash, *Safhat Min Masirti al-Nidaliya*, 150.
32 Habash, *Safhat Min Masirti al-Nidaliya*.
33 Walter Rodney, *Decolonial Marxism: Essays from the Pan-African Revolution* (London: Verso, 2022), 66.
34 Fouad Matar, *Hakim al-Thawra: Sirat George Habash wa-Nidalu* [*Wise Man of the Revolution: Biography of George Habash and his Struggle*] (Beirut: An-Nahar House, 2008), 99.
35 Matar, *Hakim al-Thawra*, 100.
36 *Filastin*, 29 January 1965. There is currently no way of ascertaining whether Kanafani wrote the unsigned article himself.
37 Carole Boyce Davies (ed.), *Claudia Jones: Beyond Containment* (London: Ayebia, 2011), 203.

The influence of Kanafani's two Chinese trips, in 1965 and 1966, also left a comparably profound mark on his thinking. Covering 150 pages, *Then Shone Asia*... charts this journey, as well as Kanafani's impressions of post-independence India. Writing after 1967, he drew on Mao's reflections of the Chinese war of liberation against Japanese imperialism, an appreciable focus on the role of the vanguard organisation, and Palestinianised the questions raised by both Mao and Hồ: "Who are our enemies? Who are our friends?" The central references of Kanafani's political work during this period included Lenin, Lukács and Stalin, along with Mao, Hồ and Giáp. Underlining the collectivist underpinnings of such readings, the PFLP cadre schools – of which Kanafani was an enthusiastic proponent – included in their curriculum many of the same works and authors, along with Marx and Engels, and readings on the Chinese, Cuban, Korean, Soviet and Vietnamese experiences.[38]

Although Kanafani was only 36 years old at the time of his assassination, he left behind a reservoir of literary, political and theoretical work. So, what were his main theoretical contributions? This book offers many indications:

- Kanafani was the first intellectual to apply Marxist class analysis to the Palestinian situation, demonstrated in his scandalously under-referenced work on the 1936–1939 revolution and shown further in his reflections on the crisis after 1967.
- The mobile, octopus-like body of imperialism was analysed in terms of regional power and what it represented, seeing Zionism as an outpost of British and later US imperialist interests in the Middle East.
- Kanafani detailed the relevance of communist-led anti-colonial liberation movements to the Palestinian case and inseparable bonds between questions of theory, organisation and practice.

---

38 Gérard Chaliand, *The Palestinian Resistance* (London: Pelican, 1972), 157–58.

- Palestine was central, in his mind, to the wider cause of Arab freedom. Indeed, he refused to see Palestine – or indeed any cause – as existing in a bubble, as shown by his references to popular movements in Denmark, Vietnam, Yemen and many other examples.

- Kanafani understood and connected the normalisation of racism in oppressor nations to the settler colonial project, beginning to critique Orientalism before its expansive application by Said.

- And, in describing the resistance movement in materialist terms, Kanafani – like Che, Fidel, Fanon, Hô and Kollontai – was able to envisage that a new human being would necessarily be generated by the revolutionary movement.

What distances Kanafani from those who came after – and, indeed from the navel-gazing academics of his time – is the conviction that the idea of revolutionary organisation must be raised alongside questions of theory and critique. Kanafani was not a rank-and-file PFLP cadre, but the Front's intellectual emissary. Like Mahdi Amel, Kanafani did not describe the Middle East in "post-colonial" terms, seeing an "ongoing process of plunder",[39] underpinning continuing imperialist interventions in the region. Zionism and Arab reaction were not the puppet masters, but rather existed to represent imperialism, which stood behind their moves. Appearing on front pages of *al-Hadaf*, Lenin was a foundational influence, whose theory of imperialism helped Kanafani to analyse such events as the 1967 defeat, the standpoints of Arab states after Black September, and the Saudi-spearheaded intervention against the socialist liberation movement in Yemen.

Kanafani was a leader in the shift by which Palestinian socialists addressed the question of the vanguard, prophetically seeing the resistance in Gaza as showing the way forward. From his place of exile in different Arab capitals, including Damascus, Kuwait and Beirut, Kanafani theorised about the absolute necessity of a constructive unity of Palestinian organisations before mounting a successful armed struggle for liberation, the culture of resistance,

39 See "The Resistance and its Challenges", Chapter 8.

the transformation of the masses, the making of new human beings to enable successful decolonisation and liberation, and transnational solidarity with other liberation movements from around the world. According to his comrade Salah Salah: "As far as Ghassan was concerned, words were bullets."[40]

A WORD ON TRANSLATION

The late writer, translator and activist Barbara Harlow reminds us of a "larger and collective political agenda" attached to the acts of translating.[41] We were reminded of this fact when looking again at the English versions of PFLP documents from 1969–1972, with omissions, selective word choices and explanations aimed at anglophone readers. Kanafani had been part of the organisation's Information Department, which led this work, and was a habitual translator himself. His translation practices ranged from columns analysing racist and biased Western press reports of events in the Middle East, to Marxist extracts into Arabic for the purpose of his studies, or, as on his epic journeys to China, carrying out interviews in English to be translated for Arab readers. His wife Anni remembers that he'd translate his novels and other writings into English for her own understanding.

The work of translation is an inexact science of infinite permutations and with justice rarely done to source-language idioms. While our collective is satisfied with the results, we remind the reader that translation is also an act of (politically) guided interpretation. To make our process as rigorous as possible, work by the initial translator was put through two thorough peer reviews, before any final editing took place. Guidance for this work also came from the seminal existing translations we were able to include in the volume, with honourable mention to Barbara Harlow and Nejd Yaziji. We also looked to the Marxist canon which had formed a bulk of Kanafani's reading since the 1950s; the noun *al-raja 'iyya*,

---

40 Salah Salah in *Ghassan Kanafani: Al-Kalima al-Bunduqiyya* [*Ghassan Kanafani: Word of the Rifle*], directed by Kassem Hawal (Palestine, 1973), Al Jazeera documentary, 16 June 2017.

41 Barbara Harlow, *Resistance Literature* (London: Methuen, 1987), 25.

for example – which he and his comrades used to describe reactionary Arab regimes – appears as "reaction" in the work of Irish socialist James Connolly,[42] as well as in the English language works of Leila Khaled,[43] and others of Ghassan Kanafani's generation. Each text presented different challenges, from locating the quotes and citations used by Kanafani in their original English or Arabic, to questions of whether or how to standardise the works' political vocabulary and syntax. "Translating and introducing Ghassan, you have to be an artist", as Khaled Barakat quipped early on in the project. So, the interpretation of his work is simultaneously political and poetic – personifying its writer. The creative approach at play between members of the translating collective raised discussions on a wide number of words, phrases and passages. The title of the 1967 article included here as Chapter 4, for instance, is *"al-muqawama hiyya al-asl"*. This could mean "Resistance is the Basis", "...the Source", "...the Foundation", and so on. Its translation as "Resistance is the Essence", we think, gets to the crux of Kanafani's argument on the 1967 defeat and its aftermath: the struggle of the masses is key, essential. This discussion hints at a central tenet of our approach: the goal was to communicate the essence of Kanafani's argument.

The collective also looked critically at previously translated works. One of our debates centred around the term *'amal fida'i*, translated in early PFLP documents as "commando action". The consensus was that we should retain the Arabic for *fida'i*, with the *fida'iyyin* representing both an enduring armed struggle and constituting a recognised emblem of the Palestinian liberation movement. Likewise, Palestinian concepts of *sumud* (steadfastness) have also entered into common use. With this in mind, we considered which other Arabic language words and phrases may be retained to better communicate Kanafani's meaning. We considered replacing the English word resistance with its Arabic,

---

42   James Connolly, "Labour and the Proposed Partition of Ireland", from *Irish Worker*, 14 March 1914, Digital version by *Marxists Internet Archive*, https://www.marxists.org/archive/connolly/1914/03/laborpar.htm.
43   Leila Khaled, *My People Shall Live: The Autobiography of a Revolutionary* (London: Hodder and Stoughton, 1973 [1971]), p. 57.

muqawama, which would set the Palestinian struggle on its own terms, identifying Kanafani with new generations utilising the same vocabulary. However – and this relates to one facet of the international battle analysed in this book – being able to openly assert one's right to support anti-Zionist Palestinian *resistance* is both an iterative and material fight, taking place in and beyond English-speaking countries. We were mindful that this right is asserted openly and unashamedly in the face of ruling-class onslaughts upon Palestinian activism, renewed venomously after the launch of Operation Al-Aqsa Flood on 7 October 2023.

Not since the prolific early days of Palestinian media committees or the vigorous translations of Harlow and Yaziji has there been a greater hunger to translate revolutionary Palestine for international readerships. Our work stands alongside the new translations by Mahmoud Najib of *On Zionist Literature* (Ebb books, 2022) and Hazem Jamjoum of *The Revolution of 1936–39 in Palestine* (1804 books, 2023), with many more translations of Kanafani's literary and political materials hopefully on the way. The reception to these works shows that the mini-explosion of interest in Kanafani's writings among Arabic-speaking Palestinians threatens to boil over into the world at large. Presenting Kanafani's Marxist works also means situating his contribution alongside newly published texts by Mahdi Amel, Amilcar Cabral, Che Guevara, Hồ Chí Minh, Claudia Jones and Walter Rodney.

Long may the Ghassan Kanafani revolution continue!

PART I

Revolutionary Routes:
Arab Nationalism and Socialism

1

On Childhood, Literature, Marxism, the Front and *al-Hadaf* (1972)

Introduction: Reflections on a Rare Interview
by *Hania A.M. Nashef*

At the end of the novel *Men in the Sun*, the poignant question posed by the driver of the tanker, "Why didn't you say anything?" reverberates throughout the still desert. In retrospect, the question was addressing a larger audience: Ghassan Kanafani is wondering why humanity remained silent in front of the suffering of Palestinians and demands that the Palestinian resistance should assume a stronger position. Furthermore, the author is requiring of his fellow Palestinians a more active role in their struggle, calling for collective action against existing Palestinian and Arab leaderships. In this article published in *Shu'un Falastiniyya (Palestinian Matters)*, an interview conducted by an unnamed Swiss scholar, Kanafani discusses his early childhood, literary work, political life and the experiences that helped shape his career as an activist and literary figure.

Describing his childhood and upbringing as traditionally Palestinian, Kanafani referred to a common plight shared by the majority of his people. Conversely, his background before the forceful eviction of his family from Akka was representative of the urbanite existence of an educated, middle-class Palestinian family. Becoming a refugee at the age of eleven, this disruption forced him to seek work at an early age for his family to survive; at the same time, he was completing his school education. Echoes of Kanafani's life are evident in much of his writing.

In the interview, he describes how his father was never able to adapt to exile and refugeehood. In Akka, he had practised law, and accepting a lower-ranked job in Damascus felt demeaning to him. It is worth noting that much of Kanafani's literary work is influenced by the early childhood experiences or observations he formed of his milieu in the camp. For example, the short story *Land of Sad Oranges*, written in Kuwait in 1958, ends with a shrivelled orange and a black gun placed on a low table near an elderly man's bed, a metaphor of a father's life cut short as a result of his inability to accept displacement, expulsion and loss in the aftermath of the 1948 Nakba, when the family were forcibly exiled to Lebanon. In this interview, Kanafani tells us that his father was also unable to come to terms with the change in his social status. On the other hand, for the young Ghassan, adjusting to a government school in which the language of instruction was Arabic after having been taught in a French missionary school in Akka, also posed a challenge. During a six-month hiatus due to a broken leg, he immersed himself in Arabic.

Many of the situations encountered in his early years as a refugee not only reverberate through Kanafani's short stories but were also instrumental in shaping his political ideology. In one incident, he explains how he became angry with a child who was sleeping in class, only to discover later that the children he was teaching worked all night as peddlers, selling sweets or chewing gum outside cinemas and on street corners. In the short story, *Ka'ak on the Pavement* (1959), young Hamid tells the teacher that he is unable to study because he sells *ka'ak* [a sweet] to crowds leaving the cinema at midnight. Realising that the students he taught could not relate to the given curriculum when asked to draw an apple or a banana, having seen neither, Kanafani asked them to draw a camp instead. The Syrian authorities reprimanded him for digressing from the official curriculum, describing him as incompetent. This incident left a lasting impression on the author, and henceforth he realised the importance of fighting for one's own rights. His political views resulted in his dismissal from the University of Damascus, which led him to Kuwait, where the impoverished conditions of many exiles inspired *Men in the Sun*.

Kanafani began writing literature at an early age, in a quest to find answers to the Palestinian Nakba. Here, he reflects how all his characters were drawn from the refugees in the camps. He reveals that the years from 1956 to 1962 proved critical to the development of his style, namely, in the way he portrays Palestine and her people. Eventually, for Kanafani, the Palestinian person portrayed in his work became the epitome of the suffering of the human race as a whole; Palestinian woe symbolised the misery encountered by many in the world. To him, Palestine symbolised humanity.

In the interview, Kanafani also notes that his short stories and novels evolved from representing raw emotion to representing reality, which the Palestinian author argues exhibits a more mature stance than his earlier political views. Kanafani recalls how he read Soviet writers extensively, and that this was a major influence in the formation of his Marxist thought. The interview ends on a note of optimism. According to Kanafani, the resistance movement had made progress, despite its challenges. He describes the period after 1967 as pivotal for the history of the struggle.

* * *

INTERVIEW: WITH THE MARTYR GHASSAN KANAFANI[1]

Original Introduction

Shu'un Falastiniyya obtained the full text of an unpublished private conversation conducted by a Swiss writer, who was a specialist in Ghassan Kanafani's literature. Conducted just a few weeks before the assassination of the Palestinian resistance martyr, this interview eventually formed part of the writer's scholarly study on Ghassan Kanafani's literary work.

Ghassan, can you tell me something about your personal experience?

I think my story reflects a very traditional Palestinian background. I left Palestine when I was eleven years old, coming from a middle-class family. My father was a lawyer, and I was studying in a French missionary school. Suddenly, this middle-class family collapsed, and we became refugees. My father immediately stopped working, since his class roots ran so deeply – continuing to work after we left Palestine no longer made sense to him and would have forced him

---

1   Original publication: *Shu'un Falastiniyya*, Issue 36 (July 1974). English translation by the Samidoun Spain collective.

to abandon his class position and move to a lower class, which is not easy.[2] As for us, we started working as children and teenagers to support the family. I was able to continue my education on my own, through my job as a teacher in one of the [UNRWA: United Nations Relief and Works Agency for Palestine Refugees in the Near East] primary schools in the village, which did not require higher academic qualifications. It was a logical start, as it helped me to continue studying and finish secondary school in the meantime. I then enrolled at [Damascus] university, in the Department of Arabic Literature, for three years, after which I was dismissed for political reasons. I then went to Kuwait, where I stayed for six years and began reading and writing.

My political career began in 1952, when I was 14 or 15 years old. In that same year, or in 1953, I met Dr George Habash for the first time by chance in Damascus. I was working as a proof-reader in a printing house. I don't remember who introduced me to al-Hakim,[3] but my relationship with him began at that time and I immediately joined the ranks of the Arab Nationalist Movement (ANM), thus beginning my political life. During my stay in Kuwait, I was politically active within the ANM, which is now represented by a significant minority in the Kuwaiti government. In 1960, I was asked to move to Lebanon to work on the party newspaper. In 1967, I was asked to work with the Popular Front for the Liberation of Palestine (PFLP), the Palestinian branch of the ANM. In 1969, I began my work [as editor of] the newspaper *al-Hadaf*, where I continue to work.

Did you start writing as a result of your studies in Arabic literature?

No, I think my interest in Arabic literature pre-dates my studies. I suspect that my interest was the result of a complex (*'uqda* – عقدة), if memory serves me correctly. Before we left Palestine, I had been studying in a French missionary school, as I mentioned before. I

---

2   Unable to practise law upon his arrival in Damascus, Muhammad Kanafani sold groceries on the streets, while Ghassan and his siblings sold newspapers and other items.

3   "The wise" or "the doctor": George Habash was also a trained physician.

was therefore an Arab not possessing the Arabic language, which caused me a lot of problems. My friends always made fun of me because I was not good at Arabic. This perception was not clear when we were in Palestine because of my social class. But when we left Palestine, my friends were of a different social class and immediately noticed that my Arabic was poor, and that I resorted to foreign expressions in my conversations. So, I concentrated on Arabic language in order to handle this problem, probably in 1954. I think I broke my leg that year in an accident. I had to stay in bed for six months. It was then that I started reading Arabic in earnest.

I think we may cite many examples throughout history of people who have "lost" their language and therefore attempt to recover it. Do you think that this process develops a person politically?

I don't know, it may be so. As for me personally, I was politicised in a different way. I got involved in politics at an early stage because we lived in a refugee camp. And so, I was in direct contact with the Palestinians and their problems through that sad and emotional atmosphere that I experienced as a child. It was not difficult for me to discover the political roots of the environment in which I lived.

When I began to teach, I faced great difficulties with the children I taught in the camp. I would always become angry when I saw a child sleeping in class. Then I found out why: these kids were working at night, selling sweets or chewing gum and similar items in the cinemas and on the streets. Naturally, they would come to class very tired. Such a situation immediately brings a person to the root of the problem. It became clear to me that the child's drowsiness was not the result of his disdain for me or his hatred of education, just as it had nothing to do with my dignity as a teacher but was merely a reflection of a political problem.

So, your teaching experience contributed to the development of your social and political awareness?

Yes, and I remember how this happened one day in a direct sense. As you know, primary school teachers teach all subjects, including drawing, arithmetic, English, Arabic and other subjects. One day,

I was trying to teach the children to draw an apple and a banana, according to the syllabus approved by the Syrian government; I was teaching [in Syria] and therefore had to stick to the book. And at that moment, as I attempted to draw the two pictures on the blackboard as best as I could, I felt a sense of alienation, of not belonging. I remember well feeling at that moment that I must do something, because I realised, before even looking at the faces of the children sitting behind me, that they had never seen an apple or a banana. So, these were the last things they would be interested in. There was no connection between them and these two pictures. In fact, the relationship between their feelings and these drawings was strained, not positive. This was a decisive turning point, as I remember that very moment clearly among all the events of my life. As a result, I erased the drawings from the board and asked the children to draw the camp. A few days later, when the inspector came to the school, he said that I had deviated from the governmentally directed programme, proving that I was a failed teacher. Having to defend myself led me straight to the Palestinian cause. Accumulating small steps like these pushes people to make decisions that will mark their whole life.

Commenting on this point, I think when you engage in art, as a socialist anyway, you connect art directly to the social, political and economic spheres. You touched on this by drawing an apple and a banana. But, as for your writings, are these works related to your reality and the present situation, or are they derived from [literary] heritage?

My first short story was published in 1956 and was called "A New Sun". It revolves around a boy in Gaza. When I review all of the stories I have written about Palestine so far, it is clear to me that each story is directly or indirectly linked, with a thin or solid thread, to my personal experiences in life. However, my style of writing fully developed during the period from 1956 to 1960, or in 1961 more specifically. At first, I wrote about Palestine as a cause in its own right, as well as about Palestinian children, about the Palestinian as a human being, about Palestinian hopes, being themselves separate things from our independent and autonomous world, as inevitable

Palestinian facts. It then became clear to me that what I saw in Palestine was an integrated human symbol. When I write about a Palestinian family, I am actually writing about human experience. There is no incident in the world that is not represented in the Palestinian tragedy. When I portray the misery of the Palestinians, I am in fact seeing the Palestinians as a symbol of misery all over the world. You might say that Palestine represents the whole world in my stories. The [literary] critic may now notice that my stories are not solely about the Palestinian and their problems, but also about the human condition of a person suffering from those problems. But perhaps those problems are more crystallised in the lives of Palestinians.

Did your literary development accompany your political development?

Yes. In fact, I don't know which preceded the other. The day before yesterday, I was watching one of my stories that was produced as a film. I had written this story in 1961.[4] I saw the film from a new perspective, as I suddenly discovered that the dialogue between the protagonists, their line of thinking, class, aspirations and roots at that time expressed advanced concepts of my political thinking. [So], I can say that my personality as a novelist was more developed than my personality as a political actor, not the other way around, and this is reflected in my analysis and understanding of society.

Does your writing reflect an analysis of your society, or do you also colour your analyses in an emotional way?

I suppose my stories were based on an emotional situation at the beginning, but you could say that my writing began to reflect reality from the early 1960s. My observation of this reality and my writing about it led me to a thorough analysis. My stories themselves lack analysis. However, they narrate the behaviour of the protagonists, the decisions they make, the reasons that motivate

---

4   The film was probably *The Dupes* [*al-Makhdu'un*], based on the novel *Men in the Sun* and produced by Tewfik Saleh (Syria, 1972).

them to make those decisions, the possibility of crystallising those decisions, etc. In my novels I express reality, as I understand it, without analysis. What I mean by saying that my stories were more developed [than my political views] is due to my sincere amazement when I followed the development of the characters in the story I was watching as a film, and which I had not read in the last few years. I was astonished when I listened [again] to the dialogue of my characters about their problems and was able to compare their dialogue with the political articles I had written during the same period of time and saw that the protagonists in the story were analysing things in a deeper and more correct way than my political articles [at that time].

You mentioned that you started your political work by joining the ANM the day you met [George] Habash in 1953. So, when did you embrace socialist principles? The ANM was not a socialist movement at the beginning.

No, it wasn't. The ANM was [directed] against colonialism, imperialism and reaction (*al-raja'iyya* – الرجعية). It did not adopt an ideological line at that time. However, the Movement took on a socialist ideology of its own during its years of activity. Anti-imperialism gives impetus to socialism if it does not stop fighting in the middle of the battle and if it does not come to an agreement with imperialism; if it does [compromise], the movement will not be able to become a socialist movement. But if one continues to struggle [it is natural] that the [anti-imperialist] movement will develop into a socialist position. The Arab nationalists realised this fact in the late 1950s. They realised that they could not win the war against imperialism unless they relied on certain classes: those classes who fight against imperialism not only for their dignity, but also for their livelihood. And it was this [path] that would lead directly to socialism.

But in our society, and in the ANM, we were highly sensitive to Marxism–Leninism. This position was not the result of our hostility to socialism, but the result of the mistakes made by the communist parties of the Arab world. That is why it was very difficult for the ANM to adopt Marxism–Leninism before 1964. But in

1967, and specifically in July, the PFLP embraced the [principles] of Marxism–Leninism and was thus the only [front] within the ANM to take such a step. The ANM changed its name to the Arab Socialist Action Party, with its Palestinian branch renamed the "Popular Front". Of course, this is a simplification of the problem. We had developed within the ANM, where there was a constant struggle within the Movement, between the so-called right and the left. In each round, the left came out on top because our position on anti-imperialism and reactionary standpoints was preferable [to the position of the right]. This resulted in the adoption of Marxism–Leninism.

I don't remember now whether I leaned to the right or left in my position on the conflicts that arose within the Front,[5] because the border between right and left was not as easily delineated then as it is now, as occurs in developed political parties, for instance. But I can say that the ANM included some young elements, including myself, who made fun of the older generation's sensitivity to communism. Of course, we were not communists at that time and were not in favour of communism. However, our sensitivity towards communism was on a lower level than that of the elders and consequently, the new generation played a leading role in the development of the ANM into a Marxist–Leninist movement. The main factor in this was the fact that the majority of ANM members belonged to the class of the poor. Numbers of members belonging to the petty bourgeoisie or big bourgeoisie were limited. Nor did [these classes] continue with the Movement and they left within two years of joining. New members [of these classes] also joined, who left in turn [shortly afterwards]. The poor classes remained and soon formed a pressing force within the ANM.

When did you begin to study Marxism–Leninism? Do you remember?

I don't think my own experience in this regard is traditional. First, I was and still am an admirer of Soviet writers. However, my admi-

---

5   The context here suggests that Kanafani had meant to say *al-Haraka*, the Movement, rather than *al-Jabha*, the Front but his contribution is revealing of the extent to which the founding group of the PFLP were already organising themselves within the ANM prior to 1967.

ration for them was absolute at the time, which helped me to break the ice between myself and Marxism. In this way, I was exposed to Marxism at an early stage through my readings and admiration for Soviet writers. Second, my sister's husband was a prominent communist leader. My sister married in 1952 and her husband influenced my life at that early stage. Also, when I went to Kuwait, I lived with another six young people in a house and, a few weeks after my arrival, found out that they were forming a communist cell. So, I began to read about Marxism at a very early stage. I don't know how much I absorbed at that time and during this period, being under the influence of those emotions with the ANM. I can't measure my understanding or comprehension of the material I was reading but the content was not alien to me.

It may have been these early influences that moved your [early] stories forward [in relation to your political ideas at the time]. I think your readings of Soviet literature and your contacts with Marxists were reflected in your writing.

I don't think these factors take precedence. I think the biggest influence on my writing is reality itself: what I see, the experiences of my friends, relatives, brothers and sisters, students, and my living in the camps, among poverty and misery. These are the factors that affected me. Perhaps my fondness for Soviet literature was due to the fact that it expresses, analyses, deals with and describes what I was actually seeing. My admiration continues, of course. However, I don't know whether Soviet literature had an influence on my writing; I don't know the parameters of this effect. I prefer to say instead that the primary influence is not due to [Soviet literature], but to reality itself. All of the characters in my novels were inspired by reality – which gave [my writing] strength – and not by imagination. Nor did I choose my heroes for artistic reasons. They were all from the camp, not from outside. The characters in my first stories were always rascals (*al-shakhsiyat... sharira* – ...شريرة الشخصيات) because of [my experiences with] my subordinates at work. So, life itself had the biggest influence.

You belonged to the middle class, but joined the proletariat as a child?

Yes, of course, my background is related to the middle class because my father belonged to the middle class before we went to Syria as refugees. My family's attachment to its [class] roots was distant from its lived reality, which had no connection to those roots. And we children had to pay the price for this contradiction. Therefore, my relationship [with the middle class] became aggressive rather than friendly. I won't pretend to have joined the proletariat. I was not a real proletarian, but I joined what we call in our language the "lumpen proletariat", whose members are not part of the productive apparatus, but on the margins of the proletariat. This helped me, of course, to understand the ideology of the proletariat, but I cannot say that I was part of the proletariat at that time.

However, from the beginning you were able to see reality from the perspective of the oppressed.

Yes, you could say that. My concept, however, was not crystallised in a scientific, analytical way, but was [simply an expression of] an emotional state.

Let's go back to 1967, when the PFLP was born. What were the beliefs of this new organisation and what were the reasons for its creation?

As you know, the PFLP was not a new organisation. It is essentially the Palestinian branch of the ANM, of which I was a member. It developed at first through members of the ANM in 1967. We created the PFLP because the Arab world [took] centre stage [in the political space]. The size of the Palestinian branch of the ANM had also expanded greatly and there had been changes in its leadership, as well as in the mentality of its members. So, we joined the PFLP. I personally joined the Front, of course, because I believe that the Front, as a party, represents a relatively advanced stage, compared to other organisations in the field of Palestinian action. I believe that the way I see the future can be realised through this organisation. This is the main reason I joined the PFLP.

How do you see your role as editor-in-chief of the organisation's newspaper al-Hadaf? *Can you tell me something about its method of mass mobilisation?*

I am a member of this organisation, which in reality constitutes a party, with its own internal system and political strategy. It also has an organisational and leadership strategy based on democratic centralist principles. When the leadership assigns me a particular position, I must therefore complete a specific programme. I am a member of the Central Information Committee of the PFLP. *Al-Hadaf* is part of the media structure of the Front, according to our understanding of the media, which is not limited to propaganda, but goes beyond, to education, etc. I am not [solely] responsible for *al-Hadaf*. The task is entrusted to the Central Media Committee, and I represent this committee in the newspaper. In practical terms, I must deal with the organisational aspect of *al-Hadaf* as an institution, while we have a committee that reads and evaluates *al-Hadaf*, writes articles and discusses editorials. Within the Front, there are ten similar institutions and departments, and our institution may be smaller than the others. However, there are circles within the PFLP that practise social and political activities inside the camps. We also have those who work in the military struggle and other camps. Each of us is an integral part of the other. Of course, those who work in the organisational field – organising conferences, the educational programme, meetings and contacts with the masses – benefit from our newspaper, in order to express the standpoint of the PFLP. They also consult us regarding the masses. Therefore, as a result of these dynamic relations between them, all circles carry out a mass mobilisation campaign together.

Can you tell me something about the newspaper itself?

Working [on the paper] is very stressful. This is how I feel now that I have completed this week's issue. I feel exhausted. It's horrible for someone to work for a paper like this. By the time you finish the last sentence of one issue, you're suddenly faced with 20 blank pages to fill. In addition, every line, title and image in the paper is discussed by [members] of the Front, detecting even the slightest error. The newspaper is then subject to criticism the likes of which are unlike working on an ordinary newspaper. In an ordinary newspaper, you are obliged to merely do your work, but in our newspaper the smallest details are read carefully and discussed by the [different spheres within the Front]. It is therefore very difficult for a person to carry out such comprehensive work in this large court, made up of [other] members of the Front. So, one feels the imperative to work harder.

In addition, we currently operate in [Lebanon], a developing country (*min al-buldan al-namiyya* – من البلدان النامية). In the resistance movement, and in an organisation like ours, every department works to attract people with talents and competencies, however minor, to fulfil the work involved, since completing work and implementing assigned programmes are essential [duties] for the individual. We at *al-Hadaf* have a small number of employees, and when we ask the Front to assign us more workers, the answer we hear is: "Give us two or three of your employees to teach the rank and file (القواعد – *al-qawa'id*), because their work is more important than working at the newspaper." So, we remain silent, lest they take employees away from us. It is hard for others to believe that only three people edit *al-Hadaf*. This situation has existed for three years. Sometimes we receive [extra] help from a fourth person, but then this person leaves us, we replace them, and the story repeats itself.

Then you have to work day and night.

Yes. I don't think any of the colleagues work less than 13–14 hours a day. This is non-stop, without holidays and without mercy from criticism. Critique comes from people in our organisation, the government and other newspapers.

Do you consider al-Hadaf *to be a progressive newspaper, and do you think it reads like a progressive newspaper from a theoretical political angle?*

Yes, and I also think that causes a problem. I am not merely singing the praises of the paper, but it is very difficult to express deep political and theoretical ideas in a simple way. Few people have this ability. In the PFLP, we have two people with the ability to express such deep thoughts in a straightforward and easily understandable way for the reader. One of them is George Habash and another is a military leader who has written some wonderful pieces. For others, it is difficult, especially if they have not practised [writing] before. We always face criticism from the rank and file, that it is very difficult to understand what our newspaper writes, and that we must simplify things and write in a straightforward way.

That is why preparing the paper takes a lot of time, as I must revise the paper and simplify some of the points it raises after the writing takes place. I think that the creation of other internal newspapers within the Front would facilitate our task and the continuation of our work in this direction. An internal newspaper has the ability to express simple things and ideas, but a central, public newspaper like ours makes it difficult for us to imitate an internal newspaper due to the necessity of taking a serious public position. To do so, we are attempting to limit the number of articles that deal with complex political ideas, so that these articles take up a smaller number of pages and focus on direct political campaigns.

Do you publish literary works, like poetry and other works, in your newspaper?

We dedicate two pages [in each issue] to literature, film criticism, theatre, art, painting and more. I think the journalists mentioned earlier are the most popular, because the leftist line of thought running through these pages is well understood by many in the Front.

Have you personally published short stories?

I haven't had time to write [short stories] since I began working at *al-Hadaf*. In fact, I only [recently] published two stories about an old woman whom I write about regularly [Umm Saad]. I don't have time for literary writing, which is rather irritating.

Would you like to write more?

Usually, when I leave work at the office and return home, I feel so tired that I can't write. So, I read instead. And, of course, I must read for two hours a day because I cannot continue [to function] without it. But after I finish reading, I feel that going to sleep or watching a silly movie is preferable if I'm unable to write [after finishing work].

Do you think that recent developments within the Front are reflected in the fact that it has become a collective where debates abound, rather than a collective that engages in military activities?

No, I don't agree with you. In fact, in the Front, we have always insisted on a certain strategic line, whose motto is that "every political actor is also a fighter, and every fighter is also a political actor". As for the phenomenon you are witnessing now, it is not limited to us. This phenomenon is due to the fact that the Palestinian resistance movement is now witnessing a state of decline, due to objective circumstances that are working to destroy us at this period in time. We have lived through this state of decline since [Black] September 1970, which prevents us from increasing our military activities. But that does not mean that we are going to stop military action. This is [true] for the resistance movement in general. As for the PFLP in particular, our military operations in Gaza, the West Bank and Israel itself have intensified over the last two years. Israel is trying to repress these operations, but we remain active. We also have bases in southern Lebanon, and we are preparing for a covert people's war against the reactionaries in Jordan. However, the state of decay in which we live and the general repressive atmosphere imposed by the Arab governments affects public opinion and people think that our military activities have ceased. This conclusion is incorrect.

In your opinion, how has this state of decay affected the Palestinian individual, without referring to a specific political line?

Political movements resemble human beings. When a person is physically well, famous and wealthy, friends gather around him, and everyone supports him. But when he becomes old, sick and

35

loses his money, the friends around him disperse. Now we are [as a resistance movement] passing through this stage, the stage of apathy, so to speak. The Palestinian individual feels that the dreams he built up over the last few years have been undermined. This is a painful feeling, you know, but I think many comrades share my opinion: that this stage is temporary. When the Palestinian discovers that we are fighting a great enemy that we cannot defeat in a few years, that our war is long term and that we will be defeated repeatedly, then their loyalty to the Palestinian revolution will not be as fragile and emotional as it is now. I believe that we can mobilise the masses again when we win our first new victory. I am confident that this victory will come.

We are not afraid of this "low period" (فترة الفتور – fatrat al-futur) as I like to call it. This is normal, since Arab leaders and media spokesmen have made many promises to the masses, praising an easily achievable victory. Now, many Arabs have discovered that these promises were misleading. I do not believe, therefore, that this phenomenon is either inherent or continuous. We know that we will overcome this stage in the future and that the loyalty of the masses to the revolution will be stronger than before.

Were you or the leadership of the Front too optimistic in 1967, 1968 or 1969? Did you make too many promises? Did you see this conflict as an easy struggle?

No. In fact, the PFLP warned the masses through its written documents that the problem was not simple. It also warned them that they would be defeated repeatedly and would face many bloodbaths, tragedies and massacres. We have mentioned it many times, but generally speaking, the [PLO] leadership of the Palestinian revolution promised an easy victory before the masses. We are very optimistic and I can say that, despite being at the lowest point of our difficult struggle, our situation now is better than in 1967, 1968 or 1969, both from a scientific point of view and as a resistance movement forming an analysis through its own historical movement, rather than the phenomena of superficial appearances.

Written when Nasserism remained the defining influence on Palestinian socialism, Ghassan Kanafani's articles for *al-Muharrir* were accompanied by columns exposing European and US media claims on the region. Source: The Palestinian Museum.

2

Yemen and Iraq: One Story or Two? (1964)

Introduction: Restoring Palestine's Arab Depth –
the Pan-Arab Holism of Ghassan Kanafani
by *Patrick Higgins*

In November 1964, Ghassan Kanafani, then a 28-year-old journalist writing in the pages of *al-Muharrir*, the newspaper of the
Arab Nationalist Movement (ANM), took rapid account of sudden
changes sweeping through Yemen and Iraq. Kanafani encouraged readers to hold up a wide-angle lens to these events and
view them as connected, not as random or isolated happenings
in countries far-flung from one another.

In Yemen, Egyptian and Saudi leaders had just established the
tenuous Erkowit ceasefire agreement, arranged during secret
talks in Sudan. These negotiations had built gradually on earlier,
cautious contacts made between Egyptian and Saudi representatives that September at the Arab League conference in Alexandria,
where communication between the two parties broke the years of
silence caused by the proxy war they had been fighting against
each other in Yemen since 1962. By 1964, the Yemen war had
claimed the lives of thousands of Yemenis and an estimated
10,000 Egyptian soldiers. After Kanafani's article was published,
the Erkowit agreement collapsed and the fighting in Yemen continued for a further six years.

The term "proxy war", however, does not do justice to the
full weight of the local political stakes of the war in Yemen. The
conflict began with a Saudi counter-revolution against the 1962
anti-colonial and nationalist coup in North Yemen, led by Abdullah
al-Sallal against King Mohammed al-Badr, bringing an end to the
Mutawakkilite Kingdom of Yemen and marking the beginning of
the Yemen Arab Republic (YAR). Al-Sallal's military education in

Baghdad and his subsequent travels to Egypt, Syria, Palestine and Lebanon had put him in contact with Arab nationalists, dedicated to raising the standard of living for the poverty-stricken Arab masses. He had formed a secret alliance, the Free Officers, whose Free Yemeni Movement first attempted to take power in 1948. Fourteen years later – after al-Sallal had been imprisoned and his confederates tortured, and in some cases executed – the Movement finally seized the royal palace. Nasser's support for the young YAR was a matter of basic affinity, as he had himself led a Free Officers Movement to depose King Farouk during the revolution of 23 July 1952 in Egypt.

Immediately after the Yemeni coup, republican leaders brought in technical and military advisors from Egypt, the Soviet Union and China, while the Kingdom of Saudi Arabia began pumping money and guns into the hands of monarchist loyalists keen on retaking power. As Nasser said in a speech to soldiers returning from Yemen in 1963, he believed the Egyptian intervention was defending the "right to revolution". At the very beginning of the war in 1962, King Faisal of Saudi Arabia had made clear to US President John Kennedy the Saudi stance regarding an Egyptian presence in the southern Arabian Peninsula: Yemen, he said, was victim to "Nasser's aggression and Sallal's insurrection". Faisal, in pushing for a more aggressive US policy against Nasser's forces in Yemen, seethed at what he called Kennedy's "material assistance" to Egypt in the form of aid programmes. Despite Faisal's consternation, the Kennedy Administration professed internally that the object of US aid to Egypt was to induce a foreign policy in line with US preferences. And despite an official posture of "neutrality" in Yemen, Kennedy continued to provide weapons support to Saudi Arabia and its covert partner in Yemen, Israel, giving credence to Kanafani's reading of the situation, that the Western powers wanted to saddle and bleed Egypt in Yemen for as long as possible.

Meanwhile, Iraqi leaders announced in September 1964 that they were strongly considering embarking on a merger with Egypt under the banner of the United Arab Republic (UAR). A project of unity between the two countries would attempt to succeed where Egypt's prior unification with Syria had failed, dissolved in a military coup against the Nasser-backed UAR leadership in Damascus in September of 1961. Iraq's prospects for unification with Egypt, led by Ba'athist Abdul Salam Arif (who also played a supporting role in the Erkowit agreement), saw increased prospects for socialism, referred to by Kanafani as a "nationalisation wave". The Iraq–Egypt unity project was threatened by Mustafa al-Barzani's assertion of de facto autonomy in Northern Iraq. Kanafani observed – presciently, if one considers the current relationships of Kurdish leadership in Iraq and Syria with Israel – that the Kurdish movement appeared vulnerable to infiltration.

In this piece, two hallmarks of Kanafani's superb journalism come to the fore. The first is his pan-Arabist outlook and Nasserist sympathies, which were, during this period, essential components of his organisational experience with the ANM. The ANM goal of Arab unity did not arise solely out of revivalist predilections pertaining to language and culture, but represented a sustained, collective analysis, showing that the division of Arab lands forced their societies into dependence, vulnerability and internecine wars over resources. For the ANM, pan-Arabism served as a form of internationalism on a regional scale and opened up their perspective to wider events in Africa and Asia.

The second hallmark that Kanafani displays here is his incisive holism: his constant highlighting of connections. Kanafani was no "coincidence theorist", to use a phrase from Michael Parenti. As Kanafani himself writes here, "it is unacceptable to attribute such things to coincidences when a coherent analytical line is at hand". At a time when holistic analysis of the Arab region has fallen from favour, so that the ongoing wars in Syria, Iraq, Libya, Sudan and Yemen are treated as isolated phenomena, a return to Kanafani's method and analysis is desperately needed.

* * *

YEMEN AND IRAQ: ONE STORY OR TWO?[1]

Perhaps the past week's events are the gravest that the Arab world has witnessed for quite some time. I mean particularly the two main and almost concurrent events: first, the Erkowit agreement[2]

---

1 Original publication: *al-Muharrir*, 9 November 1964. Translated by Asma Hussein.
2 Meeting in Erkowit, eastern Sudan, on 2 November 1964, Yemeni royalist and republican forces agreed to a ceasefire and a national conference on 23 November,

concerning the Yemen question; and then the campaign against Iraq.[3]

At first glance, there seems to be no connection between the two events and any attempt to find one is deemed a failed contrivance. Nevertheless, since these two events co-symbolise a phase in the Arab progressive movement's complex and arduous combat with the forces opposing it, the connection is fundamental. Considering the concurrency of the two events as a pure coincidence is therefore unobjective; instead, it would be better contextualised in the stream that has been exposed to constant ebb and flow since September 1961.

Yemen

The Yemeni Revolution occurred at a period of historic downturn, during which the region's progressive stream was almost fatally besieged. Hence, from the first moment of its outbreak, it was considered a restitution of the progressive forces and a verification of their logic. In addition to its essential and historical value as a successful translation of the masses' will for change, the Yemeni Revolution is a process with multiple implications that cannot be ignored: first, it is a forthright test of the resilience and seriousness of the progressive forces in the region; second, it has widely opened the door of the new round for [these forces]; and third, it presents a historic opportunity to catch a breath and tilt the balance in favour of the liberation movement and Arab progress.

For all of these reasons, the Yemeni Revolution marked a decisive turning point in the position of the revolutionary forces in the region. The available options were immediate and critical: the rev-

---

calling for UAR and Saudi support in facilitating the dialogue; Egypt and the Soviet Union had supported the republican cause, while the Saudi regime backed the royalist forces. These and subsequent talks came to little, and the war raged on.

3   During this period under the leadership of Abdul Salam Arif, Iraq had once again become closer to Egypt and the UAR, agreeing to form a joint Presidential Council and a Unified Political Command on 14 October. September had seen a failed Ba'athist coup, with its leaders Ahmed Hassan al-Bakr and Saddam Hussein arrested.

olutionary forces would either be up to their historical mission and embrace this experience or they would not. The latter case offers little room for choice, since letting the opportunity pass without a response would not only maintain the siege enforced on the revolutionary forces, but also push them further backwards, escalating the fight to its attack phase, on all levels.

On the spur of these critical choices (both equally immediate and grave), the first group of Egyptian paratroopers landed in Yemen. During the ten months that followed this landing, the Arab forces in Yemen rose in number, from 5,000 to 10,000, 20,000 and 25,000 fighters, whose supplies, from bread to munitions, were provided by the United Arab Republic (UAR). Under these circumstances, it was not claimed that the operation was a "military excursion" (*nazha 'askariyya* – نزهة عسكرية), since the simplest principles of combat showed that the case is otherwise: 2,000 miles away from their bases, the soldiers on challenging, mountainous terrains were fighting a battle-hardened enemy, bolstered by a huge financial power in the north and a foreign superpower in the south.

British intelligence reports recommended that policymakers not recognise the Republic, since its |existence| would last "merely a matter of days, or, at best, months". Israeli, US and Western press reported that, generally, the fight in Yemen is "out of the ordinary", and that things "cannot continue this way for two months". Not only have things continued, but they have also led to significant results: an insurrection broke out in the south against the British presence in Aden; the [Yemeni] Republican government adopted its constitutional and administrational principles; and the foundations of the National Army were laid. Throughout 16 months of bloody fighting, the counter-revolutionary forces failed and regressed.

Despite this, the present article does not aim to survey the context of Erkowit. The development of political reality is not governed by wishful thinking, but rather by a set of objective circumstances that surround it. Therefore, criticism should consequently be illuminated by these objective circumstances, whose complexity and realism shape a given situation.

Besides the tasks of the revolutionary forces in Yemen, there were others that could not be sidestepped or ignored:

- In the UAR itself, there is the daily, demanding process of the construction of socialism, with all its requirements in terms of material resources and manpower.

- On the UAR's eastern borders stands an enemy whose main interest is to keep the powerful Arab Army[4] far from its fronts.

- The two summit conferences have proved that any Arab anti-Israeli effort cannot be realised unless the Arab Army in the UAR is able to shift between different fronts.

- It has become evident that the Western powers and the reactionary forces at their command wish to have the Egyptians bogged down in Yemen for as long as possible, for the sake of the easy manipulation of certain tribes. They wish, in addition, to effectuate a slow and continuous exhaustion of the material and human forces [operating] at a 2,000-mile distance from their bases.

- It has become increasingly evident that the revolutionary situation in Yemen, torn between its programme and the objective circumstances in the country, will ever be subject to a stark paradox that necessitates keeping a defensive force on Yemen's side, even if the reactionary forces and the colonisers cease their offensive.

- The developing situations among the Arab powers, along with the negative historical role of the Ba'ath [movement], have confirmed that those who adopt [mere] slogans of Arab struggle will be unable to take historical responsibility towards the UAR in Yemen. Moreover, regarding the events in the east [of the country], they play an endlessly disruptive role.

- Saudi Arabia has made it "clear" that, with the continued support of the Western powers, it will not cease in causing anarchy, chaos and disorder in Yemen. Its losses are minimal in all cases, since: first, it has the money and could choose parsimony when it comes to Saudi [citizens'] welfare, or squandering when it comes to bribery and stirring unrest; and second, it has given itself license to "sacrifice" its recruits, down to the last tribesman.

---

4   The army of the UAR.

Enumerating these circumstances is not about justifying anything, but about giving a clear perspective of the situation in Yemen. This perspective would, accordingly, facilitate in following what has happened, rather than being led by pure "temperament", in the logic of many observers.

Nevertheless, the burning question has not yet been posed: having understood these circumstances, what are the benefits of the Erkowit agreement for the Yemeni Revolution and the Arab revolutionary forces?

It has been evident, ever since the Republic of Yemen announced it had "cleared" the Yemeni land of the frontal forces, that there is a tendency to "solve" the Yemeni question on the conditions proposed by the Republic. In the two summit conferences, this tendency informed the correspondence between the UAE and Saudi Arabia. There was a common feeling that the Republic was capable of surviving under any circumstances. But it was equally felt that Saudi Arabia could also sustain disruption and unrest under any circumstances. This is the ugly truth. Ignoring it is blindness.

The agreement was premised on recognising that the political front no longer exists, and that the Republic is an inevitable fact, which might not prevail in the short term, perhaps, but in the long run.

The forces that have managed to fight with arms for 16 continuous months should prove their efficacy in fighting for their principles, on a more serious level than arms, that is. Let us admit that this "compositional rhetoric" is worthless, but it at least indexes one thing: that a new battle has been declared since Erkowit. Six months of fighting have not concluded with absolute victory but has rather put Yemen on the threshold of a new phase of battle.

For Saudi Arabia and those who tail-end it (*thyulha* – ذيولها), Erkowit is a second attempt, after the failure of the "renegade wars" was publicly acknowledged.[5] For Republican Yemen, it is a "new

---

5 Dubbed the "nutcracker" campaign, the British imperialist military intervention was likewise a failure, while its spokespeople admitted to the effectiveness of guerrillas in Radfan; see Fred Halliday, *Arabia without Sultans* (London: Penguin, 1974), 195–96.

round" of implementing new mechanisms for continuing a revolution that has now been struggling for a year and a half. In this case, the odds are as even as they have ever been and as they should be in any battle.

Now, one cannot weigh one possibility over another. But there remains one reservation: revolution is a reality, and – as history has shown us in akin cases – it cannot be uprooted, whatever the ebb and flow qualities of its manifestations. Is it necessary to place a label on what has happened? We shall leave this to headline buffs. But what has happened, all that has happened, in 16 months, both within and outside of Yemen, will remain. It is what has happened through millennia in Yemeni and world history.

Iraq

The observer wonders whether the tendency towards aggravating the situation in Iraq is a plan based on the assumption that creating a crisis in Iraq, coupled with the unstable Yemeni situation, would deal Cairo a decisive blow. The counter-revolutionary forces wished that Yemen would be Cairo's end. After months of waiting, this appeared fully unattainable, but after the second summit, it seemed that escalating the Iraqi situation before settling the Yemeni question would absolutely eliminate the "aspirations" of the revolutionary forces in Cairo.

This is, perhaps, why the campaign against Iraq exploded in Tehran, Istanbul, Damascus and Geneva, unexpectedly – a few days before Erkowit. Coincidence? No, it is unacceptable to attribute such things to coincidences when a coherent analytical line is at hand. In the Iraqi case, there is more than one line:

- For the lurking forces, the military agreement between Iraq and Egypt is more than a legal issue. Having in mind that the Egyptian military force in Yemen has prevented, under extremely harsh conditions, the destabilisation of the young regime, its presence in Iraq is much more meaningful.
- The relationship between the UAE and Iraq has become more than a "legal agreement", and the nationalisation wave could now sweep the field of oil.

- Iraq, which has always been part of an alliance with Iran and Turkey, proved incapable of playing a role in the region due to the Kurdish question. Now, Iraq is on its way to stability, which will eventually threaten the rest of the alliance.
- Iraq was always a victim of the Arab and Kurdish relationships it embodied. For its enemies, its Arab connections are firm and have stronger prospects [of withstanding intervention]. Regarding its Kurdish connections, infiltration remains a possibility but, in this regard, time is on Iraq's side, since it remains open to just and socialist solutions to the Kurdish problem.[6]

The question now is whether the campaign against Iraq is based on the principle of dispersing Cairo's military and ideological efforts on two, far-flung fronts: south and east, militarily and ideologically. Or, is the plan based on the tendency to exhaust Cairo: having been done with Yemen, will [Egypt] face a new "Yemen" in Iraq?

Be it the first or the second possibility, there is no doubt that Iraq will be the battlefield of this phase unless events in Yemen abruptly dominate, once again. However, it is unmistakable that there is a strong feeling among the anti-Cairo parties, within and without, that this is the phase when they should "attack", after a long period during which Cairo took the initiative in attacking.

Have the conference summit and its governing logic any connection to this new strategy?

This is the question.

---

6 Though the Arif government had waged war on the Kurds, Kanafani's assertion of its ability to resolve these differences came as the Nasser government applied diplomatic pressure towards a settlement of the Kurdish issue in Iraq. By November 1964, a Kurdish autonomous government was operating from Bushkin, northern Iraq.

3

Fares Fares: This is the Famous Professor (1965)

Introduction by *As'ad AbuKhalil*

Little is known in the West about the journalistic career of Ghassan Kanafani. Though he was editor of the highly influential revolutionary magazine, *al-Hadaf* (1969–1972), he did not found it; the idea belonged to Wadi' Haddad, while Kanafani secured its initial funding. But Kanafani had already left his imprint in Lebanese journalism in a variety of media. From 1964 to 1967, he edited the *Filastin* supplement of the highly influential *al-Muharrir*, a staunch Arab nationalist newspaper. That supplement introduced Palestine to a whole new generation of people. Kanafani did not write in the stale style of the Arab nationalists and communists of the day. He, for one, had a sense of humour, while they had none. He did not believe that a revolutionary should carry himself too seriously, either in life or in writing. As a political commentator, he was at once witty, sometimes scholarly and always interesting.

This style and substance set him apart and was a reason for his assassination. Kanafani was a member of the Popular Front for the Liberation of Palestine (PFLP) Central Media Committee but was made a member of its politburo only posthumously, in order to honour his contribution. He edited the Sunday supplement of *al-Anwar* from 1967 to 1970 (at a time when it remained Arab nationalist in outlook), and also wrote under a pen name – and he had a few, of which Fares Fares is now the most well-known – in *al-Hawadith*, the most widely read Lebanese weekly magazine of its day. Kanafani had honed his skills in political journalism in *al-Hurriyya* magazine, the mouthpiece of the Arab Nationalist Movement, prior to the founding of the PFLP in 1967. His political column revealed a person who read voraciously, in many different fields and disciplines, and he wrote about and commented on all of them. This short article is a thinly disguised attack on the progressive leftists of the day, who he did not take seriously, and who were full of themselves. But Ghassan Kanafani had also detected a new trend that was forming: of opportunist Arab intellectuals who did not have a core belief system.

* * *

THIS IS THE FAMOUS PROFESSOR[1]

He is the "professor" of them all, and their professor in particular. He is the master of gossip and insidiousness; the writer of unsigned articles, the one who inspires them, without labels. He is the one who offers his services to both sides of a conflict, like the trader in smuggled arms, with one difference that he does not covet a salary; self-sufficiency is the salary of the masked persuader. His self-sufficiency does not come except through success in insidiousness, viewing the world turned upside down and the prevalence of talking behind others' backs, and insults, cursing and brawling.

If you agree with him, he disagrees with you, even about his own name. And if you disagree with him, he agrees with you just for fun, which is his only profession in this busy existence.

He is a "Professor", although he has not read anything in the past ten years other than his own identity card and reads it twice a day out of doubt and suspicion. If it was not for his photograph, he would have said to Nasserists that it was a Ba'athist conspiracy, and to the Ba'athists that it was a Nasserist conspiracy, and would have told both, if they were present together accidentally, that it was an Italian conspiracy.

He is the first inventor of linguistic fads, which are his special rockets in a world that still does not know that it has manufactured spacecraft that fly to the moon.

He gets his information from coffee shop tables and his political stances from the contradicting positions that he hears by accident.

---

1 Originally published in *al-Muharrir*, 19 June 1965. Translated by As'ad AbuKhalil.

He offers his services to everybody, for the price of patiently listening to him. And if he calculates that the price of listening to him is too cheap, it is because you have not listened to him yet.

His name? Unimportant: he is willing to change it, if necessary, because, to him, the changing of names and stances are way easier than you could imagine.

But if he were to change his own name, it is certain that he would keep his title, because it is the only thing that is not written on his own identity card.

PART II

War, Defeat and Revolutionary Critique

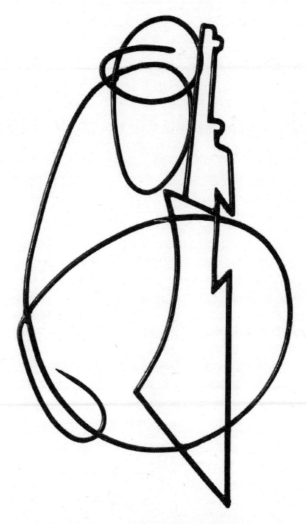

A metalwork sculpture by Ghassan Kanafani. One of a number of artworks in which the fate of Palestine is tied to the armed struggle for its liberation. Here the rifle points north, to Lebanon, with Palestinians in the vanguard of new resistance. Source: Ghassan Kanafani Cultural Foundation.

4

Resistance is the Essence (1967)

Introduction by *Louis Brehony*

Before its dust had settled, Ghassan Kanafani saw in the consequences of June 1967 a disaster more severe than 1948. Casualties
of the Naksa were numbered beyond mass Palestinian displacement,[1] the military catastrophe suffered by Egyptian-led forces
and the direct Zionist conquest of Palestinian, Syrian, Lebanese
and Egyptian lands. Arab socialism had been dealt a body blow,
with its proponents at pains to find realpolitik solutions. Though
the crisis was marked in some quarters by intellectual fatalism,
Kanafani and his comrades would take spirit from the rising
movement of Palestinian *fida'iyyin* and disembark with revolutionary optimism for the path ahead.

Nationalised by the Nasser government in 1960, the Egyptian
weekly *al-Musawwar* served as its official organ in the period to
follow. Among the magazine's leading voices was the journalist
Ahmed Baha'iddin, who analysed the Naksa crisis by appealing for the creation of a state in partitioned regions of Palestine,
now under direct Zionist occupation. Originally printed in the
6 October 1967 issue of the magazine, Baha'iddin's proposals
attracted commentary from a range of Palestinian figures. Seeing
an opportunity for Jordanian resisters to fight alongside the insur-
gent PLO, the then leading figure Shafiq al-Hout, a personal
friend of Baha'iddin, welcomed the suggestion of the West Bank
forming the crucible of a Palestinian state;[2] al-Hout would later
staunchly oppose the Oslo "peace" deal which some claimed
would do just that.

---

1 For reading on 1967, see Nur Masalha (ed.), *The Politics of Denial: Israel and
the Palestinian Refugee Problem* (London: Pluto, 2003).
2 Ahmed Baha'iddin, *Iqtirah Dawlet Filastin* (Beirut: Dar al-Adab, 1968),
36–37.

Though he did not off-handedly dismiss the recommendations, Kanafani's criticism of Baha'iddin was, in one sense, a critique of Nasserism itself, and hinted at the now heightened influence of communist-led anti-colonial movements on Palestinian Marxism. Warning against the application of "solutions" such as those that had partitioned India and Pakistan, Kanafani adopted a flexible notion of the state, as a dialectical and changing entity determined in the course of popular struggle. This argument would come full circle with the call of Kanafani and the Popular Front for the Liberation of Palestine (PFLP) for "Arab Hanois", pointing clearly to the difference between being reduced to a shrinking portion of the land or liberating it.

This critique of statehood as an end goal in itself makes for interesting reading in light of Mahmoud Abbas' UN recognition bids. In 1996, the Netanyahu government was the first Zionist administration to use the term "Palestinian state". Minister of Information, David Bar-Illan clarified: "Semantics don't matter. If Palestinian sovereignty is limited enough so that we feel safe, call it fried chicken."[3] With a Palestinian Authority (PA) apparatus seemingly geared towards making this colonialist exhortation a reality, Kanafani's scientific socialist approach contrasts starkly.

We see in this short article prismatic shards of the revolutionary Marxism that had now found its full embodiment among Palestinian socialists. Reflecting this journey, Kanafani joins twentieth-century revolutionaries ranging from Che Guevara, Hồ Chí Minh and Franz Fanon to Alexandra Kollontai in raising together the questions of socialism, liberation and the new human being. Hồ had written in 1957 that: "To transform the world and society, we must, first and foremost, transform ourselves".[4] This transformation was observed in the dynamism of the struggle in Algeria, where Fanon saw a "new humanity", unrecognisable even from its immediate history.[5]

Like Che, Kanafani saw as essential the creation of humans capable of revolutionising their conditions. Whereas, in post-liberation Cuba, Che envisaged a new man and woman emerging

---

3 David Bar-Illan, "Palestinian Self-Rule, Israeli Security: An interview with Victor Cygielman", *Palestine–Israel Journal* 3, no. 3 (Summer 1996).
4 *Selected Hồ Chí Minh*, ed. Vijay Prashad (New Delhi: Leftworld, 2022), 279.
5 Frantz Fanon, *A Dying Colonialism*, trans. Haakon Chevalier (New York: Grove, 1994), 27–28.

from party-led education in the process of socialist construction, Kanafani saw the new Palestinian as both a prerequisite and result of the movement – and organisation – for liberation. Here, his vision finds similarities in Amilcar Cabral, who observed the "new awareness" in the creation of new men, women and children as "the most important result of the struggle", in the context of a deepening anti-colonial struggle in Guinea and Cape Verde.[6] For Kanafani, ultimately, the "fighting people", not negotiations or halfway measures, would determine the shape of the future. Palestine itself would be reflected in those dedicated to its recovery. In Ghassan Kanafani, all roads lead to the masses.

* * *

RESISTANCE IS THE ESSENCE[7]

The proposal of Ahmed Baha'iddin on the issue of recreating a Palestinian state in Jordan and Gaza (*al-Musawwar*, 13 October [1967]) will appear to many as putting the cart before the horse. But I think the problem is doubly more difficult than that. If now is a suitable time to revisit old records, to make it easier for us to become acquainted with the new entries, the worst thing about these records is that the Arabs of Palestine, and the Arabs in general, rejected a similar suggestion in 1948. At midnight on 15 May of that year, as Israel announced the creation of its first government, the thought didn't cross the mind of any Arab that announcing a Palestinian government that same night would have significantly changed the course of events in the 20 years that followed.

Is it possible to right this wrong after 20 years? After a disaster even more bitter than the disaster of 1948? This is certainly possible, provided that we acknowledge from the start that it would be more difficult and less effective on this occasion than it would have been

---

6 Amilcar Cabral, *Return to the Source* (New York: Monthly Review Press, 2023), 53.

7 Original publication: *Al-Adab*, October 1967. See also Ghassan Kanafani, *Al-Dirasat al-Siyasiyya* [*Political Writings, Vol. 5*] (Cyprus: Rimal Books, 2015), 479–84. Translation by Louis Brehony and Ameen Nemer. An earlier version of this translation appeared on the website of the Revolutionary Communist Group in July 2022.

in 1948. However, all of this does not at all mean that the suggestion is not an effective gateway to a domain whose doors, at the moment, appear to be completely closed.

Nevertheless, discussion of this proposal in the first place requires us to establish several points that are related, directly and indirectly, to the matter as a whole:

First, that the greatest crime committed against the rights of the Palestinian people, after the crime committed by Zionism, in alliance with imperialism, was the crime of stripping (*khala* ʿ – خلع) the Palestinian people of their cause, then stripping them from what remained of Palestine. In actuality, this did not take place with 1948, but rather after 1936, when the waves of Palestinian revolution practically constituted a rising of the Arab movement for freedom – and when Arab regimes were still incapable of perceiving the organic link between Zionism and colonialism, and felt unashamed in appealing to the Palestinians to end the revolution, relying on the promises of "our friend Britain".[8]

Second, the isolation of the Palestinians from their cause, whether intentional or not, has led to the "dispossession of the Palestinian", after the dispossession of his land. This analogy is deliberate. Namely, that what happened on the level of the land happened to the human being. The Palestinian land was violated (*intuhkat* – انتُهكت) and the Palestinian was also violated. What is left of the Palestinian land has not been allowed to remain Palestinian and so what is left of the Palestinian people has not been allowed to remain, in the combative sense, Palestinian.

Third, and as a result of the first two points, the question of a Palestinian entity[9] remained passive and unattainable at the required

---

8 Kanafani would expand on this analysis in his seminal 1972 text *The Revolution of 1936–39 in Palestine*, quoting Saudi and Iraqi royalists lobbying on behalf of British imperialism. Based on the *effendiyya*, or urban regional elite, this role found expression in Palestine, "manifested in this bourgeoisie's role as licenced agents for British, and in some cases Jewish, industry"; see Ghassan Kanafani, *The Revolution of 1936–39 in Palestine: Background, Details, and Analysis*, trans. Hazem Jamjoum (New York: 1804 Books, 2023), 52–52.

9 Kanafani does not, at this point, use the word *dolah*, which more clearly denotes a "state", but rather *kiyan*, meaning entity or a state of being. When he uses *dolah* later in the article, he does so in parenthesis.

level. This is not because land is necessary for such an entity, no matter how small the land is, but because the Arab countries who had acted as the custodians of the Palestinian people proved incapable of ending this custodianship and allowing the people of Palestine to decide for themselves.

It is these points, in my opinion, which would necessarily lead to the adoption of the proposals of Ahmed Baha'iddin, if there existed a genuine intention to support the Palestinian people to recover themselves, their land and take the lead, again, in the decisive field of struggle. However, the Palestinian state proposed by Ahmed Baha'iddin in the West Bank, East Bank and Gaza (and, I would add, vast swathes along the Syrian borders) requires more than a mere political decision based on geographical principles.

This brings us back to the story of the horse and the cart, and I think it is a waste of time thinking about which is in front of the other when right now neither the horse nor the cart is within our reach.

The movement to create a "Palestinian state" must inevitably go hand-in-hand with the "creation" of a new Palestinian human. And for as long as they consider themselves custodians, it is a role that Arab countries must collectively take upon themselves to build, side-by-side with the Palestinian people.

After 20 years of wandering and exile, Palestinians have remained capable of *sumud* ([steadfastness] *istata' al-Filastini... in yusmud* – استطاع الفلسطيني... أن يصمد) in the face of all of the treacherous conditions that confront them. I do not think that they have given up their Palestinian identity, despite everything. Yet, there is no doubt that the relationship among Palestinians has become one of exile and displacement, rather than a revolutionary relationship. The demand for "land", in my view, should be accompanied by a demand to create new relationships among Palestinians, as well as between them and Arab states. This question runs parallel in importance to the creation of a Palestinian state, since the latter will not be created as an ordinary state, but as a "state of transition", a "state of mission", or a "state with a message". This means that the immediate demand – along with the creation of the state of Palestine – is for the creation of a people who embody the cause of this state.

Here is not the space for detailed discussion on how this would happen. However, there is no doubt that at the forefront of what needs to be done is to create a new relationship between the Arab states and the Palestinian people, in order for this state to emerge, with the Palestinian cause as the "cornerstone" for Arabism. And then to find a way, either through coercion or free will, to mobilise the Palestinian people, with all of the wasted potential that I have discussed elsewhere, to put in place a Palestinian and Arab strategy for the Palestinian state to fulfil its mission.

All of this brings to our attention the dangerous caveats contained in the following points:

First, that this state is considered the solution to the Palestinian cause. Second, that it will be an excuse for the international public opinion to liquidate the Palestinian cause, based on the erroneous understanding that the Palestinian cause is a refugee issue. Third, that this state will fail to achieve sufficient international recognition. Fourth, its ability to become, like Pakistan, split down the centre, or on the other hand, like West Germany under the imposition of the Holstein agreement.[10] And fifth, the ability of this state to remain steadfast in the face of Israeli retaliations.

It is encouraging to note that the Palestinian resistance in the occupied territories is more capable of linking the fate of the West Bank and Gaza than resistance elsewhere, and this certainly bolsters Baha'iddin's theory, giving objective justification to the suggestions. There is no doubt that this resistance, in its later stages, will be more capable of achieving two inseparable aspects of our proposal: the creation of the state with a message, and the creation of a fighting people.

---

10 The modern Schleswig-Holstein region was historically the subject of dispute between Germany and Denmark. It fell within the territory of the West German state at the time of Kanafani's writing.

Ghassan Kanafani speaks in Beirut. "Thoughts on Change" was just one example of Kanafani's public speaking. He'd confidently argue his case among comrades and in the hornet's nest of international journalists. Source: Al Jazeera.

5

Thoughts on Change and the "Blind Language" (1968)

Introduction: From the Ashes of Gaza,
a Volcano Erupts by *Rabab Abdulhadi*

The ongoing Israeli genocide in Gaza makes writing or engaging in any intellectual activities outside this context completely meaningless. This is the context within which we can understand this lecture given by Ghassan Kanafani in 1968 and which was published in *al-Hadaf* during the first months of the Intifada of the Stones, a term that I find superior to the more commonly used, "First Intifada". Why did *al-Hadaf* decide to publish these two lectures over 20 years later? What was the significance of these lectures in 1988?

Commemorating Ghassan Kanafani is not a random or an isolated act, but a radical praxis aimed at defeating the colonial strategy of imposing a collective amnesia on the colonised to effect defeatism, releasing the colonising community of any sense of responsibility and in turn accountability for historic and current genocidal crimes, including what we witness in Gaza today, aimed at removing Palestine and Palestinians from the map, destroying living proof that this land belongs to its indigenous people. Kanafani gave this lecture in Beirut in March 1968, months after the 6 June 1967 Israeli occupation of the rest of historic Palestine and weeks before the Battle of al-Karameh, in which the Palestinian *fida'iyyin* and Jordanian nationalist movement defeated the mighty Israeli military, much like what we're seeing in Gaza today.

Kanafani's writing is timeless, not solely because of the revival of his work and widening interest in the ranks of solidarity activists, spreading around the 40th and 50th anniversaries of his martyrdom. I would argue that *al-Hadaf* published this lecture in 1988 because of the debate within the Palestinian movement in general and the Palestinian left in particular on whether there was a role for a cadre organisation, amid the broadening mass movement that characterised the Intifada. Perhaps *al-Hadaf* sought to intervene in this serious debate by invoking the words of this legendary leader who is loved and revered by Palestinians, irrespective of the Western or US academy.

Another reason is the significance of the specific language we use, and the impact or detriment certain expressions can have for the Palestinian and other struggles for liberation. This assumes additional importance when we remind ourselves of the need to defy the imposed colonial strategy of collective amnesia aimed at systematically erasing Palestine, eradicating the Palestinians and erasing our narratives and traces. It might also be to instil a sense of humility and collectivism, two ingredients that represent oxygen to revolutionary movements and discourses.

To be clear, Kanafani's lecture was not published in *al-Tha'ir*, the secret pamphlet of the Arab National Movement (ANM), as the late Barbara Harlow suggests. According to Palestinian writer and intellectual Marwan Abd el-'Al, it was published in *al-Hurri-yya* magazine when Kanafani was its editor-in-chief. Abd el-'Al says that Kanafani was debating with his earlier comrades, who split from the ANM and the Popular Front for the Liberation of Palestine (PFLP) to form the Democratic Front for the Liberation of Palestine (DFLP). According to Abd el-'Al, some of Kanafani's arguments made it to the political programme of the PFLP that became known as the "August programme". Those who formed the DFLP demanded a complete break with the Arab National Movement, while Kanafani belonged to the other part of the movement that called for the development of the PFLP by building on the rich, radical heritage of the ANM, instead of throwing out the baby with the bathwater. In other words, to develop a Marxist organisation that did not exclude Arabism.

The debate was rich and serious. It grew out of attempting to address the roots of the 1967 defeat: Did the Arab defeat signal the failure of Arabism as a concept and thus the necessity to abandon *qawmiyya* (Arab liberationism) altogether? However, some of the intellectuals sought to lay all the blame inwards, attributing the defeat to subjective conditions, such as the failure of the Arabs.

Though it is clear that Kanafani did not for one minute question the sincerity of his comrades' motives, he nonetheless sharply criticised their emphasis on self-flagellation that he characterised as "excessive". He did not disagree that internal or subjective factors are essential but vehemently rejected Orientalist and colonialist tropes whereby colonised people are envisioned by their racist coloniser as "unworthy and incapable of developing and growth".

There is a generational and class distinction made, I think, when Kanafani mentions the "patriarchy", and then the "new blood" and energy of youth. What was he really arguing here? That the movement should dispense with traditionalist leaderships and build a new form of organisation? He asserts that patriarchy is "a social rule that is not easily eliminated". Defining patriarchy as "a remnant of feudalism" and the "demand by elders of total submission of the youth without questioning", Kanafani does not call for the elimination of the family as a social institution but rather stresses the need for the old to respect the young, a necessary condition for "expedited social transformation".

How to grow new leadership in general and in the face of a brutal settler colonial regime intent on plucking the life out of the leaders and intellectuals as it is among the people, from babies to the elderly? Kanafani was a committed member of the central committee of the PFLP, a Marxist–Leninist cadre organisation. Thus, he did not, nor did the PFLP, advocate a non-hierarchical structure as many of the movements demand today or as anarchist theory posits. Here, Kanafani's emphasis on the necessity of a cadre organisation and the respect for "genuine democracy" and "multiplicity of internal opinions" goes hand in hand with a party of youthful renewal that rejects sectarianism, detects all the "blind language" of repression, breaks the chains of oppression, and brings about a steadfast new dawn in universities, cultural and intellectual circles, families and communities.

What is happening now is only the labour pains of something great that will be born from the rubble of defeat like a volcano born from under the cold ashes of a forsaken mountain.

This is Ghassan Kanafani in 1968.
This is Gaza today!

* * *

THOUGHTS ON CHANGE AND
THE "BLIND LANGUAGE"[1]

This platform has seen now many qualified professors examining different sides to the reasons for the defeat (*al-hazima* – الهزيمة), its underlying circumstances, the challenge it raises, and the immediate obligations with which that defeat confronts one side or another of our society.[2] Everything that has been said until now proves one point at least, and on which there is complete agreement: given what has happened, what is happening, and what will happen, the issue must be considered from different sides, for there is no single perspective, no single mistake. The defeat cannot be summarised in a slogan nor vindicated by accusation.

This very platform then is a condensation of sorts of what is happening in practice throughout the Arab world in the aftermath of a profound crisis: discussion breaks out from all sides, reproducing the situation. The different sides cannot be expressed on a single front nor by a single individual. The effort to comprehend all that has been said will alone give the discussion its meaning, its usefulness, and its future.

But before beginning my own intervention into this discussion I want to make clear that the position from which I speak can be

---

1   Original lecture delivered 11 March 1968 at Dar al-Nadwa, Beirut and published in *Muhadarat al-Nadwa* (June 1968). It was republished in *al-Hadaf* 919 and 920 (17 and 24 July 1988). This translation by Barbara Harlow and Nejd Yaziji first appeared in *Alif: Journal of Comparative Poetics*; see Ghassan Kanafani, "Thoughts on Change and the 'Blind Language'", *Alif: Journal of Comparative Poetics* 10 (1990): 137–57, https://doi.org/10.2307/521722. Reprinted with the permission of the journal. The PFLP translation of this title is "Thoughts on Renewal and the 'Blind Language'".

2   According to Barbara Harlow, "Kanafani's examination of the multiple contradictions, of greater or lesser magnitude, confronting the Arab world in the aftermath of the defeat responds critically to Mao Tse Tung's 1957 statement 'On the Correct Handling of Contradictions among the People.'" The lecture's critique of individual leadership is linked to Gramsci, relating to debates on vanguard emerging among resistance organisations from Latin America to the Philippines, while providing a material critique of the enemy position finds confluence in the works of Cabral and Fanon; see Barbara Harlow, "Introduction to Kanafani's 'Thoughts on Change and the 'Blind Language'", *Alif* 10 (1990): 134–35, https://doi.org/10.2307/521721.

a meaningful part of the subject – if it is to have any meaning at all – only in the context of the many defined dimensions provided already by colleagues on this platform. There are points that I am omitting, reasons greater perhaps than the ones I will indicate, more important clarifications than what I see to be the order of priorities. The following pages do not negate this, however, but rather form an interconnected link in the chain of actual meaning. The role of outside forces in the story must be explored in depth, as must the role and extent of counter-forces from within. Then there are the results of the interactions of social and economic forces and the Arab style of political work over the last ten years. There are other reasons and concerns that even the enemy is unable to categorise or deny; and, since they are not categorisable, they are not pertinent.

Taken in isolation the presentation proposed here is perhaps partial, but, located within the larger story of this platform and 16 other voices, it finds, if you will, a kind of completion.

*   *   *

Periods of defeat in a people's history are witness to a rapid growth in critical spirit that can often develop into resentment and anger. Yet this critical spirit, even in the form of resentment and anger, remains an indispensable constructive capacity. The human power to rise from a fall is the power to judge and find guilty, the capacity to correct a mistake is indeed the capacity to discover that mistake in the first place. Thus, a people's periods of defeat take on a rigorous and stern examining character, an internal sort of self-punishment, its basic aim being to increase its capability of self-defence. This critical spirit in times of defeat seems all at once to awaken human feelings in times of danger, feelings that double the capacity for both self-awareness and confrontation. All this is, no doubt, a constructive phenomenon – both necessary and indispensable – as long as it is basically motivated by an exit from defeat.

Periods of defeat, however, witness not only the awakening of a spirit of criticism and re-examination, but another very closely related phenomenon as well, namely, that of the spirit of criticism gone beyond its own limits into a kind of withdrawal through an exaggerated form of self-punishment. Such a phenomenon represents a still more dangerous side to periods of defeat. In describing the awakening of a critical spirit, we are using the analogy of a human being who, confronting danger, doubles the capabilities of his feelings of self-awareness and confrontation. The description of the critical spirit surpassing its own limits may trigger in another human being who, surrounded by danger, would lose the courage of the awakening of this feeling, thereby adding the spectre of illusions to the danger he confronts. He, thus, loses not only the ability to evaluate his capacities, but that of directing them as well.

In any case, we are presently confronting a combination of the two situations: in the face of the tendency towards courageous re-examination that we observe here and there, there is another tendency towards lamentation that leads only to a withdrawal behind a veil of criticism. In the name of criticism and re-examination in periods of defeat, this latter tendency, less capable of steadfastness (*sumud* – صمود), plays a game of suicide. It thus enters into the confusion of assessing things, factors and situations and makes enormous mistakes in understanding their real weight and place within the shaky picture that it has sketched. Such a game finds fertile ground amid the ruptures generalised now by the defeat. From here it acquires its dangerous capacity for destruction.

In these critical periods, the task of the researcher takes on a deeper role than it has had at any other time in the past, requiring a twofold courage: on the one hand, a critical power; and on the other, a devotion to what must not be destroyed. The distinction between these two sides of the task is an extremely precise one. If the researcher takes just one extra step in the direction of criticism, he falls into the confusion of assessment. One step too many in the direction of devotion to traditional givens and he falls into a state of resignation in the face of the now unacceptable. The danger of a period of defeat – that carries within it both the seeds of construction and the seeds of destruction – requires a true grasp of what must be rejected and what must be defended. Only absolute rejection is easier than absolute devotion.

*   *   *

Our generation used to see in its schoolbooks an unforgettable photograph. This photograph, taken in the second decade of this century, shows a man mounted gloriously on a charger. A shining sword glistens in his hands with which he boldly confronts a Turkish airplane about to destroy him. This was a true picture – not a film, nor mere sensationalism, but a unique and terrifyingly realistic representation of how the Arabs looked on the twentieth century from within the great Arab revolution.

Exactly half a century separates this picture-symbol from our-selves. And if we step back from the maelstrom engulfing us and troubling our own time, we will see that what has happened over the last half century seems to be a miraculous development. None-theless, it has not been quite half a century, since in reality the Arabs confronted the age not much more than 25 years ago when "local men" (al-rijal al-mahalliyun – الرجال المحليون) took over the leadership of an immense territory that had only just, in the last quarter century or so, emerged from out of the middle ages.

The Arabs in this short period have accomplished for them-selves something enormous, when taken in the balance of history, in escaping from under the dark cloak thrown over them by a backward Ottoman rule. For centuries such has been the essen-tial value in the history of modern humankind, a history that has seen numerous examples of rapid awakening, as in Japan and Germany. These awakenings, however, do not spring from avoid-ance but rather from a given technological, political and military stratum (tabaqa – طبقة), even when that stratum had been shat-tered by war. The Arabs, by contrast, began their entry into the age from a complete void.

Our generation, for example, has seen an amazing develop-ment, but our closeness to it has made us incapable of estimating its true value. The basic difference separating us from our fathers is unprecedented. Only rarely has history seen such a distance between two successive generations, but it is perceptible in the face of our brothers and sisters. The wheel turns more quickly than we can grasp. This fact, however, is important only in so far as it refutes the theory of Arab unworthiness and the Arab incapacity to enter into the spirit of the age, a theory that is used not only to justify the invasion of the Arabs but that also provides the theoretical criterion for some of our authors, passing under the veil of criticism.

The difference between our generations can no longer be measured in years. The incalculable speed of development gives rise to one of the most significant contemporary problems, in fundamental contradiction with the social foundation of our life and yet inseparable from it, what we are designating principally with the term "patriarchy" (qaʿida al-ubuwa – قاعدة الأبوة). Older men, both in terms of age and by custom, demand always of the younger the right of respect and submission. If this custom formed the basis of social organisation in times of stagnation, then it forms now, in the midst of a daily intensifying dynamism, a difficult fetter with dangerous consequences. And while this does not mean abandoning the familial institution, it does necessarily mean adding to it a further vital and fundamental article: that the older men likewise respect the younger.

What we are calling "patriarchy" extends beyond just the family structure, for although family structure may appear to be the best example of patriarchy, it is not the most important. Patriarchy is reflected in the very foundations of our social and political life as well, where it serves to inhibit the emergence of young people into the ranks of the leadership. In a period of rapid social movement, however, what is required is that generation's ascent – not its shackling.

This discussion, it must be added, by no means implies a delimitation of the "younger generation" in terms of age in years, although this is important. Rather, the conventional term, "younger generation" (al-ʿanasir al-shabba – العناصير الشبة), goes well beyond such a limited identification to include the intellectual character of the younger generation or the youthful mentality in keeping with the times, irrespective – if the matter so requires – of birth certificates. And yet, in our current state of development, the youthful mentality goes hand in hand with a young age. This should not dissuade us from attending to the exceptional cases that can sometimes be of great importance. Whether this applies to one faction or another of those who represent the youthful mentality, there are still undefined obstacles on the paths of both, exhausting, sometimes to the point of surrender. Given the chance, however, to overcome these obstacles, both sides find it difficult to transfer their newly acquired position to a generation that has all too soon arrived after them. One of the most obvious results of this is the acceptance of the principle that the holder of power remains as long as possible at the head of the power structure rather than exchange his position according to the dynamics of development and the promotion of men of the age in their continuous development on different levels of leadership.

Again, we must add that what we mean by leadership is not at all the leaders of the state. The question is not, nor should it be, the question of an individual or group of individuals. The leadership comprises all those levels and functions practised by human-kind in a healthy and effective social order. In fact, the president of the state or the head of the party is the product of the whole collection of leaders present within the social and political body that they direct. It is incorrect to see it in terms of an individual. The change at the summit of the state is not at all change in the sense in which we understand the word here, since the collection of leaders forming the political pyramid is itself unsound, thus making it futile for us to ask for that change at the summit to respond somehow to our goals.

The issue behind this discussion is deeper than a mere formal movement and we cannot attend only to the superficies of forms and outward appearances. When we talk about change, we mean a profound change in the infrastructure of the social and political formation. It is this change that bestows on any president of a state, any party leader or any organisation's leadership, the ability, right, power, instrumentality and authority to realise its goals and programme. Thus, when we say that the debility in understanding the younger generation's power leads to the acceptance of the principle that the holder of power in office for a long period of time forms within it an obstacle to those generations more in harmony with the developments of the age, we are in fact simply pointing to all of our apparatus, institutions, organisations, parties, administrations and associations, in their political, economic and cultural forms.

This phenomenon constitutes an invisible barrier obstructing the transference of our strong capacities for development onto the level of daily practice. This is precisely what we see embodied in the phenomenon of emigration and exile, for exile is not only a search for material wealth, but for values as well. And it is precisely this too which makes us see the bureaucrats as older than the papers in their office archives, just as it prevents us from seeing younger faces in the seats of legal and executive power, in a way that would reflect accurately the development that we are living.

What we are here calling a lack of enterprise, imagination and invention – not the capacity for such – is what is peculiar to the moment. It is the reason for the absence of any of our programmes joining the spirit of the age, and for the absence of any administrative frameworks keeping up with the rapid pace of movement in the society. It further nullifies the willingness on the part of organisations in our political life, whatever their form, to respond to and interact with the dynamism and capacities of the young.

At a first glance at images of organisations in different countries elsewhere in the world, it might seem that the younger generations there too do not enjoy these privileges, but such an image is incorrect in two important ways. First of all, the younger generations there have in fact seized their full opportunity in political and administrative institutions. And second, our own need, given the ups and downs of our intense and rapid development, to promote the younger generations into the centres of leadership is greater by far than the need of Western societies who do not face the enormous developmental gap between successive generations that we do. This fact leads us to another essential point and that is the question of democracy.

The democratic institution is not just the translation of a parliamentary institution. Parliament is but one of the manifestations of democracy, but is not democracy itself. Democracy is a combination of equal opportunity, from parliament to the family, and continuous with the political, administrative and cultural institutions that form the blood circulation system of a democratic situation. Any replacement of that "blood circulation system" (*al-dawra al-damawiyya* – الدورة الدموية), whether complete or partial, is itself an abuse of democracy. Only when our administrative, political and cultural institutions are capable of spontaneously comprehending the youthful strength, its excitement and influence, is there a democratic situation. The opposite has nothing whatsoever to do with democracy.

A new meaning is here added to our first point about "patriarchy". Our ability to understand the younger generation is in fact subject to our capacity for accepting its influence in our institutions and submitting these to a new, collective and growing comprehension. This ability is still limited. What we call "technological underdevelopment" (*takhalluf tiknuluji* – تخلف تكنولوجي), currently much discussed, is in fact to a large extent the result of wasting the ability of our younger generation. When the holders of power are unable to keep up with the age's rapid development, they prefer to keep closed the door of current accomplishments rather than relinquish their power on account of their inability to keep up with the age.

This discussion does not, of course, mean that we are technologically advanced. It means that not only are we content with that lack of advancement, but also that we obstruct the potential for rapid change. As a result, those very capacities of ours that might form an important and basic beginning are lost without us really understanding why. The first accounts of highly educated young people obliged to emigrate warrant that we consider with alarm the massive accusation of our technological underdevelopment. And other unavailable data that might tell us just how many of our distinguished scientists work, or are obliged to work, in fields that have no relation to their specialisation, would probably warrant that we consider this issue with an even greater sense of alarm. This age is witnessing a unique phenomenon, that is, that the overwhelming majority of groups who make up the scientific and technological corpus of the society are, as a result of the rapidity of development, a younger majority. Applying this maxim to our society and its intensifying speed of development, it is easy to see just how dangerous and basic the problem is that we are now facing.

Understanding this development requires us to have an unusual capacity for agreement and an enormous capacity to replace traditional structures (*al-itarat al-taqlidiyya* – الإطارات التقليدية) in order to keep up and evolve with it. Such an ability is necessitated by the

71

twofold nature of the difficult race that we have embarked on. On the one hand, we are trying to overcome our own underdevelopment and, on the other, we are competing to catch up with the rapid movement of the age. The question is why, despite everything, this understanding has not occurred. Why, despite everything, has the younger generation not asserted its presence in the way required by this dynamic reality? Should not the replacement of the structures within which we move result necessarily from the growing speed of our development? The answers to these questions are in turn a question of time. Our society is really only in its birth phase, and it would be unwise to believe that the movement of history will not assert itself in the end.

However, we must admit that the economic reality, and the political reality resulting from it, weigh atop this movement and prevent it from a real take-off. It is hardly a coincidence that the whole region should be witnessing a series of attempts to determine this turning point with its different possibilities of success and failure, even bitter failure. Nevertheless, these attempts – in varying ways – have become once more the captive of their own self-estimation, obstructing, at whatever levels the younger generation's constant, forward-directed, rapid movement. In the midst of these difficult birth pains, at times violent and at others more tranquil, one phenomenon stands out for observation and analysis, a phenomenon that has spread in very similar ways throughout the region regardless of the different systems that prevailed. Ultimately, this was to be the inevitable result of all the contradictions concealed in and behind the numerous above-mentioned attempts in the past.

Over the last ten years, we have witnessed the birth of what we might call a "blind language" (*lugha ʿamya* - لغة عمياء) in the region and nothing has been more operative in our daily life than this blind language. The most significant words lost all meaning. There was no longer any specificity, and each writer had his own private diction, using his words according to his own private understanding, an understanding that had no consensus and which thus meant nothing. The meanings carried by such conventional terms as "revolutionary", "Nasserist", "socialist", "justice", "democracy" and "freedom" appeared in innumerable writings that we would read every day and although it seemed – from just observing these words and their widespread dissemination – as if there was some consensus on their meaning; in fact, no one agreed with anyone else on their significance.

We need urgently to re-evaluate these words, so that definite and meaningful specificities can be agreed upon. Such a step was similarly necessary for other peoples of the world at the end of the nineteenth century as they too stood at the threshold of an emergent age. The conventional terms have, however, become pure alienation for us and this mutual deafness leads only to a total absence of meaning in discourse. But the problematic has gone even farther than that and it has now become possible for someone to use language to conceal his own impotencies or to hide his intentions. We now have a lore of blind language that has managed to empty discourse of any effective value, making it possible to employ it for contradictory aims at one and the same time.

Hiding behind a cloud of words is the basic weapon either for someone who feels his own impotence to realise his goal or for someone who has no defined goal at all. Impotence and the absence of clear thinking, which themselves have become a kind of "working strategy" (istratijiyya al-'amal – استراتيجية العمل), have buried us up to our necks in what might be called "incantatory thought" (al-fikr al-ghina'i – الفكر الغنائي) that replaces clarity with sound and disguises the absence of a goal with ringing words that satisfy the emotionality in the depths of us all without ever illuminating its vision. This blind language provides, in the final analysis, a sense of security for those who are frightened by change, and provides a curtain of fog over the movement that they truly fear. Whereas the representatives of a certain class are greatly pleased to encourage this blind language that, under the veil of nationalism, they consider to be a healthy expression, it is, in fact, nothing but a shield to protect those who, by their economic and political influence, have been suppressing the beginning of the movement for change.

Might we not then, in accordance with our rejection of this exploiter class, call such encouragement itself the exploitation of language? This is, of course, possible, but only on the condition that we do not forget that the question of exploitation has two sides:

the exploiter and the exploited. And if language is the means of the exploiter, what then can serve as the defence of the exploited? And if the exploiter goes beyond the exploitation of language used to obtain his own objectives, then what is to be a strategy for the exploited? This is the operative side of the problematic that we are reviewing here, the side that focuses on the larger issue that we must now discuss. "Blind language" has gradually deprived us of the ability to establish our own clear strategy for confronting the challenges that beset us on all levels. Given, on the most dangerous level, the enemy that confronts us, and given the clear and present danger, we must subject all our contradictions to the finding of a solution to that one main contradiction and its own well-defined strategy directed against us in unmitigated malice.

Ben Gurion, the chief architect and proponent of that strategy, has proposed the following plan:

> We must use military conquests as a basis for incontrovertible settlement and the creation of a new human, economic, cultural and social reality that will force everyone to recognise it and take it into account. And the adherents of traditions and morals who attack our right to expand our borders to include the occupied areas, do they not understand that they are assisting the enemy who is still claiming those lands in our possession, one part of them with the consent of the United Nations and another, without its consent. We must change the situation in those areas emptied [of Palestinians] through Jewish immigration and settlement. There is no excuse for defending the rights of the enemy lying in wait for us. For us he has no rights.

Ben Gurion wrote these words on 20 October [1967], in the Israeli newspaper *Haaretz* where he unhesitatingly announced the Israeli strategy necessarily directed against us.

In the face of such a clear goal and a logic that wants to use military conquest as a means of justifying settler colonialism, cancelling once and for all any rights for the other side, the "blind language" engulfing us becomes more than a mere meaningless transitory phenomenon. It is a crime. It not only obstructs the arrival of a youthful vanguard, bringing new blood and influence with them into the ranks of the leadership, but it also obstructs a clear view of the enemy and a recognition of the depth and breadth of the danger it poses, as well as the establishment of a firm strategy for confronting it and meeting its challenges.

None of this has happened by chance or arbitrarily, but rather as a series of interconnected links, in all of its small circles, forms the chain that obstructs our release. What we have been calling patriarchy is really nothing but the necessary result of a feudal mentality, of a political feudalism and the logic of national capital. Nor is this patriarchy a psychological phenomenon except insofar as class itself crystallises psychological phenomena. Further-more, what we have been calling blind language is not so much a literary school as an intellectual chain whose links are forged on the anvil of narrow convention in order to impede rapid histori-cal movement. The absence of a real working strategy, an absence that resulted from patriarchy and the blinding of language, is in turn a necessary result of the absence of a democracy appropri-ate to our present conditions and functioning as the "circulation of blood" in our political body. This absence is not restricted to names alone, but arms itself here and there, in one case or another, with the blindness of language or patriarchy.

Going back over the parts of our argument, we come to the fol-lowing conclusion: we are facing an enemy that brings with it from the West the epitome of technology, scientific development and an enormous capacity for assimilating the younger generations within the organisation of its leadership, thereby utilising not only one of the forms of democracy appropriate to its requirements and tasks, to the effective rapidity of current development and adaptation, but also makes use of its natural and organic connection to the devel-opmental movement of the age. The enemy has his own clear idea with his own strategic line, one that epitomises much of the confu-sion and exposes all of the major contradictions erected, effectively and on a daily basis, between it and ourselves. The natural conse-quence of this circulation of blood is, from first to last, to redirect intellectual, political, social and technological efforts to a clear and well-defined goal, with no waste and no frivolity.

For the Arabs, by contrast, historical circumstances have not facil-itated the consolidation of the technological capacity promoted by the age. And to that we ourselves have added an amazing capacity for squandering not only our own scientific potential but even the very degree of development that this potential has managed to achieve, despite all the difficulties. The traditional social structure of our political and economic organisations displays an unusual rigidity in its inability to admit our younger generations, in order to progress, develop and transform.

Without the circulation of new blood, continuously, rapidly and automatically, to the centres of power, not only was there an increased collapse of possibilities generally but also an even greater separation from the age's developmental movement. This situation has led naturally to a sanctification of the society's superstructure, itself a major impediment to the speed of change and transformation. Even in those periods when a relatively new power would take over, its ability to influence came immediately up against those broken bridges separating it from the society's infrastructure or base, in turn retarding the process of change.

Even with regard to democracy, whether it is called revolutionary democracy or traditional democracy, the result remained the same, that the social body's circulation system was only skin-deep and thus unable to circulate the blood properly. This then empties the "dialogue" (al-hiwar – الحوار) of everything that gives it its value and forces it into what we have been calling "blind language" or what is more commonly called a "dialogue of the deaf" (hiwar al-turshan – حوار الطرشان), not unlike the slogans of the parties and states in the region, whose constitutions, in and of themselves a matter for surprise, are astonishing for the number of contradictions they contain.

All these factors of course contribute automatically to the Arabs' lack of a working strategy, a lack that nullifies any capacity for redirecting their technological, intellectual, social, political and even statistical efforts towards more useful and less futile daily goals. The lack of such a strategy annuls, too, the capacity to organise the contradictions facing the Arab societies of the region as well as any knowledge of how most appropriately to enlist these in resolving the largest and most immediate contradiction. Thus, we fought our battle, so to speak, "without proper preparation", "without using our potential", "isolated from our capacities", and citing "startling

technological underdevelopment", "rigid military and political tra-
ditionalism", and the fact that "the people didn't participate in its
battle" and so on. Such formulas, and their repeated use, however,
threaten only to express once again earlier situations and their
unfortunate chain of circumstances. The very use of these clichés
is itself a consequence that must be examined as such. Otherwise,
their use will become natural as long as their logic remains intact
and inviolable.

The dispute between Ben Gurion and Levi Eshkol traces its
origin back to 1917 and yet the two leaders managed to hang
together in a single party organisation until 1964,[3] and even then,
neither Eshkol nor Ben Gurion closed off the question of annex-
ation in 1967. Instead, the "circulation of blood" supplying the two
parties with younger generations made for a direct synchronisa-
tion with ongoing rapid developments. Directly after the June War,
and at the height of the triumph, Yitzhak Rabin was removed as
chief of staff of the Israeli Army. In a period such as this, where
speed surpassed the grasp of a single individual, the law prohibited
a chief of staff remaining in his post for more than four years. At
the time that Yitzhak Rabin left his position, the Israeli cabinet was
determined to remain a cabinet of national unity combining conflicting groups sharply opposed among themselves. This conflict
had to be subordinated to a calculated strategy for the next phase
when the Israelis anticipated other developments.

These examples are not intended to be a systematic treatment
of the enemy as a model, but rather to insist that what we have
long been calling the "distribution of roles" (*tawzi' al-adwar* – توزيع

3 Eshkol was Zionist prime minister at the time of Kanafani's lecture and had
publicly split with his predecessor Ben Gurion over the latter's call to reopen
an investigation into the so-called Lavon affair. Under the leadership of then
defence minister Pinhas Lavon, Zionist agents had failed in their 1954 attempt to
detonate bombs in Egypt with the aim of stoking instability and continued British
occupation of the Suez. Both Eshkol and Ben Gurion had joined the British
Army's Jewish Legion in the aftermath of the 1917 Balfour Declaration and its
occupation of Palestine and both worked to found the colonialist Histradut and
Zionist labour movement. Kanafani implies that their later disagreement over the
judicial transparency of the occupation state found roots in this earlier period.
Unlike Eshkol, Ben Gurion was a leading member at this point in the "socialist"
Poale Zion organisation.

الأدوار) among the Israeli forces is not really so; it is quite simply an inevitability necessitated by a pre-planned strategy that alone determines the duties and rights of each given phase. Thus, the lack of a strategy of this sort on the part of the Arabs itself would lead to what we might call an "error of judgement" (*khata' al-taqdir* – خطأ التقدير), a judgement error that is certainly not a cause but a consequence.

This brings us to the following essential question: the issue, as we have said, is not that of changing the leadership since the leadership is in fact just one aspect of the problem. Rather, we must ask, how are we to go about modernising our political and economic apparatus and our cultural institutions to make them effective enough to keep up with the speed of development in our society? The question places us at the crux of the issue, the issue of democracy, a term by which we understand, first of all, the rule of the people, by the people and for the people, irrespective of conventions used to undermine the word democracy. We consider parliament to be but one feature of democracy, not democracy itself. And since by democracy we mean that circulation of blood, healthy and reinvigorating, that must reach every part and member of the social body, what is required of us is that we transform the democratic spirit into a daily practice at all levels.

The Arab world, in the context of its dialogue with democracy, has seen various experiments that merit examination: in one case, there is parliament without freedom of the press and, in another, freedom of the press without a parliament; in still another case, there is parliament but no parties, or else parties without a parliament; or there might be a parliament, parties and freedom of the press without any of this being able to create a real democracy. Despite all this experimentation, the regimes still call themselves "democracies".

Where then is the solution?

It is wrong in fact for us to look for democracy in all these forms and opinions about its existence and non-existence, or about how many different appearances democracy has taken on in its parliamentary aspect, since we are also inquiring into democracy in its social and cultural dimensions. Furthermore, we are really asking that we look for democracy in its administrative and collective aspects, and, first and foremost, in its party aspect. The party itself is the consolidation of the democratic experiment. Thus, if the potential ability and qualifications of any party are measured by the circulation of blood in its body, we will see that the overwhelming majority of our parties suffer from an absence of democracy, both in terms of the apparatus of each of them and in terms of their relations with each other.

Within its own apparatus, the party founder assumes for himself the seal of sanctification and the small group around him forms the rampart against which the upward movement of the younger generation collides. Outside the apparatus, in its relations with other parties, accusation substitutes for dialogue, and wilful defamation replaces mutual understanding. Inside the apparatus, the leader's authority prevents the movement's growth and the fetishisation of the role of the leader as irreplaceable is reflected in his own self-esteem when he makes of himself such an irreplaceable power. Outside the apparatus, this absolute and positive self-esteem leads to a negative evaluation of others.

The social body might be compared to the human body in that each gland has its own function and that its well-being is endangered not just by a defect in one of these glands but also by a defect in its relation to other glands. As far as most of our parties are concerned, they are incapable, whether in their own internal organisational structures or in their relations with other parties, of creating a nucleus of real democratic spirit, and the absence of this spirit in turn impedes the crystallisation of a clear strategy either for itself or in its conception of the role that other forces might appropriately play.

Party formation is an invaluable experience insofar as it instructs citizens as to the best means of playing a role of public responsibility. Within the party, they acquire a new political culture and a new idea of political work, thus also enabling what might be called a democratic ethos. Our parties have been incapable of realising this indispensable task and of crystallising within their own structures a political vanguard that could play a leadership role in the society, one that would at the same time both influence and be influenced by that society. This incapacity led then to a still more dangerous consequence, namely, the incapacity of the parties to crystallise a strategy adequate to the dynamics of a society attempting either to express itself or to develop an alternative form that would replace the traditional ones that it has rejected. All of this results in two interconnected phenomena in our party experience: first, the multiplication of parties, and second, the inability to focus effective social forces.

In conditions of the kind experienced by our society, the absence of effective parties representing real forces is an incalculable loss, a destructive and horribly debilitating mistake with dangerous consequences resulting from it at all levels. There is no way out of this profound dilemma we are now experiencing except through party activism (*al-hizbiyya* – الحزبية),[4] party activism in the true, effective and productive sense, produced within an internal framework of established democratic relations, and of relations with others in a constructive and productive dialogue. These conditions of party activism cancel the unnecessary multiplication of parties which in themselves only reproduce the same previous mistakes and deficiencies rather than advancing the role of the party itself.

In their past experience, our parties have taken the form of sectarian or clan or student groups, of undefined social forces and with unclear and indeterminate boundaries, that, taken together, recreate patriarchal structures within the party formation as well as in the form and content of its relations with other parties – quantitative accumulation rather than qualitative development. The sum total of these relations leads to the acceptance of the absence of a party strategy. The need for a quick understanding of the objective conditions as well as the desire to deal with these on a practical level are ignored. Although such experiences do not cancel altogether the inherent value of the party, they do require systematic study and critique in the direction of a total developmental practice.

In past years, there has been a wide-reaching and interminable discussion on the issue of the single or multiparty system. In fact, no one criterion can be imposed, nor can any single paradigm be considered indispensable, since for every social condition there

4 Kanafani was at this point a member of the PFLP, which had been established seven months prior.

exist numerous reasons, motivations and interpretations. None-theless, the groundwork remains first of all in the ability of these parties as a whole, or of the single party individually, to realise within their organisational structures and in their relations with other organised forces, a real circulation of blood that would make it a healthy phenomenon, one not trapped in some vicious circle.

The political party is one of the forms for organising effective forces in a society but there are other forms as well that are capable of such organisation. These are represented by the labour unions, including worker, peasant and professional unions, or cultural insti-tutions that, whether intentionally or not, function as the ground on which discussion is built. Whether the organisation is a party, a union or an association, its first priority should be to ensure the circulation of blood in its body. Its primary potential should be not for discussion, but for raising the level of understanding of what is young and new and how to adapt and interact with it. The problem in the region was never in the inconceivability of development, but rather that we did not use our developmental capacity to enhance our progress.

Our dilemma is not that we failed to implement our programme but that we did not give ourselves the opportunity even to draw up a programme. And our defeat was due not only to the tradi-tional political, social and economic forces fettering us, but to the fact that the alternative forces were more oriented towards refusal rather than constructing a new and comprehensive strategy. Fur-thermore, our impotence was not so much an expression of our lack of qualification as it was the result of the prevention of new blood in our society from reaching its head and arms. The problem is not that we do not know, but that we do not permit those who do know to speak and to act. It is not that we are foreigners to the age, but that we have squandered and thwarted the younger gener-ations who are themselves the bridge to the age.

The responsibility for all of this, as we have tried to demonstrate, is not limited to this or that individual, nor to a single system or organisation, but is the responsibility of everyone to almost equal degrees. The entire region stands at the gates of a decisive historical turning point and there will be victory in this confrontation except the victory of all, and no defeat that is not the ruin of everyone.

Any objective assessment of the previous few years that the region has just passed through must demonstrate one thing at least and that is that there is no one confronting the challenge more than any other, and no one can withdraw except at an enormous collective cost. Whatever the theoretical dispute that might have been engaging ideas about the unity of the region's destiny, that unity has never at any time in the past seemed stronger than it does now, following the humiliating defeat and facing what have become life and death challenges.

This idea imposes on Lebanon a number of tasks whose circumstances are themselves a kind of preparation for the fateful role Lebanon must play in confronting the big challenge certainly, but also in confronting the smaller challenges that collectively constitute its internal issues. The Lebanese role is made up of three basic components: national duty, historical commitment and geographical standing.

From within the challenges contained in each of these three components, Lebanon stands at a historical turning point, whereby it might yet succeed in renewing its blood and moving forward with the age. This requires first of all a decisive clarification of priorities in the hierarchy of challenges making up the daily situation in the region, as well as a commitment to a programme for meeting these challenges. This clarification should not happen as mere coincidence, or on the basis of spontaneous or automatic thinking, but rather by releasing the absorptive potential through free discussion, thus focusing the rapid developmental movement throughout the entire region and providing the necessary conditions for the crystallisation of its effective powers.

The society must organise its discussion on the basis of definite strategic situations and give to the active social forces their full role in this discussion, its organisations and its parties. The movement of a healthy discussion must be such that it can create a form capable of absorbing and expressing the hidden potential of the people. The arteries for the circulation of blood in its body must reach as far as possible, deep and wide, connecting the given structures with the power to express the dynamism and vitality of development in our society.

In the present circumstances, national, historical and geographical, the Lebanese situation might yet release the constructive potential of a courageous and responsible discussion, focusing the voices clamouring from one end of the Arab world to the other, and on the basis of this discussion, release its own specific potential as well. In Lebanon, the fetters imposed by "patriarchy" could be abolished in order to give to the exuberant younger generations the opportunity to extend their dynamism and vitality and their connectedness to the age to the level of daily influence. Lebanon could extend the slogan "national unity" (al-wahda al-wataniyya – الوحدة الوطنية), in both form and content, from its purely sectarian character to its larger social, economic and political character, and deepen the democratic spirit to the level of the circulation of blood, functioning in the parliament, in the parties and universities, in the cultural institutions and in the administrative centres, reaching even to the heart of family gatherings. Lebanon could open the eyes of language so that language is not just an expression of impotence, uncertainty and incantation, but is a clear vision of values and issues, and thus abandon the debate and discussions that have been so destructive of time, potential and situation.

The Lebanese climate can be now perhaps critically important to a new dawn in the Arab dialogue, but only on the condition that we set free its full potential for understanding, effectiveness and responsible commitment. While the spirit of critique after the defeat permeates the entire Arab world, it is not by chance that it should have had its first stirrings in Lebanon, even despite the many competing discussions, slogans and intentions there. In effect, Lebanon is playing a part of its potential role, and it will doubtless play that role more fully as long as we can have faith in its possibilities for continuing, whatever the contending voices, to benefit the people.

All of this throws the burden of responsibility onto the shoulders of everyone, to differing, but nonetheless necessary, degrees. Responsibility rests on the shoulders of the younger generation, in its universities, its parties and its families, to the same degree that it rests on the shoulders of the leaders in their sphere of influence, parties, families and the centres of power that they enjoy. Responsibility rests on the shoulders of the intellectuals to be a conscious element rather than a blinding and vacillating one, to be an element of constructive commitment and not an element that sits back in its absolute rejectionism. Responsibility rests too on the shoulders of journalists and media people, responsibility towards the powerful weapon that they hold in their hands and for what comes of national duty, historical commitment and geographical standing. And finally, responsibility rests on the shoulders of the architects of state policy for building the domestic and foreign strategy required by the powers latent in the society and the younger generation representative of the blood that will renew that society and bring it to interact with the developmental movement of the age.

In the last quarter century, and as it enters the modern age, the Arab world has accomplished one of the miracles of development in history, and it has accomplished it on a land made muddy by more than 500 years of oppressive underdevelopment. The Arab world has accomplished this miracle despite its rape by contrary forces surrounding it and working away at it from inside and outside in a series of fateful challenges that continue even now in difficult daily confrontations. Nonetheless, our ambitions remain broader and greater than any retreat into silence. If there is any meaning to this at all, it is the meaning of worthiness.

The defeat came and this people discovered an extraordinary ability not only to reject it, but also to re-examine its own account with itself. The opposition to its experience is harsher even than that enabled by a courageous critique. And if that critique was sometimes exaggerated to a painful degree, it was only to satisfy the yearning and ambitions to attain something greater and better. In this present and difficult experience, the Arab has added to his desire for steadfastness the desire for liberty and critical revision. The Arab was defeated in a deadly battle in which it was not granted to him to fight as he can and should. His desire for steadfastness and liberty, however, have not wavered, but, on the contrary, have acquired additional potential for firmness and yearning for the better, expressed collectively in the unusual awakening of a spirit of criticism and re-examination.

It would nonetheless be unwise for us to imagine that the Arab is finding his full compensation in this critical awakening. Rather, this period of waiting, lived so tensely now, is not unlike that of 1949, or that experienced by the Russian people between 1904, when they were defeated by Japan, and 1905, with its first revolution, to be followed ten years later by another revolution that changed the face of the twentieth century. What is happening now is only the labour pains of something great that will be born from the rubble of the defeat like a volcano born from under the cold ashes of a forsaken mountain.

The wound opened in a dead body causes no agitation, but what has rent (*anshaqqa* – انشق) a living body increases its potential for resistance. A hidden power in the depths is stirred and its capabilities are doubled in response. The wounded Arab body is moving. It is healing, preparing itself, resisting. Its senses are redoubled, and it stands firmly on its feet, spanning a bridge of agony.

6

Will the September Settlement
Surprise Us? (1969)

Introduction by *Louis Brehony*

In this short article in *al-Hadaf*, Ghassan Kanafani commits the newly founded Popular Front for the Liberation of Palestine (PFLP) newspaper to scrutinising the political aftermath of the June 1967 Naksa, two years on. Providing a narrative of US-led negotiations, the report analyses the roles and interests of the drive towards a "comprehensive" and "peaceful settlement", through which Israel would be asked to give up none of the spoils of its conquests. At the time of writing, UN Special Envoy Gunnar Jarring had been appointed to implement UN Resolution 242, which called in November 1967 for Israel's withdrawal from newly captured territories, leaving the 1948 occupation intact. On 242, Kanafani and the PFLP were forthright:

> We reject it. If Nasser accepts it, that is his business. We are fighting today on our own and for ourselves. Any Arab leader who would recognise the existence of Israel would pay very dearly.[1]

Fighting scurrilously for the Israeli side throughout 1969 were Joseph J. Sisco, US Assistant Secretary of State for Middle Eastern Affairs and US ambassador to Tel Aviv, Wally Barbour. South-African-born Abba Eban trotted the globe to drum up support for the expanded occupation in his role as foreign affairs minister for the Zionist state. These manoeuvres faced opposition from the Soviet Union which, unlike the USA, Britain or France, recognised the legitimacy of the Palestinian liberation organisations and, like

---

1   Ghassan Kanafani quoted in Clara Halter, "The Liberation of the Occupied Territories Is Only the First Step", *New Middle East* (September 1970): 36.

China, armed them in the years that followed. Though Kanafani points out the error in imperialist claims that Soviet policy was "total" in its commitment to the Arab stance, archive materials that may shed light on the Soviet Union's diplomatic role in Egypt and other Arab states in the aftermath of June 1967 remain inaccessible. It is now known, however, that the threat of a Soviet military intervention against the Zionist state halted the latter's 10 June plan to invade Damascus, with Premier Alexei Kosygin delivering the warning directly to the US government, via channels activated for the first time since the Cuban Missile Crisis in 1962.[2]

With an election on the horizon, Kanafani pointed out that the Israeli Labour Party was once again displaying its readiness to continue the colonisation project. Having taken over as prime minister in March 1969, Golda Meir led the ruling government after 28 October; she had infamously declared that there was "no such thing as the Palestinian people" on 15 June. The September "surprise" turned out to be a failure on the part of the UN to resolve the crisis. Jarring's successor in ostensibly pushing for a peace deal was US secretary of state William P. Rogers, who in December complained of the obstacles placed in the way so far by the Soviet Union. Rogers went on:

To call for Israeli withdrawal as envisaged in the UN Resolution without achieving an agreement on peace would be partisan towards the Arabs.[3]

UN resolutions now put to one side, the goal of imperialism was – and remains – a campaign to recruit Arab bourgeoisies towards the normalisation of Zionist occupation. Standing in the way, then and now, is the Palestinian resistance.

*   *   *

2 Isabella Ginor, "How Six Day War Almost Led to Armageddon", *Guardian*, 10 June 2000, https://www.theguardian.com/world/2000/jun/10/israel1.
3 Statement by Secretary of State Rogers, 9 December 1969, Volumes 1–2: 1947–1974, Ministry of Foreign Affairs, https://www.gov.il/en/pages/9-statement-by-secretary-of-state-rogers-9-december-1969.

WILL THE SEPTEMBER SETTLEMENT SURPRISE US?[4]

The journey of the political settlement as it has recently transpired can be summarised in the following timeline:

1. On 18 July, Abba Eban concluded his European tour by meeting Gunnar Jarring, with the international mediator journeying to the Swiss capital for the sole purpose of meeting with Eban.
2. In the meantime, Joseph J. Sisco was discussing the Middle East issue with Soviet officials in Moscow.
3. On his return journey to Washington, Sisco stopped in Amsterdam to hold a quick meeting with Jarring.
4. Subsequently, Washington briefed Israel on Sisco's discussions in Moscow by arranging a meeting in Tel Aviv between the US ambassador [Walworth] Barbour and [Israeli UN ambassador] Gideon Rafael.
5. On his arrival in Washington, Sisco swiftly left to join Nixon on the Asian tour. During this tour, [Sisco] held talks with Romanian officials regarding a "political settlement".
6. Less than 48 hours after Sisco's return to Washington, he left again on a quick visit to Belgrade, where he held a round of talks with Yugoslav officials, before returning to Washington.
7. The Yugoslav Ministry of Foreign Affairs reported to Cairo the nature of the discussion with Sisco the following day.
8. Upon his return to Washington, Sisco announced that the quadripartite communication would resume by end of September, and that the foreign ministers of the four major powers may hold a conference to resume communication.

Progress In Talks?

The Israeli *Jerusalem Post*, with close ties to the Ministry of Foreign Affairs, stated that Sisco presented new American proposals in Moscow in response to the Soviet plan, with subsequent talks showing that "some development and disagreements have

---

4 Original publication in *al-Hadaf* 1, no. 3 (9 August 1969). Translated by Lena Haddadin.

been reduced" (21 August 1968). It added that Sisco's mission in Moscow centred on "drawing more effective lines for Dr Jarring", which explains why Sisco was so eager to meet with Jarring upon his return from Moscow. Likewise, Eban was also keen to meet Jarring in Switzerland "to review the conclusions they've reached, and to urge him to resume his mission". Sisco then made sure to contact Belgrade and Bucharest to follow up on this matter.

This could only mean that the period during which talks between the four major powers were suspended – and which witnessed discreet and silent contacts between Moscow and Washington – has seen some major developments, making it possible for these four major countries [the USA, Britain, France and the Soviet Union] to resume their suspended talks.

Towards a "Comprehensive Deal"

Despite the great difficulties surrounding agreement on any "political settlement", this does not mean that the efforts of the major powers are now heading towards a dead end.

On one hand, Israel claims the new US draft does not align with its perspective, while on the other, it argues that the Soviet draft reflects a total commitment to the Arab stance. While the latter claim is untrue, Israel remains sceptical of the possible outcomes since it is certain that Washington "does not wish to cut off communication with Moscow before bringing up the issue of disarmament, etc." among other issues standing between the two countries. This is a crucial indication that the international talks on the Middle East crisis are now heading towards a "comprehensive deal" that will include all issues raised between the two countries.

This may be the path that Washington insists on to reach a settlement, by considering the Middle East crisis as one aspect of the conflict between the two giants and thus imposing a solution as a result of the "comprehensive deal".

A Surprise in September?

All of this requires paying close and thoughtful attention to any surprising developments at the level of the "international effort" exerted.

During the last two weeks, Arab diplomatic circles at the UN unofficially reported that the current international action towards reaching a settlement in the Middle East crisis is far more dangerous than had been estimated in official Arab circles. They now expect that September will reveal big surprises related to this issue.

The same circles do not expect disruption to this ongoing international communication from the electoral programme of the Israeli Labour Party, which was issued recently and officially establishes its expansionist intentions.[5] This is especially true since those communications are based on the official responses provided to Jarring by the Arab countries and Israel three months ago. These answers and solutions remain the framework utilised by the four major powers to reach a peaceful resolution. They also form the foundation through which different solutions are proposed by one side or another in the framework of bilateral communications and which will, eventually, work in Jarring's favour.

An Extortive Israeli Manoeuvre

In a statement issued by Abba Eban last week, Israel claims that it "favours the status quo over any political settlement that does not meet its demands". However, this declaration is fundamentally incorrect, since Israel's anguish and intolerance of the limits of the "status quo" indicate that it, undoubtedly, prefers reaching a kind of solution that guarantees its expansionist interests, a guarantee that is ensured in the proposed US drafts.

This extortive manoeuvre – as it is dubbed by Arab circles in the UN – aims to conceal the progress made to reach a political solution. Therefore, our urgent priority lies in handling this issue with extreme caution and preparing to counter any attempts of this kind.

---

5   This policy was borne out in the subsequent government. In 1972, Meir declared: "We will not go back to our original borders in any sector. Do you suggest that we come down from the Golan Heights – since President [Hafez] Assad of Syria is such peace-loving person?"; "A Talk with Golda Meir", *New York Times*, 27 August 1972.

PART III

"The Target":
Building the Marxist–Leninist Front

Original cover for the English pamphlet of "A Strategy for the Liberation of Palestine", released by the PFLP central media committee in 1969. Ghassan Kanafani was among its main contributors. Public domain.

7

Excerpts from PFLP: Strategy for the Liberation of Palestine (1969)

Introduction: A Fundamentally Necessary Approach by *Khaled Barakat*

The Strategy for the Liberation of Palestine is both a historical document and a living political programme for the Popular Front for the Liberation of Palestine (PFLP). Issued in 1969 at the time of the Front's second congress, this document lays out the fundamental understandings and analysis of the PFLP in relation to the colonisation of Palestine, the forces of the revolution and the forces arrayed against the Palestinian people. In addition, the second section of the Strategy puts forward the organisational vision and programme of the Front. In Arabic, this document is known as the Political and Organisational Strategy; however, its English title, the Strategy for the Liberation of Palestine, lays out clearly what this document presents – a vision, analysis and understanding to guide the tasks of the Palestinian national liberation movement in working for freedom, return and liberation.

Since the original publication of this document, a great many historical developments and changes have taken place. The document contains references to a global socialist camp and the Soviet Union, which no longer reflect our current reality. Many other changes have also taken place, including some which firmly underline the analysis presented in this publication. The process of negotiations and political settlement that began with Madrid (1991) and Oslo (1993) and led to the establishment of the Palestinian Authority (PA) to represent certain sectors of the Palestinian capitalist class while undermining the Palestinian national liberation movement – including engaging in "security" coordination with the Israeli occupation against the Palestinian resistance, was a dagger in the back of the Palestinian revolution.

The development of the PA and its role well reflects the analysis originally presented here in "The Palestinian Bourgeoisie". The entire path of Oslo and the role of the PA have served to create an institutional framework for Palestinian capital as a subcontractor for Israeli occupation, while diverting the Palestinian cause from a path of resistance and revolution to a futile road of negotiations. Today, PFLP continues to uphold the position represented in this document and by leaders such as Abu Ali Mustafa, slain on 27 August 2001 by an Israeli-fired, US-made missile in the window of his office in Ramallah: "Liberation, not Negotiations!"

This document also reflects the Front's close relationship at the time of its founding with anti-colonial and revolutionary movements around the world. The document takes inspiration from the writings of Mao Tse Tung, the experience of the Chinese Revolution and, contemporaneously, the struggle of the Vietnamese people for liberation, unity and socialism. The close relationship reflected here with other revolutionary and national liberation movements has continued to be a strong reality in principle and in practice throughout the history of the PFLP – from the period of the 1970s and 1980s, when fighters in African, Asian, Arab and Latin American liberation movements all joined the ranks of the Front but also trained for their own struggles in the Palestinian camps in Lebanon – to today's ongoing joint struggles against our mutual enemies, in confrontation with imperialism, Zionism and capitalism. In addition, the analysis of Arab reactionary regimes has remained exceptionally valid to the present day. While the roles of specific regimes have shifted – note, for example, the role of the Camp David Accords in shifting Egypt towards normalisation and reaction – the analysis presented in this document continues to guide the Front's relationship with powers like Saudi Arabia, deeply enmeshed with US imperialism and playing a destructive role in Palestine and throughout the region.

The re-publication of this document in English today makes it clear that, despite the significant events that followed its publication – including "Black September" and the attack of the Jordanian regime that drove the Palestinian revolution from Jordan, the Lebanese Civil War and the Zionist invasion and occupation of Lebanon that pushed the central location of the Palestinian revolution from the refugee camps of Lebanon, to the Intifadas and the devastation of the Oslo "peace process" – the fundamental analysis presented here remains the guiding political framework of a leftist, revolutionary approach to the liberation of Palestine; it is an approach that is fundamentally necessary to achieving victory and liberation in Palestine.

Since the release of the Strategy, the PFLP position has been further developed and elaborated in response to the movement of history and the developing Palestinian, Arab and international situation. The Front's congresses and conventions have produced political documents that highlight the position of the Front, both as a political organisation and as an active revolutionary movement deeply engaged in the Palestinian resistance struggle inside occupied Palestine, in the refugee camps of the Arab world and everywhere in the world where Palestinians and their comrades struggle for justice and liberation. One of the most important arenas of struggle for the Front has been Israeli jails, where thousands of comrades developed a revolutionary school of resistance and steadfastness in the face of torture and interrogation, a trend that is represented today by Ahmad Sa'adat, the imprisoned General Secretary of the PFLP, and hundreds of imprisoned comrades held with him and with fellow Palestinian revolutionaries behind the bars of the occupier's jails.

Ghassan Kanafani, one of the founders and leaders of the Front, a shaper of its political vision, a revolutionary strategist and a creative thinker, artist and writer, participated in the creation of this document alongside his comrades in the leadership of the Front, including George Habash and the Iraqi revolutionary Basil al-Kubeisi, murdered by Zionist agents in London in 1973. For his role in the culture and practice of resistance, Kanafani was assassinated a year prior, along with his niece Lamis. However, his words from that time remain just as compelling today, and the occasion of the English re-publication of this document once again recalls their correctness and urgency: "The Palestinian cause is not a cause for Palestinians only, but a cause for every revolutionary, wherever they are, as a cause of the exploited and oppressed masses in our era."

*　*　*

PFLP: STRATEGY FOR THE LIBERATION
OF PALESTINE (EXCERPTS)[1]

The Importance of Political Thought

One of the basic conditions of success is a clear perspective of things: a clear perspective of the enemy and a clear perspective of the revolutionary forces. It is in this light that the strategy of the struggle is determined, and without this perspective, national action becomes an impetuous gamble that soon ends in failure. Thus, after decades of fighting and sacrifice, it has become imperative for the Palestinian people to assure themselves that their armed struggle this time has the required conditions for success. Our people have waged a long fight against Zionist and colonialist plans. Since 1917 (the Balfour Declaration), the masses of our people have been fighting to keep their soil, to obtain freedom, to free their country from colonialists, to assert their right to self-determination and to exploit their country's resources for their own benefit. Their struggle against Zionism and colonialism has taken every form and method. In 1936, our people took up arms in defence of their lands, homes, freedom and the right to build their future, offering thousands of martyrs and bearing all sorts of sacrifices. During that period of history, the armed struggle of our people created a state of mass consciousness no less than that in which our masses are rallying around commando action today. Nevertheless, in spite of all the sacrifices, of the long line of martyrs whose number exceeded that of today's martyrs in commando action,[2] of the taking up of arms and of the masses' enthusiasm, our people even until this day, have not triumphed. Most of them are still living in the wretched conditions of the camps and under the yoke of occupation. Consequently, to assure ourselves of the success of the struggle, it is not sufficient for us to

---

1 Originally translated and published by the PFLP Information Department, following the Second Congress of the organisation in February 1969. The excerpts here are taken from the seventh edition printed by the Foreign Languages Press, Utrecht (2017), with minor alterations.
2 Elsewhere in this book, we have blended the Arabic in what would make this phrase "*fida 'i* action". For this text, we have left the original translation intact.

take up arms. Some armed revolutions in history have ended in victory, but others have ended in failure. It is incumbent upon us to face the facts with a frank, courageous and revolutionary scientific mentality. A clear perspective of things and of the real forces taking part in the struggle leads to success, while impetuosity and spontaneity lead to failure.

This shows clearly the importance of scientific political thought, which guides the revolution and plans its strategy. Revolutionary political thought is not an abstract idea hanging in a vacuum, or a mental luxury, or an intellectual hobby for the educated, which we can, if we wish, lay aside as an unnecessary luxury. Scientific revolutionary thought is clear thought whereby the masses are able to understand their enemy, his points of weakness or strength and the forces that support and ally themselves to the enemy. Likewise, the masses should understand their own forces, the forces of revolution, how to mobilise, how to overcome the enemy's points of strength and take advantage of the weakness of the enemy, and through what organisation, mobilisation and political and military programmes, they can escalate their forces until they can crush the enemy and achieve victory.

It is this revolutionary political thought that explains to the masses of our people the reasons for their failure hitherto in their confrontation with the enemy: why their armed revolt of 1936 and their attempts before 1936 failed; what led to the 1967 defeat; the truth about the hostile alliance against which they are waging war; and with what counter-alliance they can face it and by what method. All of this should be put in clear language that the masses can understand. Through this understanding, they get a clear perspective of the battle and its dimensions, forces and weapons, so that their thinking emerges as a force around which they are united with one perspective of the battle and one strategy…

Who are Our Enemies?

In his article, "Analysis of the Classes of Chinese Society" (March 1926), Mao Tse Tung writes:

Who are our enemies? Who are our friends?

This is a question of the first importance for the revolution. The basic reason why all previous revolutionary struggles in China achieved so little is their failure to unite with real friends in order to attack real enemies. A revolutionary party is the guide of the masses, and no revolution ever succeeds when the revolutionary party leads them astray. To ensure that we will definitely achieve success in our revolution and will not lead the masses astray, we must pay attention to uniting with our real friends in order to attack our real enemies. We must make a general analysis of the economic status of the various classes in Chinese society and of their respective attitudes towards the revolution.[3]

Who, then, are our enemies?

...The time has come for our masses to understand the true nature of the enemy because, through such understanding, the picture of the battle becomes clear to them.

1. *Israel*

In our battle for liberation, we first face Israel as a political, military and economic entity that is trying to effect the maximum military mobilisation of its two and a half million nationals to defend its aggressive expansionist racial structure and prevent us from regaining our land, our freedom and our rights. This enemy enjoys a marked technological superiority, which is clearly reflected by the standard of its armament and training and by the dynamism of its movement. It also enjoys a great ability to mobilise resulting from its feeling that it is waging a life-or-death battle and that consequently it has no alternative but to defend itself until its last breath.

This ability to mobilise and this technological superiority must be kept in our minds at all times throughout our confrontation with the enemy. It is not by chance that we hitherto lost all our battles with this enemy, and it would be a big mistake to give

3   Mao Tse Tung, *Selected Works, Volume I* (Peking: Foreign Languages Press, 1965), 13.

partial or haphazard explanation to our defeats. Understanding the true nature of the enemy is the first step to strategic planning for victory. But is Israel the only enemy that we are facing in the battle? It would be a gross error to confine our view of the enemy to Israel alone, for then we should be like one who imagines that he is in conflict with one man, only to find himself face to face with ten men for whom he is not prepared.

2. The World Zionist Movement

Israel is in reality an integral part of the world Zionist movement – indeed, it is an offshoot of this movement. Thus, in our battle with Israel, we are facing, not the State of Israel alone, but an Israel whose structure is founded on the strength of the Zionist movement. Zionism as a racial-religious movement is trying to organise and recruit 14 million Jews in all parts of the world to support Israel, protect its aggressive existence and consolidate and expand this existence. This support is not confined to moral backing: it is really and basically a material support that provides Israel with more people, more money, more arms, more technical know-how and more alliances concluded by the movement by virtue of its influence, in addition to its support through publicity and propaganda in every part of the world...

It must be pointed out that the enemy facing us and represented by Israel and Zionism is naturally governed by a number of conflicts both inside Israel, as in any other society, and between Israel and the world Zionist movement. These conflicts must be for us a subject of constant study and research. The growth of the resistance movement will undoubtedly increase the acuity of these conflicts so that we may be able to channel them to serve the interest of the liberation battle. As far as the coming battle is concerned, these contradictions have not reached a degree that hampers the full concentration and consolidation taking place inside Israel and the world Zionist movement. For us, the picture of the enemy must remain that of a camp that is being strongly and efficiently concentrated and consolidated with technical skill and precise organisation with the object of fully mobilising the inhabitants of Israel and world Jewry to face us in this battle...

3. World Imperialism

World imperialism has its interests that it fights fiercely to defend and keep. These interests consist in robbing the riches of the underdeveloped countries by purchasing them at the lowest prices and then processing these riches and re-selling them at the highest prices in the markets of these same countries. By this operation, they accumulate immense profits, enabling them to increase their capital at the expense of the people's poverty, deprivation and wretchedness. The Arab world possesses many resources, mainly petroleum, and constitutes a big consuming market for manufactured goods. Imperialism wants to maintain this situation to allow the process of accumulation of imperialist wealth to continue on the one hand and our poverty to increase on the other. To this end, it is genuinely determined to crush any revolutionary movement that aims at freeing our country and its people from this exploitation.

The revolutionary movement of the masses in the Arab world naturally aims at destroying Israel because Israel is a force that has usurped a portion of this world and is a great danger threatening other portions of it. Consequently, Israel cannot but fight to the end, any Palestinian or Arab revolutionary movement. Here imperialism finds itself in the best position in this part of the world, because through Israel it is able to fight the Arab revolutionary movement, which aims at eliminating it from our homeland with Israel becoming the force and the base used by imperialism to protect its presence and defend its interests in our land. Such a situation creates an organic unity between Israel and the Zionist movement on the one hand and world imperialism on the other, because they are both interested in fighting the Palestinian and Arab national liberation movement. Thus, the protection, reinforcement and support of Israel and the maintenance of its existence are fundamental matters for the interests of world imperialism...

Imperialism here means more arms, more support and more money for Israel. It means Phantom jets,[4] atomic bomb secrets,[5] and the building of an economy capable of facing the permanent blockade and state of war that we try to impose...

4. Arab Reaction Represented by Feudalism and Capitalism

Arab capitalism, whose interests are represented and defended by reactionary regimes in the Arab world, does not constitute an independent capitalist unit and is consequently unable to assume independent political positions. In point of fact, this capitalism represents weak branches of world capitalism that are interconnected with, and form an integral part of, the latter. The millionaires of the Arab world, including merchants, bankers, feudal lords, owners of large estates, kings, emirs and sheikhs, have in fact acquired their millions by virtue of their co-operation with world capitalism. They have amassed this wealth because they are commercial agents for goods produced by foreign capital, or secondary shareholders in foreign banking establishments or insurance companies, or they are sheikhs, emirs and kings at the head of regimes that defend and protect colonial interests and strike at any mass movement aiming at freeing our economy from this exploiting influence. Consequently, they cannot keep their millions unless our land remains a market for foreign goods and foreign investments, and unless the colonialists continue to plunder our oil and other resources, because this is the only way that enables them to acquire and keep their millions.

---

4 The US Johnson government ultimately responded to Israeli military ascendency in June 1967 with a concerted effort to maintain this superiority. Its 1968 sale of Phantom jets – requested by its allies at least two years prior – was one means of preparing the Zionist state for its wars to come.

5 Labelled its "doomsday operation", the Zionist state had already readied its secret nuclear weaponry for use against Egypt and the Palestinians in 1967, with a plan for detonating an atomic bomb in the Sinai. William J. Broad and David E. Sanger, "'Last Secret' of 1967 War: Israel's Doomsday Plan for Nuclear Display", *The Independent*, 7 June 2017, https://www.independent.co.uk/news/long_reads/last-secret-of-the-1967-war-israel-s-doomsday-plan-for-nuclear-display-a7775076.html.

This means that, in a real liberation battle waged by the masses to destroy imperialist influence in our homeland, Arab reaction cannot but be on the side of its own interests, the continuation of which depends on the persistence of imperialism, and consequently cannot side with the masses.

These Arab reactionary forces – particularly the intelligent ones – may outwardly support superficial national movements with the object of using them to settle, to their own advantage, some of their side conflicts with Israel or with world imperialism, but in the end they are inevitably against any national liberation movement that aims at uprooting colonialism from our soil and building an independent economy that will serve the interests of the masses instead of going into the pockets of the few representing these reactionary forces.

The growth of the revolutionary mass movement means, in relation to these forces, the growth of the people's authority that acts to destroy the authority of these forces...

This then is the enemy camp that we are really facing in our battle for the liberation of Palestine. We cannot win this battle without a clear sight of all parties in this camp. In light of the definition of these parties and our perception of the connections that bind them together, it becomes clear that our strongest enemy, the real and main enemy, is world imperialism, that Arab reaction is but one of its offshoots, and that Israel's power lies in its being one of the bases of world imperialism that is providing it with all sources of power and converting it into a big military force possessing the technological superiority and the economy that enable it to survive in spite of the conditions under which it lives.

Thus, the struggle for the liberation of Palestine, like any other liberation struggle in the world, becomes a struggle against world imperialism which is intent on plundering the wealth of the underdeveloped world and on keeping it a market for its goods. Naturally, Israel – and the Zionist movement as well – have their own characteristics, but these characteristics must be viewed in light of Israel's organic link with imperialism.

Following the end of the First World War, the Palestinian feudal forces and bourgeoisie tried to picture the struggle as if the enemy was only the Zionist movement and the Jews in Palestine, and on the basis that British colonialism would act as a neutral force in this conflict. It was only later that the masses, through the national contingents that formed their vanguard, became aware that their real enemy was British colonialism which wanted to strengthen and support the Zionist movement in our country as a means of striking at the ambitions of the progressive masses.

Our people today are no longer in need of new experiments and improvised actions. In our struggle for the liberation of Palestine, we face primarily world imperialism, our battle is directed basically against it, against Israel which acts as its base and against the reactionary forces which are allied to it. We will not win the battle unless we have a clear knowledge of our enemy to ensure that our calculations for the battle are correct...

Forces of the Revolution

Who are our friends – the forces of revolution?

...It is essential to define the forces of revolution on the Palestinian level from a class angle. To say that the Palestinian people with all their classes are in the same revolutionary position with regard to Israel and that all classes of the Palestinian people have the same revolutionary capacity because they find themselves without a territory and live outside their country would be unrealistic and unscientific. Such a statement would be correct had the entire Palestinian people been experiencing the same material living conditions. As it is, the Palestinian people do not all live under these same conditions but rather under different living conditions, a fact that we cannot scientifically ignore. Therefore, it is necessary to stop at these different conditions and the different positions to which they give rise.

It is true that large numbers of the Palestinian people were driven outside their country in 1948 and found themselves in almost identical conditions of homelessness. It is also true that the remainder of the Palestinian people who stayed on were at all times threatened with the same fate. However, during the last 20 years, the Palestinian people have settled down into certain well-marked class conditions so that it would be wrong to say that the entire Palestinian people are without a territory, or that they are entirely revolutionary. In the course of the last 20 years, certain well-defined class interests have arisen and have become the basis for defining positions. The bourgeoisie has come to have its own interests and is consequently concerned with stability and the continuation of its preferential class conditions...

We live in an underdeveloped non-industrial community, but all the same, the masses of our people do not have the same living conditions. Thus, in Amman, to state only one example, there are people living in [wealthy] Jebel Luwaibdeh, others in [working class] Jebel Nazif, and still others in camps. All these people cannot have the same attitude towards the revolution.

As for the contention that we are now passing through a stage of national liberation and not of socialist revolution, this relates to the subject of which classes are engaged in the struggle, which of them are with and which are against the revolution at each of its stages, but it does not eliminate the class question or the question of class struggle.

National liberation battles are also class battles.[6] They are battles between colonialism and the feudal and capitalist class whose interests are linked with those of the colonialist on the one hand, and the other classes of the people representing the greater part of the nation on the other. If by saying that national liberation battles are national battles it is intended to mean that they are battles waged by the overwhelming majority of the nation's masses, then this statement is true, but if it is intended to mean that these

---

6 This line of argument would be developed contemporaneously by Lebanese Marxist Mahdi Amel, whose work made him an ally of the PFLP. Reflecting in 1968 on the Algerian experience, Amel wrote:

> The struggle for national liberation is the sole historical form that distinguishes class struggle in the colonial [structural] formation. Whoever misses this essential point in the movement of our modern history and attempts to substitute class struggle with "nationalist struggle" or reduce the national struggle to a purely economic struggle loses the ability to understand our historical reality and thus also [the ability] to control its transformation.

Mahdi Amel, *Marxism and National Liberation* (New Delhi: LeftWorld Books, 2023), 72.

battles are different from the class struggle between the exploiters and the exploited, then the statement would be untrue.

It is also from this angle that we must consider the statement that the Zionist Israeli peril threatens the entire Palestinian and Arab existence, and that this struggle is one between the Zionist axis and the Arab axis. If this statement is intended to mean that the Zionist peril threatens the overwhelming majority of the Palestinian and Arab masses, then it is true and certain, but if it is intended to deny the meeting of interests between Israel and Arab reactionaries (in spite of their numerical inferiority to the masses of the people) or to deny the difference in the revolutionary roles of the other classes, considering the revolutionary role of the petit bourgeoisie living in urban areas to be on the same level as that of the rural or camp population, then this is untrue.

To sum up, our class view of the forces of the Palestinian revolution must take into account the special nature of the class situation in underdeveloped communities and the fact that our battle is one of national liberation, as well as the special nature of the Zionist peril. This, however, means that we must adopt a scientific definition of the revolutionary classes and their roles in light of these special features, and should not at all lead to the dismissal of the class view in the definition of the forces of revolution.

Rightist thought is trying to dismiss the class view in the definition of the forces of revolution to enable the bourgeoisie to infiltrate into positions of leadership and obstruct the revolution at the limits imposed by its interests... The material of the Palestinian revolution, its mainstay and its basic forces are the workers and peasants. These classes form the majority of the Palestinian people and physically fill all camps, villages and poor urban districts. Here lie the forces of revolution... the forces of change. Here we find real preparation for long years of fighting. Here are the particular daily living conditions that drive people on to fight and die because the difference between death and life under such conditions is not much.

It is by starting from this objectivity that we are able to define the distinguishing mark between our people's unsuccessful struggle during the past 50 years and this new stage of our struggle, to draw a line of demarcation between clarity and vagueness, and to determine the great difference between a revolutionary march ending in victory and a hesitant, unsteady march ending in failure...

The Palestinian Petit Bourgeoisie

The petit bourgeoisie comprises the craftsmen, the educated groups such as students, teachers, junior employees, small shopkeepers, lawyers, engineers and medical men... It is possible for us to say in general that, during the stage of democratic national liberation, this class may be an ally to the force of the revolution and to its basic material represented by the workers and peasants, but alliance with this class must be so alert as to prevent it from infiltrating into the position of command because that would expose the revolution to vacillation and deviation or slackness...

The Palestinian petit bourgeoisie has raised the banner of armed struggle and is leading it today, and the fact that it is not in power makes it more revolutionary than the Arab petit bourgeoisie that is determined to preserve its interests and remain in power by avoiding the long and conclusive struggle with the opposing camp... The workers' radical and conclusive thought and strategy alone are capable of confronting the enemy camp; and it is the efficient leadership of the workers that is able, through its scientific tactics, to lead the petit bourgeois class along with it in this struggle – without this class being in the position of leadership and without allowing it to dilute revolutionary thought, strategy and programmes through its vacillating and inconclusive thought and strategy...

The Palestinian Bourgeoisie

The Palestinian bourgeoisie is essentially a business and banking bourgeoisie whose interests are interconnected among its members and are linked with the business and banking interests of imperialism. The wealth of this class is derived from brokerage transactions in foreign goods, insurance operations and banking business. Therefore, in the strategic field, this class is against the revolution that aims to put an end to the existence of imperialism and its interests in our homeland, which would mean the destruction of its sources of wealth. Since our battle against Israel is at the same time a battle against imperialism, this class will stand by its own interests, that is, with imperialism against the revolution...

On what scientific basis can it be said that all classes of the Palestinian people are among the forces of the revolution? Our revolution today is an armed one. Are all classes of the Palestinian people among the forces of this armed revolution?

After 5 June 1967, the young men of the camps and villages took up arms, hid in the mountains and fortified themselves in the cities.[7] They directed their bullets against Israel and faced Israeli bullets with their bodies. At exactly the same time, the traditional bourgeois leaderships were receiving [Eliyahu] Sassoon, [Moshe] Dayan and other Israeli leaders to discuss with them the Palestinian set-up that Israel had planned for the purpose of liquidating the Palestine question, thus achieving political triumph after having attained military victory. These attempts would have been successful had they not been foiled by the escalation of commando action. During that period, the young men of the camps were giving death to, and receiving death from Israel, while the merchants on the West Bank were seeking to link their interests anew with the enemy state.

In view of all this, is it permissible for us to hear such slogans as "We are all commandos", or "The Palestinian people with all its classes are taking part in the armed struggle", or "No rich and no poor so long as we remain homeless", without evaluating and criticising them and preventing their spread?

The revolution is science and scientific thought looks for tangible facts. We will not be misled by deceptive mottoes and slogans which are at variance with the facts, and which are launched by certain class forces in defence of their interests. The Palestinian bourgeoisie that now lives in Palestine under Zionist occupation is not among the forces of the revolution, although it has not manifestly associated itself with Israel and will in reality remain the class

---

7   It was also true that Palestinian *fida 'iyyin* had launched guerrilla operations into occupied territory prior to June 1967, but this confrontation escalated with the Egyptian–Syrian defeat.

force through which the enemies will always try to defeat the revolution and stop it in the middle of the road...

Organisation and Mobilisation of Palestinian Revolutionary Forces

Political organisation armed with the theory of scientific socialism is the highest form for the organisation and mobilisation of the working-class forces on the greatest scale. This is a fact that has been made perfectly clear by all revolutionary experiences in this century. The experiences of China, Vietnam and Cuba, as well as the experience of the October Revolution, all point to and confirm this fact. By clarifying and scientifically explaining the state of misery suffered by the working class, by revealing the process of exploitation of this class by imperialism and capitalism, by indicating the nature of the major conflict in which the communities of the present age are living on international and local levels, by explaining the motion of history and its trend, by defining the role of the working class and the importance of this role and by indicating the weapons possessed by this class, scientific socialist theory renders the working-class conscious of its existence, conditions and future, thus permitting the mobilisation of the forces of this class on the greatest scale...

The foregoing clearly indicates the basic lines of our position regarding the subject of relations among the Palestinian forces. These lines enable us to define our position with regard to all subjects and problems arising on this level and serve to clarify our position with regard to the existing picture of the Palestinian field and the direction in which we must exercise our efforts to establish objective relations among the forces and organisations of the Palestinian revolution.

1. We regard Palestinian national unity as a basic factor for the mobilisation of all forces of the revolution to confront the enemy camp, and on this basis, we must take an effective position to achieve it.

2. The form of national unity is the rise of a front in which all classes of the revolution – workers, peasants and petit bourgeoisie – will be represented.

3. We must take action to mobilise the workers and peasants in one single revolutionary political organisation armed with scientific socialist theory. On this basis, we must effectively endeavour to unite all Palestinian leftist organisations that, through contact and experience, can be persuaded to adopt this analysis.

4. The petit bourgeoisie will not join this form of organisation, which adheres to scientific socialism and strong political organisation, but will join those Palestinian organisations that content themselves with general liberation slogans, avoiding clarity in thinking and class view and leading an organisational life that does not demand of it anything beyond its capacity. In other words, this class will fill Fatah and the Palestine Liberation Organisation (PLO) in the first place.

5. On this basis, and on the basis of our view of the main conflict and the nature of the stage, as well as the necessity of achieving a national unity that will group together all the forces of the revolution to stand in the face of Israel, we must work for the establishment of a national front with Fatah and the PLO, which will provide the battle with the necessary class alliance on the one hand, and preserve that right of each to view and plan for the battle according to its class horizon on the other…

Forces of Revolution at the Arab Level

The strategy of the Palestine liberation struggle requires the mobilisation and concentration of all the forces of revolution in the Arab countries in general and the Arab regions surrounding Israel in particular… The "Arab Hanoi" motto [is] a revolutionary principle creating coalescence between the Palestinian revolution and the Arab revolution and forming a firm foundation for the Palestinian and Arab national liberation movement, which would enable it to stand in the face of the enemy camp and gain superiority over it…

The armed struggle against Israel and all imperialist interests in our homeland, the expansion of the armed struggle front, which stands in the face of Arab reaction and all imperialist interests and bases in the Arab homeland, and the encirclement of Israel with the strategy of the people's liberation war from every side – from Syria, Egypt, Lebanon, Jordan and inside the territory occupied before and after 5 June 1967 – is the only path that leads to victory. It is not important that the Palestinian people should register a heroic stand through commando action: the important thing is liberation and victory... The strategy of the democratic national revolution in this age has become clear through the Vietnamese experience and before it the Cuban and Chinese experiences...

The first national regime to appear in the Arab world on the basis of [post-Second World War independence]... was the Nasser regime in Egypt, and then the picture extended to include Syria, Iraq, Algeria and South Yemen... In any historical evaluation of these regimes and what they represented in the Arab field in the 1950s and until June 1967, we must not lose sight of the major revolutionary achievements realised by these regimes, particularly the Nasser regime. This regime was able to get rid of the British occupation forces stationed in the Suez Canal Zone, wage war against all the colonialist military pacts through which colonialism tried to get back into the area under the pretext of defence pacts against the Soviet peril, and do away with the colonialist-reactionary alliance that controlled the destiny of Egypt and its masses...

It set Egypt on the road of socialist transformation and accompanied these transformations with similar ones in the field of revolutionary thought. By this, it lifted revolutionary thought from the level of general liberation, unionist and socialist slogans to the beginnings of a class view of the revolutionary forces and the beginnings of the adoption of the general socialist course in viewing and analysing the movement of progress... But these regimes continued to move within programmes and plans imposed on them by their class nature. At this point, the problem of the structure of these regimes and the problems of their plans began to emerge. In the middle 1960s, the Nasser regime began to live through this problem without being able to overcome it until the June defeat, which came to reveal clearly the problem relating to the structure of this regime and its inability within this class nature to triumph over the imperialist-reactionary-Zionist-Israeli camp...

The interests of this upper class required the maintenance of the experiment within limits that do not conflict with its interests or with its thinking and view of the battle. This class is antagonistic to colonialism and reaction but at the same time wants to keep the privileges that it enjoys. It is this state of affairs that has defined the nature of the political, economic, military and ideological programmes of these regimes… Thus, the June defeat does not for us constitute a mere military defeat. It is in reality a defeat for these regimes and their programmes and their inability to effect military, economic and ideological mobilisation that is capable of resisting and triumphing over imperialism and its alliances and plans in our homeland…

When we present the Vietnamese liberation movement – which is waging a triumphant struggle against the US and Vietnamese reaction – as an example of successful liberation movements in this age, we do not at all ignore the special nature of our battle both in respect of the nature of imperialist presence, represented by Israel in our homeland, and in respect of the special nature of the land.

We always mean in fact the main strategic lines of the Vietnam War – represented by the strong political organisation that adheres to scientific socialism and mobilises the forces of the masses on the greatest scale under the leadership of the working class and the national front slogan, using the course of guerrilla warfare, the popular liberation war, the political, economic and military mobilisation resulting from all this, the protracted war, the determination to win – that determination which is embodied by the poor classes of the community, the classes who cannot continue to live under the burden of the ugly and dirty exploitation exercised by imperialism and Vietnamese reactionaries. We also mean the world revolutionary alliance established by the Vietnamese liberation movement to enable it to confront imperialism, with all its weight, forces and plans.

Forces of Revolution on the World Level

The Palestinian and Arab liberation movement does not move in a vacuum. It lives and fights in the midst of specific world circumstances that affect and react with it, and all this will determine our fate. The international ground on which national liberation movements move has always been, and will remain, a basic factor in determining peoples' destinies.

The First World War was a war among the imperialist capitalist powers themselves, and its object was to redistribute world markets among these powers. That war was an armed explosion of the conflicts among world capitalist blocs in their race for the exploitation and plunder of peoples' wealth and for monopolising their markets. That war was not a revolutionary war waged by the working class in the progressive countries and by the enslaved peoples against the exploiting capitalists. The same applies to some degree to the Second World War. Consequently, conflicts among the colonialist capitalist powers were the principal manifestation on the world stage...

In its liberation march to recover its land and freedom, the Palestinian people today face a unified imperialist camp with its technological superiority, its skill in fighting and neutralising revolutions, its ability to take over behind other forces, its readiness for direct confrontation whenever it feels that the forces behind which it takes cover are no longer capable of striking at peoples' movements, and its endeavours to isolate national movements from the world revolutionary camp and neutralise the Soviet Union's efforts through the threat of nuclear war...

Our first friends are the enslaved peoples who are suffering from imperialism and the imperialist exploitation of their efforts and wealth, or who are living in the same danger represented by the USA today in attempting to impose its influence on rising peoples. The peoples of Africa, Asia and Latin America are daily suffering a life of wretchedness, poverty, ignorance and backwardness, which is the result of colonialism and imperialism in their lives. The major conflict experienced by the world of today is the conflict between exploiting world imperialism on the one hand, and these peoples and the socialist camp on the other. The alliance of the Palestinian and Arab national liberation movement with the liberation movement in Vietnam, the revolutionary situation in Cuba and the Democratic People's Republic of Korea, and the national liberation movements in Asia, Africa and Latin America is the only way to create a camp that is capable of facing and triumphing over the imperialist camp.

The Palestinian and Arab liberation movement in alliance with national liberation movements in all undeveloped and poor countries will, in facing world imperialism led by the USA, find a strong ally to back its forces and augment its power of resistance. This ally is the People's Republic of China, which in reality is still facing the same US peril that is attempting to encircle and isolate it and impede its growth.[8]

The great People's Republic of China, which is still experiencing the effects of underdevelopment caused by colonialism and imperialism, and which is still facing the same peril and the same contradictions, adopts this analysis of the basic international contradiction that governs the march of history at this stage, and consequently adopts the same revolutionary strategy of liberation followed by these peoples in facing colonialism. This strategic congruence creates the concrete ground for a revolutionary alliance that will place us in a better position to face and triumph over the enemy. The People's Republic of China adopts the Palestinian Arab view in its analysis of Israel as an imperialist base that must be destroyed...

Imperialism and reactionary forces are today attempting to create a breach in the relations between the Palestinian and Arab national liberation movement and the Soviet Union and the powers of the socialist camp, and it is our duty through our vigilance to prevent imperialism from achieving this aim. Throughout the past period, the Soviet Union has been a major supporter of the Arab masses in their fight against imperialism and all its projects and plans for our homeland...

Along with this series of basic revolutionary alliances, we must also, through our fighting and political efforts and through the clear nature of our struggle as one of national liberation, draw to our side all liberation forces in Europe, America and every part of the world. With such strategy on the international level, we can

---

8   Having stated its position in open support of the liberation of Palestine at the 1955 Bandung Conference, China backed the Palestinian revolution militarily from 1966, providing armaments and training to various factions.

encircle Israel, Zionism and imperialism and mobilise revolutionary forces on the world level to stand with us in the struggle.

No Revolutionary Party without Revolutionary Theory

The revolutionary theory that presents all questions relating to
humanity and the age in a scientific and revolutionary manner is
Marxism. In the history of human endeavour to acquire knowledge, Marxism represents a unique attempt in understanding
nature, life, society and history. Marxism has presented a theory
(dialectical materialism) that analyses and explains nature and
its motion and the laws governing this motion through a tangible
scientific material approach that is devoid of illusion, supersti-
tion, subjective meditation and imagination, and mere verbal or
logical inferences. It has then applied this same tangible scientific
material approach to the study of society, the movement of society
and the march of history (historical materialism), stopping particularly before the formation, structure, conflicts and movement of
modern capitalist society (theory of surplus value and scientific
socialism). Through all this, Marxism has presented a dialectical
scientific approach that has elevated the study of history, society
and political manifestations to the level of science. As the natural
sciences are man's means for controlling the phenomena of nature
and using them for his benefit, so is Marxism the science that
enables man to understand the progress of societies and history
and to direct and influence them.

Lenin completed Marx's scientific efforts by applying the same
Marxist method to the study of capitalism in its evolution towards
the stage of centralisation, monopoly and colonisation, thus
explaining all political manifestations and events that attended the
beginning of the twentieth century. On the basis of Marxism and
the scientific socialist approach, he was able to lead with success
the first socialist revolution in history, to draw up its strategy, to
face its problems and to define the features of the top of the revolutionary organisation which led it on the way to victory. In this way,
Lenin gave Marxist theory its revolutionary modern applications
so that Marxism–Leninism has become the standard of revolution in this period of human history... The October Revolution,

the revolutions in China, Cuba and Vietnam and all revolutionary experiences throughout the world have arisen originally on the strength of this theory. This picture contrasts with the stumbling confusion and collapse of all revolutionary attempts that have not been based on this vision, this theory and this guide. It is not a mere coincidence that the October Revolution and the revolutions in China, Cuba, North Korea, Vietnam and the socialist countries of Europe have succeeded and stood firm in the face of imperialism and in overcoming or beginning to overcome their state of underdevelopment, against the quasi-paralysis or infirmity characterising the countries of the Third World, which are not committed scientifically to scientific socialist theory as their guideline for planning all their policies and defining their programmes...

The essence of the Marxist view of human society is that it is in continuous motion and continuous change, and consequently any analysis presented by Marxism in respect of any stage or any actuality arises constantly from the old actuality. The invariable factor in Marxism is its dialectical scientific approach in viewing things in their state of continuous motion and change. This method is Marxism in its essence. It is the revolutionary theoretical weapon that enables us to view things scientifically in their state of continuous motion, development and change...

It would be a gross error to imagine that our mere declaration of adherence to Marxism–Leninism is a fairy wand that will open before us the road to victory... The Arab communist parties that are formally and verbally committed to Marxism–Leninism have not been able to lead the revolution in our homeland because their commitment has been verbal, or because they have understood the theory in a rigid and fossilised manner, or because they have not been able to apply this theoretical weapon to our actual living circumstances in such a way as to deduce from it a clear view of the battle and a sound strategy for its leadership...

The value of our commitment to Marxism–Leninism lies... in the application of this approach to the conditions of our struggle for the purpose of formulating revolutionary strategy and tactics. Unless we raise our commitment to Marxism–Leninism to this level, it will remain a commitment of intellectuals to a theory that serves them in discussion and not the commitment of a revolutionary party to a theory that opens before it a clear view of the battle.

Criticism and Self-Criticism

Stopping to evaluate our work from time to time, placing the party and its policies and activities on the dissection table once in a while and following up scientifically all the positive and negative attitudes reflected in the revolutionary cause by the party's policies, programmes and positions are matters that furnish the scientific revolutionary mentality with which the party can overcome errors and develop work programmes in light of practical experience and eventually lead the work on to success...

The practice of criticism as regards the revolutionary party is the method whereby the party breathes in new air, breathes out unhealthy air and eventually renews its vitality and capacities in a continuous manner.

Mao Tse tung says:

Conscientious practice of self-criticism is still another hallmark distinguishing our party from all other political parties. As we say, dust will accumulate if a room is not cleaned regularly. Our comrades' minds and our party's work may also collect dust, and also need sweeping and washing. The proverb "Running water is never stale and a door-hinge is never worm-eaten" means that constant motion prevents the inroads of germs and other organisms. To check up regularly on our work and in the process develop a democratic style of work, to fear neither criticism nor self-criticism: and to apply such good popular Chinese maxims as "Say all you know and say it without reserve", "Blame not the speaker but be warned by his words" and "Correct mistakes if you have committed them and guard against them if you have not".[9]

...This does not mean that there may come a time when the revolutionary party will live without problems: Such thinking is

---

9   Mao Tse Tung, "On Coalition Government", in *Selected Works, Volume III* (Peking: Foreign Languages Press, 1965), 316–17.

unrealistic and unscientific. Our ambition is to outgrow the problems of this stage of the organisation's life to face the problems of a more advanced and more revolutionary stage.

The Arab Nationalist Movement and the PFLP

At its inception, the Popular Front for the Liberation of Palestine was formed from the Arab Nationalist Movement (ANM) branch in the Palestinian field, the Heroes of the Return, the Palestine Liberation Front[10] and independent elements which soon took the form of a fourth group within the Front. On this basis and in light of this formation, it was not designed that the Front in the first stage of its life should present a complete leftist political view of the liberation battle proceeding from and based on scientific socialist theory; what was implicitly understood actually was that the Front should present a general liberation thought bearing progressive features that would crystallise increasingly with the crystallisation of the experiment. This is with regard to the Front's political thought. With regard to the organisation, likewise, the Front was not designed, at that stage of its formation, to be a unified party organisation based on the same revolutionary organisational strategic lines that we have discussed. What was also understood was that the Front would for some time continue to consist of a group of organisations, each of which would maintain its independent existence. However, there would be a beginning made towards planning for coordination among these organisations and an attempt made to unify the educational material given to them; this was in preparation for the realisation of a climate that would pave the way for the unification of these organisations in terms of strategic planning, in light of their practice and experience.

In light of this picture, it is evident that there is a definite objective distinction between the organisation of the Palestinian branch

---

10 Founded by Syrian army officer Ahmed Jibril in 1959, the Palestine Liberation Front (PLF) became the Popular Front for the Liberation of Palestine – General Command (PFLP–GC) after its split from the PFLP in 1968. Backed by the Ba'athist government in Damascus, the group refused to condemn the Syrian arrests of PFLP leaders in March 1968 and supported the 1976 Syrian intervention against the PLO in Lebanon.

of the Movement (ANM) on the one hand and the Front on the other. The Movement, in light of what was designed by its Central Committee during the July 1967 session, possesses a socialist revolutionary concept through which it views the strategy of the Palestine liberation struggle, while the Front presents a liberation thought with progressive features. Moreover, the Movement represents a unified party organisation preparing to rebuild itself according to a revolutionary organisational strategy, while the Front represents a group of organisations that differ in their organisational structure...

The Palestine Liberation Front has [in 1968] separated from the PFLP, and, with it, a group of independents. The Front continued to exist between the Palestinian branch of the Arab Nationalist Movement and the Heroes of the Return. On the other hand, the new situation has enabled the ANM to present, through the Front,[11] its revolutionary analysis of the Palestinian situation and its full political view of the struggle for liberation, that is, its complete political thought, so that the new picture is one of almost complete identity between the ANM and the Popular Front... The Popular Front's political view of the battle is now that of the Movement...

The conception of the PFLP ceases to be that which prevailed at the time of its foundation – that is, a front in the usual political sense with regard to thought and organisational relations – and our understanding of the Popular Front and the direction that we take in building it have become something different.

According to our present understanding of the PFLP and the direction that we take in its building up, it is the revolutionary party based on the political strategy and organisational strategy set forth in this report.

During the process of complete fusion of the Movement and the Popular Front, the sound motto that guides us is:

The Movement in the service of the Front, and not the Front in the service of the Movement.

---

11   PFLP "Popular Front" and "the Front" are used interchangeably in this and other PFLP documents.

"Lenin and Leninism: 100 Years", a special edition of *al-Hadaf* 1, no. 38 (18 April 1970). From 1967, the presence of Lenin bloomed in Ghassan Kanafani's analysis of the way forward. Source: *al-Hadaf*, Gaza.

8

The Resistance and its Challenges: The View of the PFLP (1970)

Introduction: The Strategic Horizon of the Palestinian Struggle by *Max Ajl*

It is widely known that Ghassan Kanafani, belletrist, militant, martyr, revolutionary organiser and theorist, was one of the authors of the Popular Front for the Liberation of Palestine's Strategy for the Liberation of Palestine, a text which remains the high noon of Palestinian theory of national liberation. Rich with the learning of a Mao-inflected Marxist–Leninism, the text identified the friends and enemies of the Palestinian masses and crystallised a strategy for a national liberation front to break the Zionist grip on the Palestinian homeland. That text has a much lesser-known cousin, one which I here introduce: *The Resistance and its Challenges: The View of the Popular Front for the Liberation of Palestine*. Originally published as a pamphlet in August 1970, the text was a theoretical inquiry into the problem of revolutionary organisation for the Palestinian movement. It was, diamond-like, the product of the pressures of world reaction, imperialism, capitalism, Zionism, opportunism and political irresponsibility, and the Front's own political impasse, bearing down on the organisation and forcing the production of as much clarity as could be found at that moment.

I would like to focus on two interlinked aspects of this text, for they highlight the creative genius of Kanafani and the Front's organic adoption and reworking to fit the challenges of their day. The first was the question of thought, of theory itself in the Palestinian revolutionary struggle. The second is the question of nation and class in the Palestinian liberation movement. For Kanafani, thought and theory were necessary in order to arm the movement with the necessary course of action to eradicate its enemies. Such arming could neither replace nor be replaced by arms them-selves. Kanafani rejected the "trend opposing the necessity and importance of revolutionary theory"; a trend tilting in favour of pure military action. Yet, for Kanafani, military action had to be tied organically to "finite political goals", a "strategic vision", to which the tactic was not simply subordinated – which would deny its dynamic creativity – but which it had to serve and with which it helped compose an "ever-advancing dialectical process". Even war itself – a war against a behemoth like the Zionist state which filled the horizon of politics and strategy – understood as politics extended to the realm of kinetic violence, was indeed not just the shooting of bullets or the assault on tanks but was itself a "strate-gic vision". War required a holistic theory.

What was that theory? Here is the second facet of this daz-zlingly cut text I want here to raise: the dialectic of nation and class in the Palestinian, and by extension Arab, national libera-tion struggle. Like others at this moment – Mehdi Ben Barka and Amilcar Cabral – Kanafani was forced by dint of historical experi-ence, by the weaknesses of the Arab national movement in state power, by onrushing neo-colonialism – to reckon with the class elements of national struggle and the national elements of class. And still, Kanafani had to make clear – as much to the bourgeoi-sie who sought to direct the national struggle in Palestine and to a lesser extent to those dismissing the national question – that national liberation was not pitter-patter designed to meet "the search of the bourgeoisie for a framework to justify its presence in authority". National liberation concerned the interests of the Arab working classes, against their "tripartite enemy: Israel, impe-rialism and reaction".

On the one hand, this reflected a temporally bound and con-textual critique of the Arab national movements and the regimes in which they were nested. The latter were not friendly to internal democracy, nor to internal organisational work, weakening the living forces of Arab patriotism. The 1967 defeat exposed the "petty bourgeois" governments, who still retained residual loyalty due to their coexistence with the "far more reactionary Arab bourgeois regimes, more deeply entrenched in clan, feudal, or monopolistic control".

Kanafani did not draw from this tableau an abandonment of the nation in favour of class. This was particularly the case when one section of the Palestinian people lived directly under colonialism and the other remained "uprooted from their land" by that same colonial force with its imperial-buttressed borders. Nor did he seek to abandon class when "one section is tied to the limb of imperialism, while the other languishes under the chains of exploitative regimes tied more or less to the wheels of imperialism" – for him, Israel was a force for imperialism and therefore a class force par excellence. He, therefore, sought to use the historical experience of defeat to enliven and enrich the thinking of the defenders of the cause. This meant rethinking class and nation, drawing and developing the dialectics of each as they interpenetrated. Palestinian revolutionary forces could capitulate neither on the class question nor on the national question, as a strategic capitulation on one was the "reserve force" towards capitulationism on the other.

Yet, here the resistance encountered a desperate dilemma, theretofore unresolved: would the Palestinian intifada, with its resistance against the open wound of colonialism in the Arab region, lead to a broader Arab revolution? Was this necessary? One way Kanafani broached this question was through the contemporary landscape of settler colonialism and the historical landscape of national liberation. Again, drawing on the Chinese experience, he considered geographical sweep and demographic depth central to successful liberation warfare. Neither obtained when looking at the borders of historical Palestine. Kanafani concluded that there was "no non-Arab way out". Thus, merging with the "toiling Arab masses", embedding itself in the geography of the "Arab continent", would lead to the Palestinian "Great Revolution" being a kind of political catalyst, a "sign of the people's greatness in their arduous struggle". This thinking would illuminate the strategic horizon of the Palestinian struggle. It demanded the creation of "Arab Hanois", and the strengthening of Arab and Palestinian "national and progressive forces", within the context of an Arab national project. Such clarity, the child of "Marxist–Leninism fused creatively with the militant coherence of Arab nationalism" was the gift of the PFLP, and Kanafani as its theorist. It is a gift whose value has diminished not a whit with time.

* * *

THE RESISTANCE AND ITS CHALLENGES[1]

1

Since its emergence, the Popular Front for the Liberation of Palestine (PFLP) has been exposed to a media counter-attack whose reasons must be explained over many pages. However, from the October 1967 foundation of the Front – with the unification of three branches (Revolutionary Youth[2] [the Palestinian branch of the Arab National Movement], the Heroes of Return and the Palestinian Liberation Front) – until January 1969, when the split with the group which later called itself the Democratic Front was almost completely confirmed,[3] the scale of the counter-attack against the Popular Front[4] was on a much lower level than the onslaught that multiplied subsequently and which has continued in one form or another to this day.

Since the formation of the Popular Front, it has been clear that this vanguard grouping in the armed resistance movement represents a "ploughable land" (*ard harth* – ارض حرث) susceptible and sensitive to many accelerated developments that have led to immediate political, organisational and military repercussions within

---

1 Original publication: *Kitab al-Hadaf*, Vol. 5 (Beirut, 1970). Translated by Louis Brehony. An earlier version of our translation titled this essay "The Resistance and its Problems" and, while the word *m`adilat* more clearly denotes "challenges" or "issues", Kanafani draws heavily on texts by Lukács and Mao which refer specifically to "the organisational problem" in Marxist political parlance. We therefore use the words interchangeably in this final translation.

2 The name of this organisation is sometimes translated as Youth of Revenge or Avenging Youth.

3 Led by Nayef Hawatmeh, differences with what came to be known as the Democratic Popular Front for the Liberation of Palestine (DPFLP, later DFLP) came to the surface in the aftermath of the first PFLP congress in August 1968, with the split coming to fruition in the following February. Though it saw the Habash-led current as rightist, the DFLP's "transitional plan" – for a state on any territory withdrawn from by Israel – became PLO policy and the basis for entry into negotiations with the Zionist leadership. Both organisations came to oppose the Oslo Accords, though the DFLP softened its stance in the late 1990s.

4 Kanafani uses Popular Front and "the Front" throughout as shorthand for the Popular Front for the Liberation of Palestine. We use Popular Front and PFLP respectively in this translation.

the Front. It is conceivable that this is precisely what has led to the following three fundamental consequences:

First: the sense of various sides towards the possibilities of "danger" posed by the accelerationist trend developing within the Popular Front, which they therefore work to besiege.

Second: the two splits that occurred within the Front. The first of these was the Palestinian Liberation Front, tending towards a purely military approach, and which – now faced with a rapid advance in the process of adherence to Marxism–Leninism – found it favourable to end the organisational relationship convened in October 1967 with Revolutionary Youth and Heroes of Return. The second split came with the departure of a group which considered its "leftist" loyalties to be too broad to be accommodated within the PFLP's organisational framework. The Heroes of Return group, however, made a decision in December [1967] towards complete organisational unity within the Front.

Third: the hugely accelerated commitment to the ideology of Marxism–Leninism and the reflection of this commitment in questions concerning political relationships, education, organisation and military activism within the Popular Front. This is exemplified in the publication of the *Political and Organisational Strategy* [Strategy of Liberation] of the Popular Front, following the February 1969 conference: the report setting out the clear commitments of the Popular Front, as well as towards realising revolutionary developments in organisational relations, in political and military activity, and initiation of the Cadre School, which follows a military, pedagogical, political and cultural programme on the highest levels. The latter is the first of its type, worthy for the graduation of ranks of political fighters at the level required for the tasks of revolutionary work.

However, all of this remained unknown to the majority of those following the events, in the face of the unparalleled media onslaught against the Popular Front. Those participating in this attack, on an equal footing, included Arab regimes: left and right; organisations of the resistance movement: left, right and centre; and international party associations: liberals, Marxists and Trotskyists!

In the midst of all of this flowed an extraordinary process of encirclement and siege, to the extent that when the US plane was hijacked [in August 1969],[5] for example, a tip-off to *al-Ahram* [newspaper] was enough for it to attribute the operation to the PLO! The PFLP was not at liberty to respond to this counterattack. First, because its missions as a revolutionary organisation carry such organisational, political and military immensity that render any attention paid to meeting non-duties a mere waste that benefits no one. And second, because the organisation has always considered the formation of a Palestinian national liberation front to be an urgent task upon which the fate of the revolution depends, while [considering] bickering, the trading of accusations and a tense atmosphere as serving as mere impediments to such a direction.

A single glance at the nature of the media counter-attack directed against the Popular Front is enough to show us the rarity of finding a charge that has not been levied against it: rightist, fascist, subversively destructive, "robbing the efforts of revolutionaries", ultra-left, regionalist, Arabist, anarcho-Marxist, national chauvinist, reactionary and atheist. From Rabat to Kuwait, the same accusations are repeated. Meanwhile, the PFLP newspaper [*al-Hadaf*] is banned from entering Syria, Saudi Arabia, Egypt, Algeria, Morocco, Tunisia and, occasionally, banned in Jordan, while its activities – with the exceptions of Aden, Amman and Baghdad – are sanctioned, banned and censored. Its men have been subjected to the contours of prison in every Arab capital without exception. However, it is the PFLP alone that drives the foremost glories of the resistance (Gaza), has more than 500 fighters in the prisons of the enemy, and has lost the largest number of military officials. The PFLP is the Palestinian force most capable of striking the inside [of historic Palestine]. Above all, it remains the only Palestinian

---

5 On 29 August 1969, PFLP activists Leila Khaled and Salim Issawi led the hijacking of a US Trans World Airlines flight, boarding in Rome and diverting its path from Tel Aviv to Damascus. There were no fatalities.

organisation to have a clearly declared strategy, with total commitment to putting this strategy into practice.

For all of these reasons, the Arab and Palestinian right reject the Popular Front, and works towards its siege and isolation. Similarly, the "infantile left" dedicates almost all of its time towards the work of distorting its reputation and spreading rumours and accusations against it. In the midst of all of this, the Popular Front continues to tread its path, becoming increasingly aware not only of the range of forces confronting it, but also of the crisis engulfing the Palestinian and Arab national movement. This is why it commits its course towards the first and most urgent task, namely, the work needed to overcome this impasse, in order to confront the enormity of the forces mobilising against the Palestinian resistance movement. It is convinced that, as a matter of duty, such a confrontation may only take place through a Palestinian national front, linked to an Arab national front. Immersion in polemics thus constitutes a distortion of the revolutionary trend, which, more than ever, demands diligent work as the bare minimum of responsibility to the battle.

This is doubtlessly a quick introduction to the subject but, without it, this discussion will fail to serve its essential purpose.

2

It has become common for any discussion of the resistance movement in its present stage to fall into a field of traps: we are not talking here about traps set by an emotional or sectarian outlook; or the view that puts the demands of the media ahead of a critical approach; or that limits itself, voluntarily or forcibly, to tactical details. Rather, we mean here the more dangerous traps associated with assessing the resistance movement through the critical approach itself.

This [critical] approach routinely falls into "eclecticism", but also into rigid doctrinairism and, most importantly, avails itself of commitment to the scientific method and the objective basis of scientific criticism, which forms an inseparable part of revolutionary work as a whole, if the revolution is – and indeed it is – compelled to interpret the world and change it at the same time.

The reality of the resistance is like that of any other movement, made up in actuality of many component parts, linked together through dialectical and continuing threads. There is no doubt that a fatal, critical sin is committed when a state of silence is imposed upon one part of that reality. Doing so only means the immediate repetition of a series of mistakes: separating this component arbitrarily from an infinite number of others, before pacifying it forcibly, then studying, criticising or assessing it in isolation from the dialectical relationship between action and knowledge.

From this vantagepoint, we see how masses of critical articles have emerged over the recent period, evaluating the Palestinian resistance through the lens of its armed actions alone. Meanwhile, other writings analysed the resistance through purely doctrinal analogy, turning the issue into a pile of formulas and literatures. Such are the diametrical analyses which isolate the Palestinian resistance, just as chemotherapy isolates a live cell in the laboratory.

Any critical view of the resistance in its present stage evidently requires an awareness of the totality of the parties to this dynamic relationship as they relate to the issue as a whole. It presupposes a view of the reality faced by this resistance from the angle of its mutual relations, and of its movement, modification and development. The dialectical method is itself, in its essence, both critical and revolutionary, as Marx says,[6] and undoubtedly continuous. Hence, the critical process is merely one component of a totality whose mutual, strained or contradictory relations constitute the continuous movement of history.

The fundamental error begins with the separation of theory and practice, and of erecting barriers between the two, for this leads

---

6 Kanafani is paraphrasing Marx's "Afterword to the Second German Edition of Capital", written in January 1873, where the dialectical method is described as, "is in its essence critical and revolutionary". Marx concludes:

> The contradictions inherent in the movement of capitalist society impress themselves upon the practical bourgeois most strikingly in the changes of the periodic cycle, through which modern industry runs, and whose crowning point is the universal crisis.

Karl Marx, *Capital: A Critique of Political Economy, Volume 1* (London: Lawrence and Wishart, 1970 [1867]), 20.

to doctrinal stagnation on the one hand, and, on the other, to a mechanistic understanding of history, and practically empiricist attempts to change it.

This brief preamble was necessary in order to outline a critical approach: there is no doubt that a method of criticism that does not allow practice to correct theory, thus enriching it and enabling it to influence reality, must be rejected. We must therefore identify the main features of the issue from the outset; these are the polarities whose interlinked relations form the underlying basis and real essence of the current revolutionary process, and whose artificial separation leads only to anarchy.

First, therefore, comes the issue of political thought in the Palestinian resistance. Second, the issue of practice, of which the combative practice is most evident. But what gives these two issues their depth and effectiveness is the third matter, which focuses on the organisational question.

Mao Tse Tung sums up this triangular question by saying:

> If our task is to cross a river, we cannot cross it without a bridge or a boat. Unless the bridge or boat problem is solved, it is idle to speak of crossing the river. Unless the problem of method is solved, talk about the task is useless.[7]

We therefore stand before a threefold problem: theory, practice and method, which consists essentially of the organisational issue. This means that any critical research into the resistance movement cannot absolve itself of any of these three polarities, or isolate it, making it the only measure of what transpires. If it does, its errors will be immediate and fatal.

It is no longer acceptable, nor worthwhile, for "revolutionary action" to be merely experimental practice fought without the weapon of political thought. Likewise, without its actualisation in practice, political thought or theory usually leads to the vicious

---

7 "Be Concerned with the Well-Being of the Masses, Pay Attention to Methods of Work" (27 January 1934), Mao Tse Tung, *Selected Works, Volume I* (Peking: Foreign Languages Press, 1965), 150. The quoted text also appears in the *Selected Quotations of Mao Tse Tung*.

cycle of idle chatter. However, the distance between theory and practice cannot be covered mechanically. The relations of political thought and practice, between theory and application, raises a third issue of parallel importance, namely, the issue of organisation.

If "organisation is the form of mediation between theory and practice",[8] then the political issues emanating from theoretical outlook and praxis cannot be separated mechanically from organisational issues, as Lenin says. And there is no doubt that the reverse is also true, since organisation consists not merely of technical questions, but forms one part of the growing dialectical relationship between theory and practice: when the organisation is not born of revolutionary theory, it results in a conspiratorial formula, and when this theory is not mediated through the execution of practice, it results in the isolated sect.

It is political ideology which decides the form of the organisation and its tasks (relations among members and their relations with the masses, the relationship between the leadership and base, bodies emerging from the organisation and their relations, tasks, etc.). And it is the organisation which is capable of carrying out rectification and enrichment procedures towards the revolutionary process, through its continuous ability to measure practice against theory. From this perspective, [organisation] provides the best guarantee in preventing the spread of diseases that have become apparent when confronting revolutionary experiences throughout history (the cult of the personality, adventurism, militarism, left-wing childishness, opportunism, individualism, bureaucratism, etc.).

Theory results in aimlessness if it is not linked to revolutionary practice. Likewise, operational practice will become directionless if revolutionary theory does not light the way;[9] this is the formula-

---

8   György Lukács, *History and Class Consciousness*, trans. Rodney Livingstone (Cambridge, MA: MIT Press, 1972 [1923]), 299. Kanafani's source was an Arabic pamphlet consisting of Lukács' final chapter, "Towards a Methodology of the Problem of Organisation", translated by Syrian *adib* George Tarabishi: György Lukács, *Fi al-Nitham al-Thawri* [*On the Revolutionary Organisation*] (Beirut: Dar al-Talia', 1969).

9   Joseph V. Stalin, *The Foundations of Leninism* (Peking: Foreign Languages Press, 1970 [1924]), 13.

tion in which Stalin, it seems, interpreted Lenin's famous sentence that: "Without a revolutionary theory there can be no revolutionary movement".[10] Yet, these words are no magic formula, for "Marxism emphasises the importance of theory precisely and only because it can guide action".[11] The main factor in this equation is organisation.

The emphasis here on the organisational question is, in reality, due to the degree of neglect that this issue has suffered in the development of Arab politics during the past half century, and to the ruinous consequences of that neglect. Therefore, any evaluation process aimed at an examination of Palestinian resistance activity during its past experience must be armed with a method, or else amount to mere subjectivities and feelings that are subject to varying degrees of emotionality towards the details, and thrash aimlessly at the totality of the complexities surrounding the current experience.

There are those who now view *fida'i* actions as merely military practices and attack or applaud them on this basis. There are others who see this stage merely as an occasion to race to build theoretical positions, or to immerse themselves only in the process of political theorising. And there are doubtless those who take both practice and theory as a basic background for their assessments. However, all of this remains inadequate, with no doubt that it leads to a violation of the correct balance of the necessary critical process; this process, no matter how daring, may lead to opposite results when its vision focuses on a singular part of the image, overwhelming the remainder of its interconnected parts. Concerning the present stage traversed by the Palestinian resistance movement, it falls

---

10 Lenin added that, "This idea cannot be insisted upon too strongly at a time when the fashionable preaching of opportunism goes hand in hand with an infatuation for the narrowest forms of practical activity"; see Vladimir I. Lenin, *What is to be Done?* (Peking: Forcign Languages Press, 1973 [1902]), 28. A critique of opportunism, for Kanafani, meant looking closely at other Palestinian and Arab trends labelling themselves socialist, revolutionary and Marxist, with much of this criticism aimed indirectly at the DFLP and other factions who had split from the PFLP.

11 Mao Tse Tung, "On Practice", "On the Relation between Knowledge and Practice, between Knowing and Doing", July 1937 (Peking: Foreign Languages Press, 1966).

upon the responsible, critical view to confront a set of essential issues by means of their dialectical character. There is no doubt that the process of "separation" (*taskin* – تَسْكِين) will lead to the drawing of incorrect evaluations on the nature of what transpires: by assessing the Palestinian resistance by military communiqués alone, or by merely theoretical political positions, or only by the form of organisation. The results [of this separation] involve duping the masses and constitute self-deception. In awareness of its dialectical relations, this threefold problem must be examined as a whole.

It must be admitted that such work is difficult and that the difficulties arise in the first place from the organically interrelated composition of the three subjects: theory, practice and organisation. However, it is clear that study requires a separate view of each, as long as the inevitable overlap between these subjects is allowed to reach its full extent.

Political Thought in the Resistance Movement

Lenin's statement that "without a revolutionary theory there can be no revolutionary movement" is no longer a matter of discussion or dispute. Yet, this case does not end here, nor does this slogan become a magic formula. Rather, it may represent the starting point of a more complex issue. On this matter, the Communist Party of China declares:

> Marxism–Leninism is not a dogma, but a guide to action. It demands that in striving to build socialism and communism we should proceed from reality, apply its principles in a flexible and creative way for the solution of various problems arising out of the actual struggle, and allow its theories to continue to develop.[12]

---

12   It is unclear whether Kanafani accessed the English or Arabic translation of this document. The English report published in China suggests slight differences (and carries a different date) to that referenced by Kanafani:

> Marxism–Leninism is not a dogma, but a guide to action. It demands that in striving to build socialism and communism we should proceed from reality, apply the principles of Marxism–Leninism in a flexible and creative way for

THE RESISTANCE AND ITS CHALLENGES

Mao Tse Tung himself, as we have mentioned, concluded that Marxism's emphasis on the necessity and importance of theory is precisely and entirely due to its capability to direct action. It was also Mao Tse Tung who described attempts to directly graft Soviet models onto the Chinese revolution as "cutting the feet to fit the shoes",[13] indicating without a doubt that loyalty to revolutionary theory is a question of creativity, or the issue of dealing with objective reality through the dialectical process in which action and theory exchange their common richness. It was Lenin, perhaps, who placed the highest emphasis on this point.

In the Palestinian arena, there is opposition to this subject from two directions. On the one hand is a trend opposing the necessity and importance of revolutionary theory in the revolution, and on the other, is a trend pushing to raise its head to fit the hat of a ready-made Marxism. It is useful to note the consequences of these two contradictory tendencies: the first negates the importance of revolutionary theory in the revolution, increasingly tending towards demonstrating its weight in the field of action, in an attempt to give

---

the solution of various problems arising out of the actual struggle, and thus continuously develop the theory of Marxism–Leninism.

The Constitution of the Communist Party of China, adopted at the 8th National Congress of the CPC, 26 September 1956, in Albert P. Blaustein (ed.), *Fundamental Legal Documents of Communist China* (South Hackensack, NJ: Rothman and Co., 1962), 55.

A similar phrase was used earlier by Lenin, attributed by comrade and wife Nadezhda Krupskaya to Marx and Engels: "our teaching is not a dogma but a guide to action"; see Nadezhda K. Krupskaya, *On Education* (Moscow: Foreign Languages Publishing House, 1957), 66.

13 As Mao Tse Tung writes:

They say that it is enough merely to study the experience of revolutionary war in Russia, or, to put it more concretely, that it is enough merely to follow the laws by which the civil war in the Soviet Union was directed and the military manuals published by Soviet military organizations. They do not see that these laws and manuals embody the specific characteristics of the civil war and the Red Army in the Soviet Union, and that if we copy and apply them without allowing any change, we shall also be "cutting the feet to fit the shoes" and be defeated.

Mao Tse Tung, "Problems of Strategy in China's Revolutionary War", December 1936, in *Selected Works, Vol. 1* (Peking: Foreign Languages Press, 1965), 180.

GHASSAN KANAFANI

it utmost, if not sole priority. Its existence took on military character in the first place, while the second tendency immersed itself
in "theorising" – in the name of the left – at the expense of actual
revolutionary practice, and sometimes contradicting it, basing the
essential value of its own existence upon plagiarising formulas,
conventions and positions from the literatures of the Marxist–
Leninist left. Why, then, is there this repeated emphasis, reiterated
by teachers of revolutionary strategy, on the necessity of revolutionary theory and, particularly, its fundamental role as a guide
to action? The revolution, even in its everyday details, cannot
advance if it is not equipped with a strategic horizon. The essential
value of tactical dynamism – political and military – is ultimately
to serve this strategic horizon.

It is well known, even military, that tactical causes appear distant
from finite political goals. Yet, it seems difficult, if not impossible,
to separate political goals from strategic vision. If we are convinced
that the tactic represents but one part of an ever-advancing dialectical process, then it is impossible for this tactic not to become a
broad strategic framework.

Because an understanding of the whole facilitates the handling
of the part, and because the part is subordinate to the whole, the
view that strategic victory is determined by tactical successes alone
is wrong, as it overlooks the fact that victory or defeat in a war is
first and foremost a question of whether the situation as a whole
and its various stages have been properly taken into account.[14]

This clarifies that war (usually defined as politics in its violent
state) represents, in the first place, a strategic vision, and like the
vision itself, can only be provided by the working guidance of revolutionary theory. The different stages of the revolution, from their
infancy to their last, are therefore subject by nature – like all other
things in our world – to continual dialectical movement, and, in
particular, are governed primarily by the decisions of humanity,
responsible for its own destiny. In our era, such decisions are no
longer subject to empiricism or dogmatism. Thus, still absent from
the Palestinian resistance in its present stage – in this organisation
or that, and to this degree or that – is a strategic horizon taking into

---

14 Mao, "Problems of Strategy in China's Revolutionary War", 183–84.

account two extremely important dimensions: the national dimension and the class dimension.

There is no contradiction in emphasising the importance
of these two dimensions together on the same plane, as may be
imagined by those plagiarising artisans (*harfiyyin al-nassakhin* –
حرفيين النسّاخين). Discussing the dimension of national liberation
is not a discourse of chauvinism, or on the search of the bourgeoisie for a framework to justify its presence in authority and
control over productive relations. Rather, the discourse concerns
the shared historical characteristics and common destiny of the
Arab working classes, who share a primary interest in the battle for
liberation, and in the defeat of their tripartite enemy: Israel, imperialism and reaction. Discussion of their singular battle is not only
an objective reality imposed by their affiliation with one nation but
is also a reality determined by the battle itself.

Together, these dimensions of the revolution, of nation and class,
represent the fundamental depth of the future Palestinian struggle,
yet they remain shrouded, despite the longevity of the Palestinian armed struggle so far. The issue, at the national level, results
largely from the loss of the class horizon for analysing and discern-
ing objective conditions. This deficiency has led to the fall of some
factions into a regional trap. It is possible to look briefly at this issue
in the following way: that objective realities and their developments
have led to a leap achieved by the Palestinian national movement,
generally in advance of those for which the forces of Arabism have
proved capable. However, if the Arab national movement is partly
responsible [for this state of affairs], it follows that imposing blame
to the point of alienation means a failure to understand the nature
of reality and its developments: that the petty bourgeois Arab
regimes proved incapable of ensuring conditions for the ripening
of these Arab national movements, or of creating an atmosphere
practically conducive to the growth of other forces, because the
majority of these regimes were not merely petty bourgeois, but,
further to this character – by the nature of their emergence and
practice – also embodied military and police-like characteristics.
Thus, their limited conception of partisanship and organisational
action (including even the organisational action that it attempted
to build to serve its own purposes) weakened the Arab patriotic

parties and abandoned them to the battle when it reached a more advanced stage, with their formations strained, shaken and worn out in the extreme, both ideologically and organisationally.

The petty bourgeois regimes were undoubtedly surprised by the [June 1967] defeat before they could fulfil their role. This defeat overthrew their impotent and insufficient programme, not to mention completely and nakedly exposing it. However, the presence of more reactionary Arab bourgeois regimes, more deeply entrenched in clan, feudal or monopolistic control than the petty bourgeois regimes, practically impelled the fall of the latter, whose previous and subsequent programmes did not match the scale and swiftness of their defeat. Yet at least some of them still attract popular loyalties – on a mass scale – and contend with the resistance movement over such loyalties.

This blurred picture of reality, which the defeat has created, has not only allowed the petty bourgeois regimes to proceed in weakening the local national movement, destroying it and blocking its path with various pretexts, it has also led to obscuring the strategic horizon of the revolution among some Palestinian resistance factions, which sometimes blamed "the Arabs" (just like that, without specifying) for a failure to liberate Palestine. And other times, towards contradictory deals with these "Arabs" (this time meaning the regimes), without seeing in this a deal with those who failed to liberate and who still practise the most powerful means of suppression, against the creation of an environment conducive to the growth and maturation of a popular revolutionary force, which is the only natural ally of the resistance movement.

Realistically, there are two essential and interrelated questions arising in this context: can the people of Palestine alone (or must they alone) liberate Palestine? And, if the answer is no, then with whom must the Palestinian revolution be fought alongside and against? The two questions immediately raise a strategic issue, in which combative and political lines appear to completely merge. The importance and necessity of revolutionary theory cannot be underestimated, as these two questions do not necessarily push towards defining the national horizon, but also require the resolution of a series of important issues, of which the most important may include the identification of the enemy and the identification of the friend, identifying the means of the prolonged revolution itself, the issue of determining the method of liberation, or of identifying the vanguard organisation, its tasks and relations, etc. There are many issues that cannot be resolved without the guide of theoretical work, which interacts with ongoing revolutionary practices and leads towards exploring the class horizon of the battle.

It would be a grave mistake to situate these two issues mechanically within the ideology and practice of political resistance. Rather, it is necessary to realise their dialectical overlap to the fullest extent, and in light of the objective conditions surrounding the Palestinian issue. Historically, realistically and in view of the future, the national horizon seems essential and inevitable and, if the scale of this fact is represented in the intellectual, organisational and combative position of the Palestinian resistance, then the national horizon of this battle is one expression of this reality. All of this makes any strategic concession in the class struggle "susceptible to immediately reflecting itself as a concession in the national struggle".[15] If "Class capitulationism is actually the reserve force of national capitulationism in the... national revolutionary war",[16] it follows that, "for the struggle against national capitulationism to become a strong and powerful struggle, it must be opposed to the tendency towards class capitulationism".[17]

If this statement was correct for China during the war against Japan, it holds greater truth in comparison with the present Arab reality, when imperialism and its agents in [Arab] regimes prey upon the masses' instincts towards national and class liberation on

---

15   *Mao Selected Works Vol. II* (Peking: Foreign Languages Press, 1965), 200. Mao adds: "The same is true of the relationship between the class struggle and the national struggle... We do not deny the class struggle, we adjust it."

16   Mao Tse Tung, *Selected Works Vol. II*, 70.

17   Here we translate the Arabic version of the text quoted by Kanafani; Mao Tse Tung, *al-Mu'allifat al-Mukhtara, al-Majallad al-Thani* (Peking: Foreign Languages Press, 1969), 93. The same section in the English version reads:

We must fight this tendency inside the Communist Party and the proletariat and extend the fight to all spheres of our work, in order to invigorate the struggle against national capitulationism, and in order to achieve the liberation of the Chinese nation and the emancipation of the toiling masses.

Mao, *Selected Works Vol. II*, 70.

an equal footing. And, if Mao's thesis in China was that class capitulationism represents the reserve force for the tendency of national capitulationism, then national capitulation in the Arab world – meaning the consolidation of the domination of the feudal and comprador bourgeoisies (al-burjwaziyya al-ʿamila – البورجوازية العميلة), linked to colonialism or imperialism, and benefitting from the fragmentation and regionalism, splitting the united struggle of the toiling Arab masses in their various arenas – is, in turn, a reserve that serves to reinforce the tendency of class capitulation.

All of this raises a question that has yet to be resolved by the Palestinian resistance movement, namely, whether the revolutionary Palestinian *intifada* is the gateway to the Arab revolution, or whether it is, indeed, necessary for the cause of Palestinian liberation to become this revolutionary Arab gateway. In reality, the answer to this question will be imposed through action, as such an assumption cannot be realised arbitrarily or by chance, and continual critical perspectives are required to find the most effective formula. It is true that the Palestinian armed resistance presents a daily example to the Arab masses and that, in this field, it often engages in agitation. But it is incorrect to believe that this kind of "daily example" constitutes a complete goal in itself, for there is no escaping the fact of the experience itself reaching a point where the demand for resolution is increasingly urgent. And perhaps this resolution depends on the ability to escape – or not – from the impasse.

Which Impasse?

A failure to see the impasse of the resistance during this stage and to continue ignoring this crisis – whether through stubbornness, or through reliance on "media solutions" – should be considered non-revolutionary. It is our belief that this impasse now constitutes, and will constitute in an increasing and escalating manner, the historical point at which the revolution must resolve the issue with a scientific answer, and with real revolutionary solutions. The armed resistance movement took shape in crystallised form in the aftermath of the June [1967] war. There is no doubt that the occupation and the shock of the rapid defeat, created in the armed

Palestinian resistance a kind of healthy lung in the atmosphere of suffocation that prevailed in the aftermath of the defeat. However, except for the reality of the occupation, the objective conditions for the revolution were still immature, and the revolutionary apparatus (*al-adat al-thawriyya* – الأداة الثورية) that rushed to perform the tasks of the revolution was both quantitatively and qualitatively unable to perform them.

Many factors undoubtedly led to this reality. And, if it is unfair for the Arab and Palestinian national movements and their aims to bear full responsibility and label their experience as an impotent failure, then it is also unfair to hold the petty bourgeois Arab regimes alone responsible for this reality. Responsibility in this field is mutual and is unavoidably shared by each party. Disavowal of this fact is gravely equivalent to the charge that both have avoided the process of rectification that alone can determine the horizon of the future and its method of struggle. Even more dangerous, however, is that the petty bourgeois regimes – which were surprised by the defeat, whose impotent programme was interrupted before it was completed, and who were completely exposed before our masses – found that they could utilise their support for the armed resistance movement at least as "a fig leaf", in an unexpected type of self-defence. We have mentioned that the existence of reactionary Arab regimes that play the role of direct agents of imperialism was one of the reasons preventing the practical fall of the defeated petty bourgeois national regimes, as they were still able, amid that loss, to represent something that would attract the spontaneous loyalty of the masses, and this led to their rush to seize more of this loyalty by racing to endorse the actions of the *fida'iyyin*.

Driven by tactical incentives, this contest first took the form of clamour, exaggeration and hype. The Palestinian resistance lacked a popular, strong, vanguard party, leading to its inability to capitalise on the vacillating atmosphere in which it was surrounded and, as a result, a major defect in its image arose. On the one hand, the Palestinian resistance rises within an environment in which the objective conditions for revolution have not yet matured to the level of its slogans, and therefore the tools of this revolution are not applicable to the level of the tasks in which its engaged. On the other hand, it is surrounded by a broad and loose framework of mass loyalty that it is, as yet, unable to mobilise and organise. Undoubtedly, the impotence and shortcomings of the Arab national parties, and the earthquake that hit them in June (when they were already strained from the burdens imposed by military, reactionary and police regimes, in addition to their own diseases), have added to a chaotic scene for the Palestinian and Arab arenas alike. However, none of this could prevent the arising of the first revolutionary impulse, which was mobilised by the limited frameworks of the resistance movement at the time and proceeded bravely to the battlefield. This surge was able to work magic within the Arab masses everywhere. However, such magic and its miracles remain subject to the ability of the revolution to organise and mobilise it according to a strategy of revolutionary guardianship.

This first revolutionary impulse reached its climax in the Battle of al-Karameh in March 1968, the battle that offered a wonderful example of the ability of a small force, unarmed with modern weapons, to confront and wound a large force through its fightback, to a large extent igniting the flame of the Arab and Palestinian masses. But this battle also led to other results on the enemy front: on the one hand, it alerted Israel to the ferocity of this phenomenon, which it had underestimated in the beginning, and, on the other hand, alerted the Arab countries – at different levels – to the danger posed by such a rising force if it were able to continue expanding. One result of this was that Israel developed a political and military strategy to confront the Palestinian armed struggle, while the Arab countries – each according to their needs – developed plans to safeguard their own "security borders". The architects of Israel's strategy decided to "coexist" with the resistance, by gradually pushing it eastwards, so that it would be concentrated on the eastern bank of the Jordan River, and by working, sometimes with violence and sometimes with bribery, to "neutralise" the West Bank as much as they could. Thus, it would constitute – even if it served as a smaller theatre of operations – a human barrier between the Israeli forces clashing with the resistance on the western bank of the river and the geographical body more susceptible to shock, where the densest Israeli population is located, in occupied Palestine. In this, Israel has been relatively successful (except for its blatant failure in Gaza), and received the support of a military and security apparatus, a modern and technologically more advanced population, and a society trained in war. But it was also aided by the almost complete lack of mobilised, organised, cultivated and trained national and progressive activity [among Palestinians] in the West Bank, throughout the years preceding the 1967 occupation.

In the months after the Battle of al-Karameh, [Palestinian] media related to the guerrilla action reached a level that the media of the South Vietnamese Liberation Front has still to attain. This led to a widening gap between the tasks that this media was assigned to fulfil by the nascent resistance movement and the real ability and maturity of a movement and revolutionary apparatus governed by objective conditions. Last winter, the Israelis accomplished militarily what they had begun in the months following the Battle of al-Karameh. They installed a sophisticated barrier on the western bank of the river in an attempt to mobilise the sum total of technological colonial expertise in preventing the movement of guerrilla groups to the western bank of the river. Thus, and compared to the level reached by the first revolutionary surge that climbed to a climax in the aftermath of the Battle of al-Karameh, *fida'i* actions are now passing through a period of relative stagnation. This stagnation is not only due to military conditions, but also primarily due to the fact that Palestinian and Arab media, which had intended – or so we thought – to mobilise the Arab masses, doped them (*khadruha* - خدرها) yet again and, on different levels, followed the same flawed paths that were taken by the [Arab] regimes before June. This is the path that results in considering mass enthusiasm from the standpoint of the spectators, as an alternative to fighting alongside them, in front of them and in their midst, and which dispenses with redoubling efforts to mobilise, educate and organise them.

Periods of stagnation that come with the waning of the initial revolutionary surge are considered a natural phenomenon, witnessed by most revolutions in the world, and do not necessarily constitute a dangerous sign. This is undoubtedly a period in which the revolution faces many factors that govern its entire destiny, resting upon the method which must be followed in confronting such phenomena.

Do we face such a period by ignoring it?
Or choose a media outlet through which to express it?
Or continue obstinately without modifying the strategy and
tactics of action?

What is it that brings an end to this stage, that allows the resistance to begin its second surge and that moves it from one stage to
the next? This stage appears to take on a primarily military [form],
but its causes and results are undoubtedly political. That is, exactly,
on a practical and concrete level, the point at which the military
issue, isolated from political thought, appears as a mere dot floating
in the air and the unknown. Precisely here, revolutionary theory
speaks its word, where it becomes apparent and absolutely correct
to say that revolutionary theory is not a closed doctrine, but an
interpretive guide to action, and so becomes capable of change.

As historic revolutionary experience tells us, when revolutions pass through periods of stagnation, they usually witness the
extraordinary development of remarkable phenomena. This is
because continuing to ignore this state of stagnation leads organically and necessarily to the emergence of "explanations", causes
and "symptoms". This period of stagnation then witnesses the
growth of subjectivity at the expense of objectivity, the emergence
of small, partial problems in different guises, the trading of accusations, the occurrence of splits, the dominance of theories, verbal
formulas and biddings, side conflicts, changes of leadership personalities and so on. There is no doubt that the persistence of such
phenomena for a longer period exhausts and fragments the revolution, or creates an opening for the lurking enemy, which realises
that this is, in practice, an open door for an attempt at final liquidation, which it tries to execute against the revolution. The way
out is undoubtedly in advancing through a necessary rectification process, which then must be practised on an equal footing
and dialectically, at the political, organisational level, and at the
level of political and military practice simultaneously, and to share
any achievements arising from any of these three levels, reflecting them in the organic interdependence between the three issues.

We say: advancing forward – in the sense of a living realisation
of that firm, dialectical relationship between the national struggle

and the class struggle – means, at the same time, that giving up on one is giving up on the other. This constitutes a strategic imperative that should build a framework that accommodates sufficient flexibility in tactics. Here, the phrase *national struggle* does not mean the necessity of waging the immediate battle for Arab unity, just as the phrase *class struggle* does not necessarily mean here waging immediate and bloody fighting against the exploiting classes, but these two phrases undoubtedly mean the adaptation of the Palestinian liberation march in the footsteps of its destiny, fate and necessities.

We say: advancing forward means real awareness of the dimensions of the current confrontation – confronting the dense camp of the enemy that has been mobilised amidst the actions of the armed Palestinian resistance – supported by technological superiority, the capabilities of imperialism, and the complicity of reactionaries, in contrast to the millions of Arab masses and the crippled Arab capabilities that stand waiting. We say: advancing forward means a real awareness of the stage of the current phase of Palestinian resistance, the stage of tireless work to create a revolutionary climate and ripen the objective conditions that endow the revolution with apparatus capable of accomplishing missions of this seriousness, in quantity and quality, and replacing loose propaganda media with revolutionary education and national awareness, replacing narrow sectarianism with revolutionary organisation, and replacing classical and semi-classical military practices with columns of the organised, armed and fighting masses.

The way out of the current impasse can only be found through an objective assessment of the characteristics of the stage the resistance is going through during this period. This evaluation is a very important issue from a strategic and tactical point of view because, without it, the resistance will not be able to achieve the ability to understand the problem, interpret it and then change it, let alone to its fullest extent. Without this [evaluation], the resistance will not be able to utilise the tasks and methods of this stage at its specific moment, and would instead borrow the tasks, methods and tactics advanced and applied at an earlier stage.

We heard, for example, much talk at the beginning of this year by the officials of one resistance organisation, on beginning the stage of clearing and liberating the occupied land, and on its supposed ability to make large strides over a short period. Similar talk had spread before regarding the stage of "big operations", while relatively small organisations, from a military point of view, went so far as issuing war communiqués on major battles in which more than four hundred fighters were dispatched over tens of kilometres. All of this, and other similar examples, lead us to raise a question about how we characterise the current stage of the resistance movement, the programme it is the process of implementing during this stage and that it intends to advance in the period we are yet to witness.

Objective evidence and the sum of the subjective and objective conditions that now surround the resistance movement indicate that the present stage is, in reality, nothing but a continuation of the stage characterised by the ripening of conditions for revolution, and for mobilising the revolutionary apparatus capable of waging guerrilla warfare. Any scorching of this essential stage will undoubtedly be reflected in the degradation of stages to come.

This outline is important because it demands immediate reflection on a number of political, organisational and military issues: it is inconceivable, if the current stage is essentially a preparatory stage (*marhalat i'dad* – مرحلة إعداد), for political practices to then become emotional and rhetorical practices, and military practices governed by the principle of tactical excess, which the laws of guerrilla warfare suppose can only be adopted at an advanced stage; it is inconceivable for this stage to be a preparatory stage while the question of organisation in the resistance is not given first priority; it is inconceivable for this stage to be a preparatory stage while not becoming a period for defining the strategic political framework, as a matter of the standing and importance of whether or not we revolt, or whether or not we are victorious. None of these political, organisational and military issues can be resolved except through revolutionary theory, guided by revolutionary action. It has become commonplace to state that the specificity of the Palestinian problem makes it too broad to be contained within the framework of a revolutionary theory, but the truth is quite the opposite: it is precisely because of this specificity that the need for a revolutionary theory is most acute, and because of the complexities of the Palestinian cause, the need for a guide to revolutionary action becomes more urgent than anything else.

It follows that because of the specificity of the Palestinian issue, that is, one section of its people live under colonialism and the other remains uprooted from their land, the national dimension of the battle becomes a pivotal issue. And because of the specificity of the Palestinian issue, that is, one section is tied to the limb of imperialism, while the other languishes under the chains of exploitative regimes tied more or less to the wheels of imperialism, the class dimension in the battle becomes a pivotal issue as well. And because of the specificity of the Palestinian issue, that is, one section falls under a vanguard of the rich, technologically advanced, exploitative world, and its other is shackled in the Arab region by the restrictions of backwardness, the war of popular liberation becomes a pivotal issue as well. And because of the specificity of the Palestinian issue, that is, one section exists under a racist, fascist entity, supported by imperialist powers that turn feudalist, tribalist, reactionary and puppet regimes in the Arab world into mediators in the ongoing plunder of the Arab revolution and the Arab toiling classes, the issue of struggle against these regimes indirectly becomes a Palestinian front as well. None of these strategic issues can remain suspended in the air while the battle rages. What is the battle if not all of this together? What is liberation if it is not based on a strategic vision that takes all of this into account?

It is precisely here that revolutionary theory has its say. All the characteristics and phenomena specific to the Palestinian cause and its complexities require a scientific confrontation by finding a response at the level of its ramifications. This is enabled only by linking the sum of these phenomena and their specific characteristics with one revolutionary logic, with a comprehensive vision and with a scientific explanation, so that change becomes possible at the level of this interpretation.

The Organisational Problem

Organisation in revolutionary action is not a process of technical structure, but rather the reflection of an ideological standpoint, without the guidance of which, it will end up as a conspiratorial, rather than revolutionary formula, amounting to sectarianism at best. Organisation is the means to implement theory, and it is the indispensable boat or bridge that Mao Tse Tung spoke of for crossing from the shore of decision to the shore of practice. When the battle is delineated by political thought as the battle of the masses, it is thus illogical for the organisation not to be an organisation of the masses. When political thought acknowledges the battle as the battle of the poor, exploited classes, it is illogical for the organisation to be woven from bourgeois cloth, or to submit to the leadership of the bourgeoisie. When political thought accepts the dialectical relationship between thought and action, and that there is no abstract thought that is not reflected by practice or fortified by experience, it becomes illogical for the organisation not to place the issue of democracy at the core of its structure. When political thought sees that the phase and tension of the battle call for quick and flexible decision-making, it is then illogical for this not to be reflected in the organisation, by adopting the principle of democratic centralism.

When revolutionary theory acknowledges that knowledge and practice represent two poles of unceasing dialectical movement, exchanging their gains continuously, and continuously requiring additions, corrections and modifications, then the organisation cannot disregard the principles of criticism and self-criticism as a basis for its relations. When revolutionary theory confesses that class surrender is the auxiliary of [Arab] nationalist surrender, and that nationalist surrender provides the conditions to impose class surrender, then the organisation cannot avoid ascribing priority to its worker and peasant extensions, and proceeding with this priority at the level of the [Arab] nation. And when revolutionary theory, by virtue of being a guide to action in the first place, is able to capture the nature and character of the period through which the struggle is passing, then this should be immediately reflected on the organisation, on the priorities of its tasks, and on its working method at that stage.

We could continue endlessly to list aspects of this dialectical relationship, between theory and its organisational repercussions. But what concerns us in the first place is the tracing of this issue through the specific field of the Palestinian resistance movement in its current stage: the revolutionary organisation, as a vanguard faction, is necessarily required, in order to effectively play the role of preventing the diseases of the reality that it seeks to change from being transmitted into the movement itself, by individuals with roots in that reality and who are necessarily loaded with its habits, temperament and mentality. In the underdeveloped world (*al-'alam al-mutakhallif* – العالم المتخلف),[18] this question takes on a more serious aspect than anywhere else and constitutes one of the first active tasks of the revolutionary organisation.

It is well known that the culture of a society is the culture of the ruling class. Yet, customs and traditions form a more fixed and deeply rooted heritage, whose dominance is more profound and, therefore, getting rid of its rotten part is a more difficult task. However, ignoring all of this can lead to decay in the revolutionary organisation if it is not dealt with consciously from the start, when threatened by the transmission of the diseases of the backward society (*al-mujtama' al-mutakhallif* – المجتمع المتخلف) to the organisation itself. The organisation would thus fail to present a living model and microcosm of the future of the struggle. But it also fails in achieving its basic tasks when personal relations replace objective relations, subjective vision replace scientific vision, sectarian, familial or tribal clashes replace comradely interactions, reverence for personality replaces collective leadership, loose chaos replaces centralised democracy, transcendence over the masses replaces interaction with it, stubborn opposition replaces criticism and self-criticism, and individualism and moodiness replace discipline. A backward society is capable of transmitting its diseases to any revolutionary organisation, if this organisation, armed with scientific theory, cannot settle the organisational issue. Without

---

18 As with the works of Mahdi Amel and other Arab Marxist thinkers, Kanafani's use of the term *mutakhallif* could denote both underdevelopment or, often viewed more negatively, backwardness. In translating this chapter, we take our cue from Barbara Harlow and Nejd Yaziji and use both English terms depending on context. When the phrase references social "diseases", for example, we have used the word "backward society", as Kanafani's view is clearly pejorative. This is also seen in "Thoughts on Change" and other writings, where Kanafani takes the view that Ottoman rule had a paralytic effect on the development of Palestinian and Arab society.

this [guiding theory], the organisation loses its ability to act as a vanguard faction involved in carrying out the tasks of a historic process of struggle. Rather, it loses its basic meaning as a mass organisation that moves among the masses like a fish moves in water, exchanges with them friendliness and understanding, knows its own problems and the scientific methods of solving them, and teaches [these methods] to others without ceasing to learn. How can these complex problems be solved?

When we say that the Palestinian organisations at the heart of the armed struggle have become bureaucratic, a few years after their establishment, this statement not only means their organisational problems on a direct level, but also their lack, in the first place, of the revolutionary theory without which the organisational issue cannot be resolved. Although this deficiency has led directly to clear and visible results, organisationally and otherwise, its form resembles the problem itself. There is no doubt that these problems diminish in the midst of practice itself, provided that such practices are able to do their work in modifying and correcting the theoretical vision. It is precisely here that the crucial importance of organisational work emerges, and it may not be an exaggeration to state this as a primary reason for the opening of that vast gap between programmes and action among many Arab parties. This occurred before or after they came to power, or even in the field of struggle within a position of power, due to the failure of those parties to solve the problem of organisation. As it relates to Palestinian armed resistance in the present, a danger of this kind must not be underestimated, not only because of the extreme sensitivity of this stage – characterised by a working to ripen conditions for the revolution – but also because of the continuous combat practices in which the Palestinian organisations are engaged, the continuation and escalation of which depends largely on the possibility of making the programme of liberation a reality.

Due to such combative practices, an initial organisational issue emerges, which must occupy priority among resistance circles. This issue is summed up in the need to avoid falling into the "rocky" or "fetishistic" (*sanamiyya* – صنمية) situation in building an organisation, because this organisation is required now, in particular, to arm itself with an organisational dynamism that is compatible with their surrounding dangers and expectations. We notice with ease, unfortunately, that this organisational dynamism, and the flexibility it entails, is to a large extent an issue that is not properly taken care of by some resistance organisations, which behave as if they are "legitimate" movements – when measured against the regimes around them and the enemy which stalks them daily – while, on the contrary, such organisations require a level of dynamism and flexibility capable of elevating them to multiple levels of activity, clandestine or open, direct or indirect, visible or hidden, cumulative or diffuse. These levels constitute inevitable necessities and must be expected at any moment, not only because of the nature of the political and military activity of the resistance organisations, but also due to surrounding Arab and international conditions, which are subject to change at any moment.

In most of the organisations, many of those leading the resistance lie totally exposed, along with their methods of work, movement, contacts and – largely – formations, centres and offices. Indeed, some Palestinian resistance organisations may be unique among their kind internationally in that covert names are used openly, and the real names of members kept secret, often despite the identity of the person bearing the two names being widely known! Under the pretext of propaganda activity, some resistance organisations have opened their doors widely to journalists or curious individuals, reporting their locations and paths, now distributed everywhere, on training methods, the sizes of patrols, the distribution of raiders in the raiding group, the types of weapons used, the methods of laying mines used, and the physical competencies of fighters. It is surely short-sighted to think that the enemy needs more than this to know the nature of the competencies and methods of the elements that its patrols will face. And under the pretext of the "international struggle" that some resistance factions clung on to by the tail, so-called "internationalists" were able to spend months in the camps of the fighters, and to examine, with sufficient and quiet opportunities, their methods of thinking and planning, and to discover with utmost freedom the problems, weaknesses and working methods of leading and military personalities, along with their planning capabilities and organisational or personal aspirations.

No matter how slim the chances may be of these components leaking into the hands of the enemy, all of this greatly weakens the flexibility of the resistance organisation to shift to a different organisational form which may be imposed at any moment by developments in the battle. If we add to this that the original structures of most resistance organisations are unprepared for enacting such a necessary transformation at any moment, and that they frequently move towards a rocky or fetishised organisational structure that is not qualified for such a transformation, then we immediately realise the seriousness of this problem.

However, there is another problem which may carry equal importance, namely, the effect of "emotionalism" (*al-infaʿliyya* – الانفعلية) in the organisation. This effect often leads to dangerous results because it governs an organisation through a reaction complex, so that the activity of the leading elements of that organisation, and subsequently its non-leadership, deviates away from the core of the revolutionary tasks that the organisation had originally assigned itself to carry out.

Such a danger is naturally more likely in the organisations that emerge from the process of a partisan split, as the first move of the dissident party (which is usually more aware of the thing it does not want than the thing it wants) is to prove the justification for its split and, consequently, to vindicate its daily existence. If the objective facts fail the organisation in this field, it begins unconsciously to fabricate them: gradually losing a scientific vision of the stage, and resorting to theoretical and media excesses, and then – to corroborate its justifications – works consciously, or unconsciously, to focus on attempts to smash the organisation from which it defected. In many cases, this phenomenon not only takes on the nature of daily, foremost and urgent concerns, but is also gradually forced towards fabricating an artificial campaign of lies, rumours and accusations to assist in these tasks. The original party, as the scene of the defection, is exposed to a similar danger, as this campaign leads by nature to a convulsive reaction, while the elimination of its effects depends to a large extent on the integrity of organisational structure, which is usually better able, by virtue of its conviction of its firmness and time-rootedness, to overcome the effects of the emotional burden. There is no doubt that this emotional phenomenon leads to dangerous organisational repercussions if it is allowed to grow, by destroying the struggle's hierarchy of priorities, and by diverting the entire organisation towards a factional battle whose foundations are fabricated, at the expense of the battle's centre of gravity. It goes without saying that the occurrence of such a split in the leftist camp would lead to a wide opening of the door, consuming not only the forces of revolution that nominate themselves to lead the process of change, but inevitably entering the patriarchy of the right and centre as well.

However, the origins of this organisational phenomenon of emotionalism are not limited to organisations that are party to a partisan split process (witnessed by the resistance movement in the past year and now seen at its tail end). It also constitutes a possibility for other organisations that were not party to the split, which induce numerous particular phenomena, with incentives of secession and tutelage, fuelled by inciting forces from outside the revolution. All of this reflects itself organisationally, not only on the political and combative competencies of the resistance movement and on the scale of the mass assembled around it, but also on the tasks and methods of dealing with extremely important strategic issues, such as the national liberation front, unity of the armed struggle, confronting current and potential enemies, and so on.

This is one aspect of the crucial importance and centrality of the organisational issue, and its repercussions on the course of the revolution, although, during the initiating stage of the armed struggle, other aspects appear to be more important in terms of practice and its organisational relation. This is because, in a case of this kind, organisational errors are not merely a breach of the rules, but also result in immediate and practical consequences pertaining to the fate of the revolution as a whole, and the lifeblood of its elements. We will take one example capable of epitomising the issue we are dealing with on a practical level. This is the issue of the military base, constituting the important and exact meeting point at which the theoretical, organisational and military issues crystallise on a material level.

What does the military base now constitute in the Palestinian struggle? What is its role, besides being a springboard for combat? It is of course an organisational form, charged with performing its role of putting theory into practice. Is it, therefore, a military barracks for a group of regular, semi-regular or irregular fighters? The main axis of this mighty and complex shield, which we call in short form "the struggle for the liberation of Palestine", is located in this case at the main juncture of the whole matter. During this stage of the battle, where scientific theory as a guide to action is defined by its nature and dialectical form, the military base of a group of *fida'iyyin* cannot be anything but a revolutionary centre. As such, it is entrusted with performing its combative and political role through the current, primary task of the Palestinian revolution, namely, the task of combat action and the policy of ripening the objective conditions that lead towards the people's liberation war. This means, by revolutionary necessity, that the base should not merely be a barracks in Palestinian translation, but should be a revolutionary cell, military and political at the same time, volunteering its political and military work to build more thoroughly and broadly revolutionary conditions.

Its military action is dialectically linked to the organisational role [of the base] as a revolutionary focal point, engaged in a tireless process to convey the combative ideal it presents to the masses, to establish dialogue between them and its activity, and to "contaminate" – so to speak– the static reality surrounding it, and to draw it into battle. How can military action play this role? How can it practically generalise the theoretical and organisational position that calls on every fighter to be a political actor and every political actor to be a fighter? This question brings us back to the crucial point in all of this, which stresses to the end the dynamic, dialectical relationship between the theoretical question and its necessity, between the organisational question and its importance, and between the question of practice and its strategy.

The Military Problem

The preceding passages may have practically led us to a discussion of the military problem in the Palestinian armed resistance before we had reached its position in the "impossible categorisation". In fact, our deliberate choice of example, the issue of the military base in *fida'i* action, constitutes one aspect of this problem, as its solution is a fundamental issue, resolving the question of whether or not the resistance reaches the stage of implementing the slogan common to all its organisations: the people's liberation war. War, as Mao Tse Tung defines it, is "politics with bloodshed",[19] and therefore neglecting political mobilisation for those who desire victory makes it tantamount to "go south by driving the chariot north".[20] Hence, Hồ Chí Minh perceives that "a military without politics is like a tree without roots, both useless and harmful".[21] A just war aims to achieve peace, which happens through the simultaneous crushing of the enemy and self-preservation, which are two contradictory issues in their essence, and it is here in particular that strategy and tactics intervene to tip the scales towards one factor. As far as this is the goal of war, it is natural that its ferocity will intensify as the force obstructing true peace becomes more brutal and capable. This phenomenon appears especially during the phases of stagnation, discussed previously, as these stages are prolonged or shortened according to the importance and solidity of the goals for which this or that party struggles. This issue conveys the increasing importance of the political aspect, and of political mobilisation during the war.

However, before proceeding with the details, it is necessary to generally and briefly familiarise ourselves with the objective characteristics of the two sides of the confrontation. Without specifying these characteristics, any analytical progress will be tantamount to divination.

---

19   Mao, "On Protracted War" (May 1938), *Selected Works Vol. 2*, 152–53.
20   Mao, "On Protracted War".
21   Hồ, "Remarks from a visit to the Military Political High School," 1951. Quote adapted from Duong Trung Quoc, *Saigon News*, 25 October 2009, https://www.sggpnews.org.vn/hochiminh2009/october-25-20287.html (accessed 27 January 2023). The imagery of trees was a repeated motif in the works of Hồ. This is from his "Stimulating Poem":

Only when the root is firm, can the tree live long
And victory is built with the people as foundation.

Hồ Chí Minh, *Selected Hồ Chí Minh* (New Delhi: LeftWorld, 2022), 137.

First: the main arena of battle, if we view it as an Israeli–Palestinian confrontation,[22] is distinguished by the small geographical area that is its subject, and this specificity produces critical military results. The small size of the area gives the repressive Israeli military force the ability to move quickly, manoeuvre and take cover. On the other hand, the Palestinian armed resistance is deprived of flexibility, along with the contours that guerrilla warfare assumes as necessity for manoeuvring and moving freely.

Mao Tse Tung considered the vastness of China an enormous advantage for revolutionary military capabilities in the protracted war of liberation waged against the Japanese occupation. There is also no doubt that this peculiarity is reflected in another and somewhat similar way in Vietnam, where the land is covered by natural phenomena that weigh in favour of the revolution.

Second: the arena of confrontation – if we consider it Palestinian–Israeli – is characterised by the presence of Zionist settler-colonisation, which replaced a large part of a people who were expelled from their land and turned into refugees in an area outside of their indigenous land. In this case, the Palestinian revolutionary fighter loses the advantage of the fish that swims in the sea of the masses. With the exception of the territories occupied after 1967, the Palestinian resistance fighter faces, in reality, a hostile audience, each of whose elements constitutes at least an "alarm bell". The theories surrounding popular wars of liberation have always relied on that numerical superiority of the oppressed people whose mobilisation leads to a breach of the enemy's military and technical superiority, and to transform this quantitative superiority of the masses into qualitative superiority. However, in the arena of the Palestinian–Israeli confrontation, the quantitative reality of both sides is almost equal. Thus, facing this reality, the Palestinian resistance is without an essential component for victory in its wars of popular liberation.

Third: in addition, there is now a characteristic important to both sides of the confrontation. While the Israeli side is distinguished so far by its strict adherence to the Herzlite theory, which

---

22   The word *sira'* (صراع) also means "conflict", but Kanafani elsewhere warns against labelling the Palestinian liberation as such (Chapter 11).

defines the nation as "a group of people united by the existence of a common danger against it",[23] this is faced on the Palestinian side by the dispersion and fragmentation of national factions, in addition to the resultant geographical dispersion and fragmentation suffered by a large part of the Palestinian people.

Fourth: the Israeli side enjoys technological superiority, with the support and contribution of the imperialist camp as a whole, and the effort of the global Zionist establishment, while the masses of the Palestinian people belong to the developing third world, with all the repercussions of underdevelopment. This backwardness is, in many cases, augmented by parasitic phenomena, sometimes expressed through the many elements climbing on the husks of the relative economic and technical progress that the Arab bourgeoisie is reproducing, linked to the interests of imperialist corporations and institutions.

These main contemporary features, whose negative form seems clear, are the same features which impose strategically imperative assets towards which the Palestinian resistance movement must be situated.

It is necessary and scientific to summarise the two titles of this new strategy in two basic slogans to tip the balance of power in favour of the resistance:

- The national character of the Palestinian resistance in its vanguard class content.
- The slogan of the national front, Palestinian and Arab.

The negative results at which we have arrived in presenting the four characteristics governing the field of confrontation were due

---

23   Theodor Herzl had declared in *The Jewish State*, "Let the sovereignty be granted to us over a portion of the globe large enough to satisfy the rightful requirements of a nation; the rest we shall manage for ourselves"; Maccabaean, New York (1904 [1896]), 23. Those "granting" the supposedly rightful claim of the Zionists to Palestine were, of course, the British imperialists. Indeed, the reality of managing "for ourselves" – as hinted at in "Resistance is the Essence" (Chapter 4) – meant dealing with the indigenous population, a violent path that relied heavily on British training and counter-insurgency to put down the Palestinian revolutionary movement, paving the way for the Nakba.

to our choice of a hypothetical point of view, which considered the battle a purely Palestinian–Israeli battle. In reality, such negative results are inevitable if the basic hypothesis is false. However, these negative characteristics can be turned upon their heads, into positives for the revolution and its prospects of victory, if the matter is considered as an essential issue for the Arab masses, in confronting imperialism, Zionism and the tools they possess, as well as their direct or indirect allies.

There is therefore no non-Arab way out, so long as the current historical confrontation provides its class dimension. Recognising this, the picture is transformed, and a power capable of overcoming and destroying the vast enemy camp stands up against it. When the geographical characteristics of the Arab continent as a whole come to favour the revolution, and when Arab numerical superiority becomes capable of jumping towards a qualitative characteristic, capable of exceeding the strength owed to technical superiority by an opponent who is few in number, and when the toiling Arab millions, who have the most urgent interest in undermining the occupation, defeating imperialism and cutting off its limbs, which are spread outside the occupied land:

- It is then that the enemy's military strength – derived from the small area on whose lines it manoeuvres – turns into weakness, as its total presence is reduced to authoritarian camp, or into a mere barracks surrounded and attacked from every side.
- Its superior ability to mobilise its own forces and attract imperialist support turns into a suicidal operation in front of a significantly greater mobilisation of millions of Arabs.
- Its ability to resolve battles by means of its regular striking arm is a fatal contradiction in the face of a protracted popular war, whose road is deepened with every military strike it undertakes.

If we view the Palestinian resistance, in its current situation, through this strategic horizon, it does not lose importance, as some imagine. On the contrary, and in complete contrast, it becomes doubly important and of historic urgency in the context of an inevitable revolution, having the potential to be a sign of the people's greatness in their arduous march.

The Palestinian resistance, which derives its qualification for this historic mission from the situation and from Palestinian vanguard initiatives, is called upon, through this strategic horizon above all others, to launch the Great Revolution.

Without such a strategic horizon, which is essential to set the direction of tactical action, the Palestinian resistance will likely remain in a period of stagnation. The prolongation of a period of this kind would undoubtedly lead to a waning in the fervour for resistance, with its support from Arab national and progressive forces gradually turning into a "fig leaf", partly covering the nakedness of these forces in front of their masses, absolving them of practical, revolutionary practices at the level of the resistance programme.

Just as the Arab regimes made a "fig leaf" of the Palestinian resistance in order to conceal their own nakedness in the defeat of June, the Arab national parties, factions and formations are likely to follow the same path if the relentless, onward movement and strategy of the armed struggle does not open a door for them to a practical relationship. The strategy sets the horizon for the Palestinian cause in the Arab mass struggle, or moreover pushes it – by presenting an example, argument and a programme – to fulfil its historic role.

Hence, it is required of the Palestinian resistance movement to prevent its own exploitation by Arab regimes, factions and parties as a "fig leaf" that exonerates those regimes from their defeat, and from bearing their future responsibilities before their masses. This alone is the value of the daily example provided by the resistance movement. Through this example, it presents a binding level of struggle, an analogy to the programmes of national and progressive Arab parties and forces, and calls on them to take up arms, within the strategic horizon that overlooks a major Arab revolution. At this point, the Palestinian battle becomes organically linked to the principle of building Hanoi, or Arab Hanois, and the two causes become inseparably tenacious.

This dialectical process must be pushed towards its climax by the armed struggle, requiring action with utmost force to tip the current balance of power in favour of the Arab and Palestinian national and progressive forces. We must admit from the beginning that all of this becomes impossible and illusory if it does not proceed from the belief that the battle is a long-term war, led by the vanguard forces of the masses, at the level of the entire Arab nation.

It seems clear that there is no situation that necessitates the initiation and realisation of this programme more than the current situation. Nor is it evident that there is a more suitable entry point for this realisation than the current situation, or that there is a more qualified instrument to initiate this shift than the armed Palestinian resistance movement. And it is apparent that there is no guide to action clearer and more effective than Marxism–Leninism, fused creatively with the militant coherence of Arab nationalism.

The confrontation in its present situation is nothing more than a "state of endurance" over those hundred miles in the Jordan Valley (even if we exclude the great value of the violent resistance raging in the Gaza Strip). It is moreover so, if we do not consider it as the capsule of an effective and enormously powerful mine planted in the heart of this vast Arab continent and have not yet used this capsule to detonate such a mine.

How can all of this be achieved, in light of the current military situation of the resistance? Or rather, preceding this question, what is the real military situation of the resistance now, compared to its missions and slogans?

Militarily, armed resistance aims, like all popular wars of liberation, at creating numerous fatal contradictions in the enemy camp:

- To force it to assemble so as to strike the resistance, which then disperses and hits the enemy everywhere, compelling the latter to fragment and induce a striking at its weakest link.
- To compel it to advance in order to retreat, while, if weakened, being hit further. Seeing an enemy retreat, the resistance would gnaw at its rear lines and, if it stood still, would besiege it; if besieged itself, the resistance would disappear.
- To deny the enemy as much assistance as possible and to widen the chasm of its contradictions with the masses of the

lands it occupies. Its losses, and the climate of anxiety and exhaustion in which it lives, lead to the expansion and intensification of the contradictions in its own society. In exchange for this disintegration, the resistance mobilises its strength and energies by consolidating its relations at all levels with its masses. All of this disturbs the balance of power, and turns few into many, weakness into strength, and strategic defence into a strategic attack.

The Palestinian resistance of today has not yet reached the point of provoking the necessary scale of these contradictions within the enemy. It is true that it has forced the latter to disperse to some extent, but at the same time [the enemy] maintains a ferocious, accumulated force, capable of carrying out major operations if necessary.

The reality of the resistance as an armed but young movement – and through an objective assessment of the difficult conditions out of which it has grown, and which deprived of any opportunity for organisation and mobilisation before the June 1967 defeat – suffers from essential weaknesses, which can be summarised generally as follows:

- Fixed military bases, a phenomenon that almost clings to some factions of the resistance movement. Stability in position not only provides the enemy with an easy target, but also important information about the training and arming of personnel, their fighting competencies and methods of activity. There is no doubt that sites of *fida'i* action must be mobile and flexible, not only for reasons of protection, but also for the ability to accomplish its tasks as a cell in its surroundings, playing a mobilising, organising and educational role.
- Israel aims to corner the resistance and deprive it of the initiative that characterises the action of armed guerrillas, and this is precisely what is now forcing the resistance into a defensive position. However, this situation hinders the realisation of the principle of strategic defence, characterised in

wars of liberation by mobile war, supported by guerrillas,[24] and forming a component of positional warfare.[25]

And if this stage is usually characterised by heavy losses inflicted on the guerrillas, it is also characterised by the corresponding need to build the national front, utilising the situation to its maximum extent for political mobilisation.

By that measure, the first task of the resistance at this stage is to adopt mobile warfare more decisively, and to build the broad national front.

- The level of education and training within the resistance is in a position where it is less capable of the rapid development it needs. It is absolutely necessary now to abandon the mechanical and classical programmes of the military training process, and raise the resistance towards producing new leadership and field competencies, to create fighters capable of initiative, with increasing capabilities to confront a rapidly moving and evolving enemy.

This is reflected, for example, in the sluggishness of the armed resistance movement in responding to the enemy's tactics, in comparison to the latter's speed in changing its methods, tactics and traps. This kind of dialectic in connection with the enemy must be turned upside down, so that when the enemy loses initiative, this initiative is turned over to the resistance, where it is reflected in speed in changing tactics, traps and methods as soon as the enemy discovers them, and always forcing the enemy into a position of a delayed reaction to flexible and constantly evolving action.

The magazine *US News and World Report* stated on 6 March 1967:

---

24 In this section, Kanafani uses the term *'asabat* (عصابات) rather than *fida'iyyin*, making clear his advocacy of guerrilla warfare, following the particular influence of the Chinese and Vietnamese experiences.

25 Mao Tse Tung, "On Protracted War", May 1938, *Selected Works Vol. 2*, 113–200.

American officers admit that the danger of Vietnamese traps cannot be avoided, while an American officer stated that in every operation his forces carry out, he discovers new traps invented by the men of the Vietnamese National Liberation Movement. He says that he has barely finished telling his soldiers about a new trap before they fall into a newer, more serious trap.[26]

Depending primarily on the level of training and initiatives of the resistance movement, this [flexible] character is not yet present [in the Palestinian case], and must be given more attention. In reality, it is the enemy which still largely maintains this kind of initiative.

Another point of weakness is summarised by the viewpoint that inadequate attention is given to the causes of organisational mistakes. The first of these consists of organisational behaviour that could lead within the Palestinian resistance to the creation of a militaristic class, connected to rank and salary, at a time when the resistance should be dedicated and the character of revolutionary guerrilla factions deepened. The former mistake was perhaps most prominent in the Palestine Liberation Army,[27] which was formed and has remained to a great extent within a classical framework.

The second of these organisational errors is summed up in the need for discipline over a fighter's behaviour, so that he presents himself to the masses as a model of the new person he is fighting to create.

In addition, or rather as a precursor, a basic weakness in the fragmentation of resistance factions is the lack of a unified military plan, and the lack of coordination and creative cooperation among them.

Perhaps this particular point is the hinge of the whole issue, and the starting point towards finding real solutions to all of the problems that, to one degree or another, emanate from it.

---

26 *US News and World Report* (New York), 6 March 1967.
27 The military wing of the PLO, founded by the Arab League in 1964 and now – and at the time of Kanafani's writing – led by the Fatah majority in the organisation.

The demand for a broad national front, whose parties adhere to a minimum programme and clear revolutionary relations must become the essential basis for any revolutionary action aimed at obtaining real and escalating results. It is certain that without such a united front, the resistance will lose many of its own capabilities, while at the same time greatly losing its ability as the nucleus of a united national front, between all national and progressive factions in the Arab world. This front will inevitably form the core of the strategic horizon of the Palestinian resistance movement.

Of course, the opportunity has not been lost, but awareness of the value of this opportunity is something that must be stressed and actively practised. Any serious revolutionary trend can only spin in a vicious circle if it does not put at the heart of its current slogans the slogan of building, consolidating and expanding the national front. And when we say a national front, we mean an expression of its actuality, that is, far from spontaneous growth, but rather having maximum commitment to a minimum programme, consolidated and developed through its practices, experiences and lessons.

This slogan returns us dialectically to the true meaning of political thought in the resistance movement: its necessity and prospects as a guide to action. Likewise, it returns us to the true meaning of the question of organisation: its necessity, prospects and value as an indispensable tool for transferring that programme to the levels of application and practice.

It is necessary, once again, to stress the historical value of this threefold key, which alone makes it possible to open the door towards the victorious prospects for our masses, who deserve it to the extent that their vanguard factions are aware of the reality of the battle and its dimensions:

- There must be a broad national front, integrating the Palestinian national factions.
- There must be a strategic horizon at the level of the Arab nation.
- There must be a progressive dimension based on class.

Of course, realising this programme will not be easy. History is not produced by a magic wand but is transformed by the masses who understand it and are determined to change it. This path is difficult and arduous but deserves the blood of those who fight valiantly for the sake of victory. Our loyalty to those who preceded us and were martyred for our sake means our rising to the level of the cause for which they unhesitatingly gave their blood. And in order to be loyal to future generations of the Arab vanguard, we must rise to the level of the tasks it entails, advancing bravely, breaking through the wall, to be deserving of the flag for which the masses have shed their blood for the last 50 years.

التركيبُ التحتي للثورة

وثيقة عَن السِّلاح التَّنظيميُّ

لينين ، ماوتسي تونغ ، هوشه منه ، ستالين ، جيلب ، لوكاكس

"The Underlying Synthesis of the Revolution", on the lessons of Vietnam and the anti-colonial struggles of twentieth-century communism for the Palestinian and Arab revolution. Ghassan Kanafani wrote its introduction. Public domain.

9

The Underlying Synthesis of the Revolution: Theses on the Organisational Weapon (1971)

Introduction I. Ghassan Kanafani and the Organisational Question in Historical Context by *Wisam Rafeedie*

This long article by the martyr Kanafani should be placed in what we see as its specific and defining historical context. By my reckoning, there were two divergent contexts, so to speak: on the one hand, the particular historic moment and level of development in the Popular Front for the Liberation of Palestine (PFLP), with all the political, ideological, organisational and military projections of that juncture. On the other, the historic context faced by the Arab left: the Palestinian left in particular and the Arab liberation movement more generally.

It goes without saying that if Kanafani had lived – and this is no small epistemological assertion – he would have led the development of the PFLP into the next millennium. What he grappled with would have enriched him with a vast and worldly experience of different locations and ranges. He would have, therefore, further deepened the observations of this text in the direction of the pivotal issue with which he dealt, namely, the link between questions of organisation, political orientation and ideology. He was, however, to deepen this subject with reference to Lukács and Mao, and through the experience of the Front itself, which had confronted such questions, practically deepening their associations in the practice of political organisation on the march of history.

Naturally, during that period, both comrade Kanafani and the Front quoted repeatedly on the leading work of Mao. He wrote this article in 1971, when Marxist-Maoism had become influential, while drawing on Vietnamese experience, recognising similarities between the Palestinian, Chinese and Vietnamese experiences, and noting that the building of the Chinese and Vietnamese communist parties rested on Leninist principles of collective leadership, criticism and self-criticism, and democratic centralism. For Gramsci, the organisation was the mediating point between theory and practice, and on this his viewpoint differed little from Mao, drawn on by Kanafani to illustrate the passage of a vessel between the shores of knowledge and practice. Both Gramsci and Mao reveal that, from behind the proverbial curtain of Marxism, theory constitutes an awesome power if it is actualised by the masses. And the masses cannot take possession of theory except through organisation.

Kanafani's genius is manifested in two essential points: first, in capturing the web of relations and contradictions between tangible phenomena, particularly relating to building the organisation; and second, his ability to Palestinianise the organisational question, if somewhat briefly, to the nature of cultural experience in which the party operates. If Lenin had assumed the party to be a militia-like organisation in order to be able to confront the regime's attempts to liquidate it, and in order for the party to seize power – and the latter is central to all of Lenin's thought – then the organisation needed in the context of an existential struggle with the Zionist project (it is either us or them) must be a militia-like party par excellence, especially since it carries weapons. Kanafani did not, therefore, lose sight of the issue of raising the political and fighting apparatus of the PFLP, which has continued to be an issue of discussion and critique.

Introduction II: Revolution as Science – Organisation as Key by *Ahmad Baha'iddin Sha'ban*

It is apparent that this study accurately expresses the maturity and crystallisation of Ghassan Kanafani's thought as a seasoned political leader. His key belief was that revolution is a science, and that victory in the struggle against Zionism and imperialism depends on the fighting forces in Palestine and the Arab world – and beyond, in the world at large – mastering the mysteries and secrets of this science. This mastery ensured victory for all of the revolutionary forces who understood and practised it, with a message written in easily grasped, simple and clear language, without riddles or prior knowledge. Its goal is clear: to reach and positively influence the awareness and consciousness of the recipient. Here lie the characteristics of Kanafani as a political leader, polished by experience and the bitterness of the confrontation, despite his relative youth, resulting in his ability to penetrate the depth of the idea and grasp the essence of the truth.

Kanafani touches in the opening of his study on the importance and centrality of the issue of organisation in the revolution, and reaches, in one stroke of the pen, the crux of the crisis of the Arab revolutionary movement as a whole, whose results have exacerbated and intensified, 50 years after his death. Namely, that the need for organisation is doubly valuable in the "Third World", in combating national and class enemies, as well as striking deep at the social roots and foundations of underdevelopment. So far, he wrote, the organisational issue had proved the fatal weakness in the struggles of the Arab world. Half a century on from his departure, it is clear why we must reread this heritage and act upon Kanafani's teachings.

* * *

THE UNDERLYING SYNTHESIS OF THE REVOLUTION: THESES ON THE ORGANISATIONAL WEAPON
Lenin, Mao Tse Tung, Hồ Chí Minh, Stalin, Giáp, Lukács[1]

To the Palestinian resistance,
the way to the Arab masses
Who are solely capable
of carrying the revolution to victory

---

1 This chapter reproduces Ghassan Kanafani's introduction to a pamphlet of the same name, printed in 1971 by the Progressive Library and Dar al-Awda, Beirut. Edited by Kanafani, the pamphlet dealt primarily with the lessons of Vietnam, drawing out the conclusions for communists around organisational, theoretical and revolutionary tactics in the anti-colonial struggle. Alternative translations of the title could include Infrastructure of the Revolution, which is used in archival documents of the PFLP. However, as the introductions to this chapter highlight, Kanafani's concern here was to show the fundamentality of revolutionary organisation and its synthesis with the conditions experienced by the oppressed masses, as arising from this Vietnamese case study.

Evidence grows, day upon day, that the question of organisation in the revolution occupies a decisive position: for Lenin, it is one of the basic conditions for the revolution; for Mao Tse Tung, the bridge or boat that connects the shore of theoretical knowledge to the shore of practice. And, as Stalin concluded, "Without such a (fighting, revolutionary, brave, experienced, flexible[2]) party, it is useless even to think of overthrowing imperialism."[3] The Americans acknowledge that the strongest weapon confronting them, particularly in Vietnam, and in South-East Asia more broadly, is a form of organisation flexible and courageous enough to ensnare the aggressors in one trap after another.

For the so-called Third World, the need for organisation is doubly valuable, for the task of this instrument of organisation is not only to confront and defeat the national and class enemy. At the same time, it must be fortified against the torrents of diseases and vices present in underdeveloped societies, and to be immune in the face of such diseases, with deep roots in society, penetrating their structure and eroding their foundations, operating basis and pathways.

During the march of Arab struggle, the organisational issue has invariably been the fatal weakness. In regard to the organisations claiming a progressive ideology, along with groupings whose path has sometimes led them take up arms against the imperialist enemy, a looseness of organisational structure has always allowed their leaders to deviate from the revolution, to abort it or haggle with it.

It is not our intention that this discussion suggests that the organisational issue in every revolution is a merely technical issue, having nothing to do with ideological commitment or with practical action. On the contrary, the organisational structure necessarily reflects committed belief. It follows that its composition must enable continuous harmony between theory and practice.

2 Kanafani adds the words in brackets.
3 Joseph V. Stalin, *The Foundations of Leninism* (Peking: Foreign Languages Press, 1970 [1924]), 103. Kanafani translates "party" here as *tanthim*, or organisation.

Lukács says that: "Every Communist Party[4] represents a higher type of organisation than every bourgeois party or opportunist workers' party." Perhaps this reality explains the Leninist principle that: "Politics cannot be separated mechanically from organisation."[5] There is no doubt, therefore, of what Lukács meant when he said, "Every 'theoretical' tendency or clash of views must immediately develop an organisational arm if it is to rise above the level of pure theory or abstract opinion, that is to say, if it really intends to point the way to its own fulfilment in practice…".[6] This phrase brings mountains of complications if applied to the reality of Arab struggle in its present stage and if we apply it to assess the experience of this struggle in previous stages. For this means, precisely, that Marxism is at its peak, at the organisational moment that is its role between the past and future.

This particular stage, the organisational stage, in the history of the Arab march has faced unlimited fluidity, especially in political parties and groups, and has witnessed countless acts of opportunism. This manifested at times in fascistic forms of discipline, and often by the dominance of a bureaucracy that benefits from and controls the "form" of the organisation. At other times, we observe a tendency towards "cronyism" (al-shalaliyya – الشللية) and militarism. Stagnation leads many organisations to fragmentation but, in a few innumerable cases, a healthy organisational reality has meant that the party was able, relatively speaking, to arrive at a true reflection of the debates erupting within it, with these developing into more advanced formulas on the level of the political plan, or in the direction of ideological commitment.

And at the present moment, as the vanguard of the Arab national march, represented by the Palestinian resistance, has raised the banner of the popular war of liberation, being the highest form of revolutionary political struggle, the need to be doubly focused on the tasks of the organisational question, as an essential trend

---

4   György Lukács, *History and Class Consciousness*, trans. Rodney Livingstone (Cambridge, MA: MIT Press, 1972 [1923]), 316. Diverging slightly from the original quotation (and based on his reading of the Arabic translation by Georges Tarabishi), Kanafani uses the phrase "Marxist, revolutionary workers' party".

5   Lukács, *History and Class Consciousness*, 295.

6   Lukács, *History and Class Consciousness*, 299.

in the dialectic between organisation and the masses (which form the material and goal of the protracted war), we say: the need for a doubled focus on the question of organisation becomes urgently important to the extent that a large and essential part of the future struggle rests upon it.

In this epoch, when imperialism is desperate to hold onto its positions, and when the world is witnessing the fierce counter-attack by world imperialism upon the so-called underdeveloped world, the only weapon that can be utilised by the colonised and oppressed peoples to resist the war of aggression that has been forced upon them, and which dominates and dictates their future – and the only possible weapon in the face of the technologically more advanced imperialist countries – is the weapon of the masses themselves.

And when we speak of the masses, we do not mean merely their quantitative accumulation. Rather, we mean the specific process of organising a vanguard party, leading the masses into the struggle, in front of, with them and for them.

The question of organisation is hereby a question of relationships and their dynamics:

- Relationships between theory and practice, so that one area of the dialectic is not separated from the other, leading the work to fall in idle talk or adventurism (al-mughamara – مُغَامَرَة).
- Relationships between members of the organisation, as to express their common will.
- Relationships between the members of this organisation and its leaders and cadres.
- Relationships between the organisation and the masses.

And then, relationships of an opposite type:

- Relationships of the masses towards the battle and the enemy, in terms of escalating the contradiction between them and resolving it in the interests of the revolution.
- Relationships between the organisation and a legacy of cultural, social and political backwardness, which burdens society from within and influences it daily.

These relationships at once raise ideological, technical and educational issues, on the levels of strategy and tactics. Such issues can only be resolved through ideological commitment, that is, in a scientific manner, at a distance from improvisation, amputation and experimentation.

This is precisely what brings the question of organisation into such a close relationship with the question of ideological commitment.

Organisation in revolutionary action is not a process of technical structure, but rather the reflection of an ideological standpoint, without the guidance of which, it will end up as a conspiratorial, rather than revolutionary formula, ending in a sectarian formula at best. Organisation is the means to implement theory, and it is the indispensable boat or bridge that Mao Tse Tung spoke of for crossing from the shore of decision to the shore of practice.

When the battle is delineated by political thought as the battle of the masses, it is thus illogical for the organisation not to be an organisation of the masses.

When political thought acknowledges the battle as the battle of the poor, exploited classes, it is illogical for the organisation to be woven from bourgeois cloth, or to submit to the leadership of the bourgeoisie.

When political thought accepts the dialectical relationship between thought and action, and that there is no abstract thought that is not reflected by practice or fortified by experience, it becomes illogical for the organisation not to place the issue of democracy at the core of its structure.

When political thought sees that the phase and tension of the battle call for quick and flexible decision-making, it is then illogical for this not to be reflected in the organisation, by adopting the principle of democratic centralism.

When revolutionary theory acknowledges that knowledge and practice represent two poles of unceasing dialectical movement, exchanging their gains continuously, and continuously requiring additions, corrections and modifications, then the organisation cannot disregard the principles of criticism and self-criticism as a basis for its relations.

When revolutionary theory concedes that class surrender is the auxiliary of [Arab] nationalist surrender, and that nationalist surrender provides the conditions to impose class surrender, then the organisation cannot avoid ascribing priority to its worker and peasant branches and proceeding with this priority at the level of the [Arab] nation.

And when revolutionary theory, by virtue of being a guide to action in the first place, is able to capture the nature and character of the period through which the struggle is passing, then this should be immediately reflected on the organisation, on the priorities of its tasks, and on its working method at that stage.

We could continue endlessly to list aspects of this dialectical relationship between theory and its organisational repercussions. But what concerns us in the first place is, precisely, the tracing of this issue[7] as it is reflected of the reality of armed struggle in the "Third World", where the tasks entrusted to the resistance organisation have taken on their highest and most succinct form.

Three points stand out in this discussion:

- First, the relationship between the political and fighting apparatus.
- Second, the development and expansion of the process of political and military awareness, both within the organisation and in the environment and mass movement in which it surrounds itself.
- [Third], the availability of opportunities for rectification and democratic monitoring.

The highest forms that have been advanced to find the solution to these overlapping questions are found clearly in the experience of the Vietnamese revolution. On the other hand, there is no more obvious reality presenting the consequences of an inability to

---

7 At this point, Kanafani departs from the section also used in *The Resistance and its Challenges*, where he had outlined the concern of the PFLP to trace the organisational issue through the Palestinian revolution. Kanafani now makes a much broader statement tying the revolution in with the movement of oppressed and exploited nations fighting imperialism, with more concerted focus on Vietnam.

resolve these issues than the experience of the Palestinian revolution in the period 1967–1971.

This explains the importance of the documents contained in this book. In this regard, we must record the following observations:

1. The documents [to which we will refer] originally formed part of a research project among American groups studying within the Ministry of Defence, to learn the mechanism and structure of the force it is fighting in South-East Asia. Since waging war on Korea – and, in all probability, since their intervention in the Second World War – the Americans have known the importance of intelligence on the organisational structure of the forces of national struggle in Indochina.

"Research laboratories" created to support the US military machine at its Ministry of Defence have become independent brains upon which US aggression essentially depends, with the aim of fragmenting and rolling back the armed national movements. The documents in our hands form part of the production of these brains.

However, dealing with the issue as it is analysed by the Americans would constitute a fatal error leading to an erroneous and mechanical portrayal of the organisational issue in political action.

Indeed, we will have, through rearranging the information, presented an account purified of any US analysis. As such, this introduction aims to place the theses which follow in their natural political context.

2. It is however necessary in reading these documents to abandon any notion that we are dealing with a merely technical question: a fascinating, superior organisational structure is the essential secret to the power of the Vietnamese revolution, its roots and incredible energy to not only strike but defeat the most powerful force known to history. We say that this structure was accomplished and developed through the astonishing convergence of theoretical commitment and objective material conditions and their repercussions. The organisational form before us is, therefore, the result of a dynamic dialectic between the party and the

masses, in a particular place, at a particular moment, with all the political, economic and cultural features of this reality. Its study must therefore be subject to all of its context and interactions.

3. The overwhelming majority of studies have placed the question of organisation into three categories:

- The essential studies establishing the major principles of the organisational issue (Lenin, Mao Tse Tung, Gramsci, Lukács, etc).
- Critical research articles produced for or against conditions for political parties specific to this or that country, ranging between negative, renegade (*murtad* – مُرْتَدّ) criticism to positive revolutionary critique.
- A set of declared internal laws and systems of communist and non-communist parties, which draw general structures for relationships between various units and ranks within the party.

These three types of study differ in their importance and fundamental characteristics from the [US] studies we have dealt with. For the study in our hands is the only form – within the parameters of our knowledge – that may draw the details of a map towards the reality of the underlying synthesis present in the Vietnamese revolution. [We mean this] in terms of the structure of the cells and the relationships among them, then the relationship between these cells and the leadership, and their relationship with the masses, their paths towards performing their duties and tasks, and their political, military and cultural activities. All of this is possible due to a detailed presentation of real experiences for one of these cells or relationships.

The organisational reality of a party is not limited to its attachment to general rules and the repetition of specific organisational slogans. Rather it resembles the complex and overlapping structure which characterises the movement of sap within a colossal tree. It follows that our study appears as a microscopic dissection of that secretive and particular world existing in one ring among many in this giant tree.

It is possible for idealistic organisational models – including democratic centralism, collective leadership, criticism and self-criticism, or the mass line – to become hollow idols, if we lose sight of how they came about and how they are transmitted into reality. The studies in this book aim to uncover the enormous and expansive world existing within the depths of these organisational foundations.

* * *

This study covers all details important to the Arab fighters who have become aware, from studying their reality, of the growing importance of organisational work. And whose awareness of how disregard for organisational perspectives in nationalist action has become one of the most essential reasons for the great chasm between theory and practice. This [chasm] has led in many instances to a shaking of trust between the organisation and the masses, for example, and also between specific organisational leaderships and their mass memberships.

Revolution is a science, with its own fundamentals, experiences and lessons. It is doubtless that without comprehending these fundamentals, experiences and lessons, "intentions" alone are like a broken compass, which subject the march to error and confusion, not to mention fatigue and deviation.

Recognising the depth of the Vietnamese revolution, its vanguardism[8] and success means objectively acknowledging and absorbing the lessons by which this revolution deepened, became rooted and proved its worth. This is naturally something different to merely singing the glories of this revolution, going beyond

---

8 Demanding the militarisation of the Việt Minh Front on 1 March 1947, Hồ Chí Minh heralded the organisation as "the vanguard unit… Not only must our organisation be single-minded, but the army, the people, and the administration also should be of one mind." The context here was a sprawling French occupation in Vietnam, which had forced the partial retreat of the forces led by Hồ and the Indochinese Communist Party. Kanafani was aware that from this position of weakness, the Vietnamese liberation movement organised itself under this vanguard to pave the way for the stunning and hard-fought victory to follow. Hồ Chí Minh, *Selected Hồ Chí Minh* (Delhi: LeftWorld, 2022), 134–35.

this into the depths of studying the ideological and organisational weapon used to confront the power of imperialism in a prolonged battle of attrition, before a tipping of the balance towards the struggle of the armed masses of Indochina.

This study forms a thesis inseparable from the theses that Arab fighters must study, absorb and use to their benefit in their struggle to conquer their Zionist, imperialist and reactionary enemies.

10

On the PFLP and the September Crisis (1971)

Introduction by *Thomas Hofland*

Carried out in May 1971, this interview with Fred Halliday is one of a number of exchanges in which Ghassan Kanafani displays his political and literary brilliance. The interview took place in a period of hyper-intensity for the Palestinian resistance. The Jordanian army had massacred thousands of Palestinians in September 1970 and, just two months after the interview, the remaining 2,000 *fida'iyyin* were captured in the Ajloun-Jerash forests and expelled. Placing the September events in their historic context, Kanafani motivates his people and comrades to continue the armed struggle.

One of the myths Kanafani sought to combat in the interview is the view that the famous PFLP airplane hijackings from 6–13 September 1970 had provoked King Hussein to attack the Palestinian resistance and halt their raids into occupied Palestine. The fact that the Jordanian regime had "nearly succeeded" in preventing these operations prior to September, he argued, was a factor leading to Black September, rather than solely being its result.

Together with the United States, Israel and Egypt, the Jordanian regime attempted to liquidate the Palestinian presence in Jordan. The hijackings were part of the PFLP's attempt to stop this liquidation and protect the Palestinian people's inalienable right to struggle for national liberation. In the narrative Kanafani and his comrades developed during this phase of battle, the confrontation between these two diametrically opposed forces saw Arab reaction collaborating with Zionism and imperialism to attack the Palestinian people, while Palestinian self-defence formed part of the fight for freedom and liberation.

Since 1971, many Arab governments have continued along the path of normalisation. They have attacked the Palestinian resistance through their military and intelligence services, by committing massacres and arresting Palestinians, by discriminating against Palestinian refugees and by strengthening the Zionist presence in the region through political, economic and military collaboration.

However optimistic Kanafani's evaluation was at the time that the idea of a Palestinian state on the West Bank was a "shock reaction", the Madrid–Oslo process of the early 1990s saw the realisation of a bourgeois Palestinian Authority (PA) in complete coordination with Zionism, imperialism and Arab reaction. Yet the words of Kanafani teach us that the setbacks faced by the Palestinian people are by no means the final nails in the coffin of the cause for liberation. On the contrary, the current situation presents many reasons to be optimistic. As in the immediate post-1967 years in Jordan, the fire of the Palestinian revolution burns through daily protests and operations in the face of a genocidal Zionism. At the time of writing, new armed resistance groups such as the Lion's Den and Balata Brigade have reorganised the armed struggle in ways unseen for decades.

There now also exists a strong armed resistance in Gaza and Lebanon, led by national and Islamic forces, while victories over the Israeli invasions of Lebanon in 2000 and 2006, and of Gaza in May 2021 remain fresh in the memory, as well as the daring actions of 7 October 2023. Resistance is enduringly popular and very much alive among millions of Palestinians and their supporters.

It is in moments of political upheaval and the threat of liquidation that new generations of Palestinians step up and assume their role in the liberation movement. To paraphrase Kanafani: in an atmosphere of Palestinian submissiveness, something must be done. In this sense, we can expect any new Zionist government and their attacks on the movement – including thousands of Palestinian political prisoners – to be met with a stubborn resistance that will not back down in the face of a technologically superior oppressor.

At the same time, decades of all-out attacks on the Palestinian liberation movement, both in Palestine and the diaspora, have left their marks. According to Kanafani, "[In] periods of relapse, there are always divisions, exaggerations, romanticisation, tendencies to individualism and to turning the revolution into a myth".

These sober yet optimistic words offer the morale-boosting implication that internationalists have no other option than to join in the struggle for the liberation of Palestine. Writers, fighters, workers, students... We all have a duty and a role to fulfil.

* * *

ON THE PFLP AND THE SEPTEMBER CRISIS[1]

Fred Halliday: *The Popular Front is best known in the non-Arab world for its hijackings in September 1970. A lot of criticisms of the hijackings have been made. Some of these are bourgeois criticisms. But there are two others which I would like to pose here. The first criticism has been made both by people within the Palestinian resistance, such as the [PLO] Central Committee spokesman Kamel Radouan, and by people outside: it is that the hijackings gave [King] Hussein an excuse to attack the resistance at a time when he would not otherwise have done so. The second criticism is made mainly by people outside the resistance movement. This is that the hijackings gave an illusory sense of power and confidence to the Palestinian masses, which was far in advance of their real organisational and military strength. The hijackings were thereby a substitute for organising the masses and were a theatrical event that encouraged fantasy. This is not to deny that the hijackings had the positive effect, of giving you a world audience on television, to whom you could explain the purpose of the Palestinian resistance. This point is not in question. But do you now defend the hijackings?*

Ghassan Kanafani: First of all, I appreciate the fact that you reject bourgeois moralism and obedience to international law. These have been the cause of our tragedy. Now, I would like to answer your questions. I want to talk in general about this kind of operation. I have always said that we don't hijack planes because we love Boeing 707s. We do it for specific reasons, at a specific time and against a specific enemy. It would be ridiculous to hijack planes at the present moment and land them in Cairo, for example, or in Jordan. It would have no meaning now. But you have to analyse

---

1 Original publication: *New Left Review* 1, no. 67 (May/June 1971). Reproduced with kind permission from the journal.

the political situation in which we carried out these operations, and the aims we wanted to achieve. Let us recall the situation. On 23 July [1970] Nasser accepted the Rogers Plan, and a week later the Jordanian government did so too. Once again, the Palestinians were put on the shelf. If you read the Arab and international press from 23 July to 6 September, you will see that the Palestinian people were again being treated exactly as they were from 1948 to 1967. The Arab papers started writing about how "heroic" the Palestinians are, but also how "paralysed" they were, and how there was no hope for these "brave heroes". The morale of our people in Jordan, the West Bank and Gaza was extremely low. On top of that, a delegation from the leadership of the Palestinian resistance movement, the PLO Central Committee, went to Cairo to negotiate with Nasser and his government; they spent days and days discussing whether [the Egyptians] would allow us to restart broadcasts from Egypt again, after the closing down of our radio in mid-August. The delegation then complained to the Arab League and tried to get them to discuss the question. Before 23 July, the Palestinian resistance was pictured in the Arab press as the great hope of the Palestinian people; at the same time, all Arabs consider the Arab League to represent the lowest form of politics, the most paralysed political body, in the Arab world. Now we had the highest form of politics approaching the "dirty shelter" of the Arab League. This showed that the revolution was threatened with liquidation, whether Hussein smashed it physically or not. Everyone – including those who criticised the PFLP operations – was convinced that the destruction of the resistance was an essential part of the Rogers Plan.

You agree that Nasser and the Egyptian regime supported this?

The Egyptian regime was one step removed from direct participation in this liquidation, since it had no direct contact with the Palestinians; it was in a safer position. The only way the Egyptian regime could help Hussein was by keeping silent: and that it did, to the extent that it could resist the pressure of the Arab masses. For the first three days of the fighting in September, the Egyptian government, and all the other Arab governments, were silent, because they thought that the resistance movement could not survive for more than three days. Then they were forced to move, because the people in the streets of Egypt, Syria and Lebanon were angry at the massacre; but the first 5,000 Palestinian victims fell in Amman in silence, and no one complained.

The Rogers Plan presupposed the liquidation of our movement, and this was now approaching in an atmosphere of Palestinian submissiveness. Therefore, something had to be done; first of all, to tell the world that we were not going to be put on the shelf for the second time, and second, to tell the world that the days when the USA and reactionary Arabs could dictate to our people were over. Moreover, there was the question of the morale, the fighting ability of our own people. We could not let things remain like that when a massacre was on the way, even if we had sat down quietly on the steps of His Majesty's palace and kissed his hand.

So, you don't accept the notion that Hussein himself was unsure of what to do, but that the army forced him to move.

Absolutely not. This is complete rubbish. It is true that there are still parts of the resistance movement who think it is possible to "neutralise" the Jordanian regime; but this is nonsense.[2] As for the argument that the hijackings provoked and accelerated Hussein's attack, the short answer to this is that the Jordanian regime had already stopped guerrilla actions south of the Dead Sea, blocked forces moving towards Eilat,[3] and prevented our units attacking the Naharin dam in the north of the West Bank. At the same time, the Jordanian army put mines at most of the points where guerrillas crossed the Jordan River and forced the guerrillas to go through certain specific corridors; these corridors were ambushes. They

---

2 Kanafani may be referring here to the forces who came to constitute the Black September organisation, which formed within Fatah and broke off to carry out a strategy of high-profile assassinations and militant attacks, including the assassination of Jordanian prime minister Wasfi Tal on 28 November 1971. The Syrian-backed al-Saiqa also retained an active confrontational force within Jordan during this period.

3 An Israeli city built upon Umm al-Rashrash, in the southern Naqab region of historic Palestine.

were sending us to be killed anyway. This was all happening before the September massacre; it was a massacre in another form.

Thus, the real clash was taking place all the time: they were forbidding us to practise our *raison d'être*. They were preventing us making raids against Israel and suppressing our political activities in the cities. So, our own actions, including the planes, were not provocations; they were the movement of a revolution trying to escape from a circle in which it was trapped.

How was your action going to do that?

All our activities were an attempt to get out of our situation. For example, we held demonstrations in Amman shouting "Down with Nasser" and "Down with Egypt"; perhaps they were a mistake, but they were one of the many ways in which we tried to break out of the circle.

It was obvious that Hussein was going to attack the resistance once he had accepted the Rogers Plan. You then had a choice: either you waited for him to attack you, or you could attack him first. Yet, in either case, it seems that you never intended to overthrow Hussein, and never imagined that you could. Wasn't your aim essentially to preserve the organisational position of the resistance, and wasn't this the idea behind the hijackings?

You mustn't isolate the hijackings from the total political context. For example, Fatah sent rocket-launchers to Ghor-Safi below the Dead Sea and blew up the potassium factories. We were all trying to break out, to give the Palestinian masses more hope, and to say that the battle was going on. We wanted to put pressure on the Jordanian government to postpone its attack on us. Our relationship with the Jordanian government is not based on common convictions, only on pressure; we have no common ground with them. It was a question of a balance of power. All our actions, from the great error of going to the Arab League to the hijackings themselves (which were the highest form of pressure) were forms of pressure. Some of them were miscalculated negatively, and some positively. On the other hand, there certainly were individuals and organisations within the resistance who did believe there was a possibility of overthrowing the king. They were in error.

Yet, even then, didn't you believe that you could overthrow the king, by waiting for him to attack you? It was thought that the people would be united by the initial adoption of a defensive position.

That was our dilemma, and we were in crisis. The resistance, and all the Arab military governments, were in a crisis which was the price of the Rogers Plan. If we had decided to fight Hussein, we should have chosen the time and the place. But as Hussein attacked us, we had no choice, we had to fight at a time and place of his choosing.

Thus, the hijackings were part of an extremely dangerous ceramic that made up the Arab and Palestinian map from July 1970 until now. There were a lot of other factors too. We were in a corner, and we had two possible ways of getting out. Either we could defend ourselves till victory, against Hussein, or we could "lose the battle by winning it" if we attacked Hussein. But the outcome was not decided only by us, it was also decided by the other side; they had more plans than we did. You should remember that Hussein had to prove to the Americans that they did not need to create a Palestinian state. The Americans were wondering whether to bring in a Suharto-type officer to replace King Hussein with a coup in Amman, which would usher in a Palestinian state there.[4] The Israelis were also discussing this. Hussein wanted to win back his prestige, and this he did; Nixon has now changed his mind, and the Americans once again believe that Hussein is capable of handling the situation.

---

4 Under Nixon, National Security Council document produced in January 1969 were revealing of how disposable such allies were to the US imperialists: "The risks to [king] Hussein are recognized, but the gamble is advocated because the present trends, if continued, probably mean he will be eliminated in any case, and also because our arming of both Israel and Jordan becomes harder to explain and defend." See *Middle East Region and Arabian Peninsula, 1969–1972*, Source: Jordan, September 1970, National Archives, Nixon Presidential Materials, NSC Files, NSC Institutional Files (H-Files), Box H–126, National Security Study Memoranda, NSSM 2. Secret, 8.

As for the hijackings, their psychological importance was much greater than their military importance, at this stage of the revolution. Now, if we had been at the final stage of the revolution, or even at the advanced first stages of the revolution and we had hijacked planes, I would have been the first to denounce it. But in the preparatory phase of the revolution, military operations have their psychological importance.

You still think you were correct to carry out the hijackings, therefore?

I think that, generally speaking, these operations were correct. Maybe we made some tactical mistakes. Perhaps we should have made the whole Palestinian resistance share much more in responsibility for them, and then if they had decided two hours later to release the planes, perhaps we should have released them. Maybe we should not have been so stubborn. But you can't imagine what this all meant to the people at that time. You raised the question of whether the hijackings created an atmosphere among the Palestinian masses which the resistance movement was unable to absorb and organise. This may have been the case. But even if it is true, we fought for twelve days in September, and we obliged the Jordanian army to fight the longest war in its history because of what we had done.

In September, many commentators believed that the Palestinian resistance could only win, either if the Jordanian army itself split and a section of it went over to the resistance, or if an outside Arab regime – Syria or Iraq – intervened and helped. Did you expect either of these eventualities to occur?

I don't think either of these would have given the resistance a victory. In a guerrilla war, conditions are different, and what is important is the aim of a particular action. The aim of the Jordanian regime was to finish the resistance completely. However, the aim of the Palestinian resistance was not to overthrow the Jordanian regime, but merely to put pressure on it. Neither of these two aims succeeded, so nobody really won. Of course, to some extent, we had to surrender certain points and go underground. But the battle is still going on; the retreat to underground activity or to the mountains is only a tactical aspect of regulating the balance of power.

You don't deny that both the possibility of operations against Israel from Jordan and the politico-military room for manoeuvre of the resistance within Jordan have been massively reduced by the September events? Isn't the Hashemite monarchy continuing to try to disarm the militia in Amman and to win direct control of your refugee camps, and other strong positions?

I know. I don't deny that the Jordanian regime has won some ground and forced us to retreat. But I would like to point out two things, to put the September events in their context. The Jordanian regime had nearly succeeded in preventing us from making any raids against Israel before September; this was not a result of September, but one of the factors that led to September. We had to tell our people we were doing something; we couldn't sit in Amman and do nothing. Now we are in the mountains, in a preparatory stage, and the revolution has taken a more realistic form than it did when people thought it was at a very advanced stage. I am against saying that we were defeated, because in the past, our real strength was exaggerated, and we now have a size proportionate to our strength. We never had room for manoeuvring in front of our own people and world public opinion, and some leaders had no such room even in front of their own militants. It will take a long time to restore the previous balance of power with the Jordanian government and we will continue to retreat until we have a correct understanding of our own strength. There are plenty of examples in history of people with rifles living in the mountains, ambushing a truck and shooting the odd soldier, and achieving nothing else. This is our problem, and there is a debate going on within the resistance about it; indeed, the PFLP is being accused of not wanting to surrender the militia's arms. In fact, I don't believe that a Fatah fighter would surrender his arms.

To what extent has the Popular Front changed its strategy since September? George Habash was reported in January to be saying that the time had come to overthrow the Hashemite monarchy. Is this true?

The Popular Front has always insisted that we have four equal enemies: Israel, world Zionism, world imperialism led by the USA, and Arab reaction. The overthrow of these reactionary Arab regimes is part of our strategy, part of liberating Palestine. The overthrow of the Jordanian regime must be a part of the programme for a Palestinian [popular front]. We have to do it, but not necessarily tomorrow. We have always insisted on the need to do this, but it must form part of a general strategic line.

It is now five months since the events of September. What, in your opinion, have been the effects on the Palestinian people?

It is normal for some to leave during periods of hard fighting. Advanced periods of struggle are attractive to people, who join because there is no price for joining the revolution. They stay at home, they continue going to their jobs; if someone is studying at Damascus university for example, he can take a year off and work with the resistance. On the other hand, shocks like September crystallise the strength of the revolution, because they have forced it into the mountains. There are now commandos living in the Ajloun forests of north Jordan; they are living in caves, with limited water and food, and little ammunition. In this situation, we can't expect that the thousands who went around Amman in khaki carrying their Kalashnikovs will live this kind of life. In the cities, organisation and recruitment are different. We used to have a known office, and we could recruit and train people openly in the camps. Now we have a different relationships with the masses: we are not wearing khaki and walking down the street, and we are not making speeches in the camps. We have to operate in a different way, and that is exactly where a party is necessary. Although it is difficult in the mountains, the situation is even more difficult in the cities. A lot of people had a bourgeois sense of haste, but we are now in a stage of retreat. Militarily and politically, this is not a mistake, and it is not dangerous. But it does pose psychological problems, because of the need to keep the people with us. Some elements on the West Bank are now calling for a Palestinian state. We knew that they were discussing this plan in private among each other for three years after the June war and that they were in contact with the Israelis, with the Arab reactionaries and with the imperialists. It is only since the resistance movement was forced backwards, that they have dared to raise this project openly. At the same time, the events in September made the masses on the West Bank aware of what it would mean to have Hussein back again, and the resulting reaction of a people under occupation and without a proper organisation is to say: "Anything, except Hussein again". For the West Bank, a Palestinian state would be better than having King Hussein's regime again. This is a very temporary reaction, resulting from a psychological shock.

Gaza is another story altogether. The resistance was on the defensive on the West Bank and on the East Bank, but it escalated suddenly in Gaza in a remarkable way. The Popular Front has the strongest influence in Gaza, so we acted. Let me mention one specific case, that of Youssef al-Khatib Abu Dhumman. He was the head of Popular Front military operations in Gaza, and he was killed at the beginning of December. For six days, there were continuous strikes and mass demonstrations in Gaza; so, everyone knew that men were still fighting. This raised the level of action in Gaza, although it made our casualties higher than they had ever been before.

What has created the greater militancy in Gaza?

The population of Gaza is 360,000; the majority are Palestinian refugees. In Gaza, people are familiar with arms. They were trained by the PLA,[5] under the Egyptian administration, unlike the West Bank. Another factor is that the Arab Nationalist Movement (ANM) was suppressed in Gaza by the Egyptians, but never to the extent that it was in the West Bank. When Gaza was occupied, the ANM had its cells there; whereas Hussein handed the West Bank to the Israelis in a "clean" state, as he has put it himself – there

---

5   The Palestine Liberation Army were trained and armed by the Egyptians from 1964–1967, largely in Gaza.

was not a single ANM cell there. So, we had the minimum base to start with in Gaza. There is also a psychological factor: Gaza is surrounded on the west by the sea, on the south by Sinai, on the east by the Naqab, and on the north by the Israeli state. The Palestinians there are psychologically besieged and used to difficulty. On the West Bank, contacts were much easier in the first months of occupation; it was simpler to send money, men and weapons into the area. The people on the West Bank got used to easier methods, and they weren't able to resist Israeli counter-measures. In Gaza, they were tougher and more professional. Another factor was that the Jordanian regime in Amman kept on paying the salaries of teachers, detectives, state employees and the like; this is the only way a reactionary regime can keep the loyalty of these people. The Israelis also paid salaries to these people. It is not true that most of them were against the resistance, but they were certainly not in a hurry; in the Gaza Strip, people were under greater pressure.

I would now like to make some more general comments. In every revolution, there is an initial wave of enthusiasm which peters out after a time, because it is not deeply rooted. I think that our first wave reached its peak at Karameh, in March 1968; after that, we started to decline, because we were returning to our real proportions. In such periods of relapse, there are always divisions, exaggerations, romanticisations, tendencies to individualism and to turning the revolution into a myth and so on. These are the illnesses of the underdeveloped world, and they express themselves in a period when one is not engaged in real revolutionary work, but one is nevertheless regarded as making a revolution. If the revolution doesn't develop out of this, if it doesn't do something like Mao's long march, or acquire more force from outside through the liberation of an Arab state, then defeats will have a dangerous effect on the morale of the masses. The period of decline did not begin in September, it began after Karameh.

Can we now come to the question of Israel itself? Do you think there is such a thing as an Israeli nation? The Matzpen[6] group and others

---

6 There were limits to the perceived anti-Zionism of Israeli "socialist" organisation Matzpen, which – though it called for the right of return for

inside Israel have argued that there may not originally have been a Jewish nation, but the Jewish immigrants who have come to Palestine have established there a new community, which can be called the Israeli nation.

That is the Maxime Rodinson solution. It is a fantastic intellectual compromise; it means that any group of colonialists who occupy an area and stay there for a while can justify their existence, by saying they are developing into a nation.

So, you don't think the Israelis are a nation?

No, I don't. It is a colonialist situation. What you have is a group of people, brought for several reasons, justified and unjustified, to a particular area of the world. Together, they all participate in a colonialist situation, while between them there are also relations of exploitation. I agree that Israeli workers are exploited. But this is not the first time this has happened. The Arabs in Spain were in the same position. There were classes among the Arabs in Spain, but the main contradiction was between the Arabs in Spain as a whole and the Spanish people.

So, you do see contradictions within the Israeli population which can divide them in the future, and provide the Palestinian resistance with allies within Israeli society?

Of course. But this will not happen easily. First of all, we must escalate the revolution to the stage where it poses an alternative to them, because up to now it has not been so. It is nonsense to start talking about a "Democratic Palestine" at this stage; theoretically speaking, it establishes a good basis for future debates, but this debate can only occur when the Palestinian resistance is a realistic alternative.

Palestinian refugees – called for a "socialist revolution in Israel", rather than supporting demands for Palestinian national liberation.

You mean it must be able to provide a practical alternative for the Israeli proletariat?

Yes. But at the moment it is very difficult to get the Israeli working class to listen to the voice of the Palestinian resistance, and there are several obstacles to this. These include the Israeli ruling class and the Arab ruling classes. The Arab ruling classes do not present either Israelis or Arabs with a prospect of democracy. One might well ask: where is there a democracy in the Arab world? The Israeli ruling class is obviously an obstacle as well. But there is a third obstacle, which is the real, if small, benefit that the Israeli proletariat derives from its colonialist status within Israel. For not only is the situation of Israeli workers a colonialist one, but they gain from the fact that Israel as a whole has been recruited to play a specific role in alliance with imperialism. Two kinds of movement are required to break down these barriers, in order for there to be future contact between an anti-Zionist Israeli proletariat and the Arab resistance movement. These will be the resistance movement on the one hand and an opposition movement within Israel itself; but there is no real sign of such a convergence yet, since, although Matzpen exists, what would be necessary is a mass proletarian movement.

PART IV

Kanafani and the Media

11

"A Conversation between the Sword and the Neck" (1970)

Ghassan Kanafani Interviewed
by ABC Journalist Richard Carleton

Introduction by *Romana Rubeo*

Two years before being assassinated by the Israeli Mossad on 8 July 1972, Palestinian leader and intellectual Ghassan Kanafani was interviewed by Richard Carleton who, at the time, worked for the Australian Broadcasting Company, ABC. The interview took place in the Lebanese capital, Beirut. This conversation with Carleton, though brief, is remembered as one of Kanafani's most revealing interviews In it, the Palestinian intellectual spoke about history, politics, resistance and even language.

The history of the world, Kanafani said in his first statement, "is always the history of the weak people fighting strong people", immediately framing his analysis around a Marxist view of history as a dialectical process that leads to class consciousness and, ultimately, a class struggle. Kanafani, of course, widened the scope of this struggle so that it includes the everlasting conflict between the oppressed and the oppressor, the occupied and the occupier, the colonised people and the colonial powers. After all, the liberation of Palestine through an anti-imperialist and anti-colonial struggle had always been at the centre of his personal agenda, in terms of both theoretical analysis and pragmatic action.

This is why, from the onset, Kanafani immediately drew a line between the two parties involved: the people versus the oppressive regimes. In his mind, this distinction applied not only to the Palestinian people and Israel, but to every other situation in which oppression takes place. For example, in reference to Black September, 1970 – which saw the Palestinian *fida'i* organisations standing against the Jordanian Armed Forces of King Hussein – Kanafani rejected the Australian journalist's definition of a "civil war", seeing the confrontation as part of the liberation struggle.

Throughout the interview, Kanafani showed himself to be perfectly aware of the ongoing war of narratives, and of the subsequent need to choose and select suitable words to rightly frame the Palestinian struggle for freedom. It reveals how Kanafani's framing is still applicable to the current situation in occupied Palestine. When Carleton defined the Jordanian war as "fruitless" and wondered what kind of achievement the Palestinian fighters had obtained, Kanafani was prompt in responding: "We achieved that our people could never be defeated." This remains the case until this day.

The suggestion made by the ABC journalist, in reference to the Jordanian conflict, can be juxtaposed with similar liberal opinions on the supposed few benefits reaped by the current Palestinian resistance movement. Kanafani's words still apply to what is currently happening in the occupied West Bank, where the Palestinian people have not given up on any form of organised resistance to the occupying power, despite the unfortunate choices of the Palestinian Authority "leadership".

Being very clear on the true priority for the Palestinian liberation movement – the fight against the injustice resulting from Israeli colonialism – Kanafani did not even engage in debate about "peace talks" with the Israelis. Well before the so-called peace negotiations that led to the Oslo Accords in the early 1990s, the Palestinian intellectual framed such talks as "a conversation between the sword and the neck", "capitulation" and "surrender".

When the journalist Carleton insisted on the potential loss of lives resulting from the resistance, claiming that stopping fighting would mean an end to death, misery and destruction, Kanafani's theoretical conflict between the colonised and the colonisers, the oppressors and the oppressed people manifested itself with defiant clarity: liberation meant something as essential as life itself.

* * *

INTERVIEW: "A CONVERSATION BETWEEN THE SWORD AND THE NECK"[1]

Voiceover by Richard Carleton: Taking the place of the timid business executive in Beirut, a new business has developed: revolution. Palestinian revolution. Palestinian guerrillas in Beirut are not like the Viet Cong. Here, they are in no way illicit; they are totally legitimate. In Beirut's main street, the biggest group has a three-storey office building, complete with all amenities. It's as modern as any in Sydney but the machinegun-toting guerrillas standing outside told me, "no photos". And there was no arguing. Of the most radical of the eleven Palestinian guerrilla movements is the Popular Front for the Liberation of Palestine, the PFLP. The Popular Front is now so well organised that it now has its own daily [sic] newspaper, with a claimed circulation of 23,000.[2] It was the Popular Front that highjacked and blew up three aircraft at Revolution Airport in the Jordanian desert. And it was the Popular Front that dynamited the Pan American jumbo at Cairo. The Beirut leader of the Popular Front is Ghassan Kanafani. He was born in Palestine but fled in 1948, as he puts it, from Zionist terror. Since then, he has been plotting the destruction of both the Zionists and the reactionary Arabs.

Ghassan Kanafani: I know… what I really know is, the history of the world is always the history of weak people fighting strong people. Of weak people who have a correct case fighting strong people who use their strength to exploit the weak.

Turn to the fighting that has been going on in Jordan in the recent weeks. It is your organisation that has been one side of the fight. What has it achieved?

---

1   The interview was carried out in late September 1970. This video transcript is transcribed with thanks to the late interviewer's son James Carleton, who released the footage online on 15 August 2017. James describes finding this recording in the dusty box of a family garage and believes that it was never actually aired by ABC (conversation with the editors, January 2023).
2   *Al-Hadaf* was produced weekly, not daily.

One thing, that we have a case to fight for. That is very much. This people, the Palestinian people prefer to die standing than to lose [their] case. We achieved proving that the King is wrong. We achieved proving that this nation is going to continue fighting till victory. We achieved that our people could never be defeated. We achieved teaching every single person in this world that we are a small, brave nation who are going to fight till the last drop of their blood to put justice for ourselves after the world failed in giving it to us. This is what we achieved.

It does seem that the war, the civil war has been quite fruitless...

It is not a civil war. It is a people defending themselves against a fascist government, which you are defending because King Hussain has an Arab passport. It is not a civil war.

Or a conflict?

It is not a conflict. It is a liberation movement, fighting for justice.

Well, whatever it might be best called...

It is not "whatever", because this is where the problem starts. Because this is what makes you ask all your questions. This is exactly where the problem starts. This is a people who is discriminated [against], who is fighting for [its] rights. This is historic. If you will say it is a civil war, then your questions will be justified. If you say it is a conflict, then of course it will be a surprise to know what is happening.

Why won't your organisation engage in peace talks with Israelis?

You don't mean, exactly, peace talks. You mean capitulation. You mean surrendering.

Why not just talk?

Talk to whom?

Talk to the Israeli leaders.

That is a kind of conversation between the sword and the neck, you mean.

When there is no sword and no guns in the room, you could still talk.

No. I have never seen any talk between a colonialist case and a national liberation movement.

But, despite this, why not talk?

Talk about what?

Talk about the possibility of not fighting.

Not fighting for what?

Not fighting at all, no matter what for.

Ya'ni, people usually fight for something, and they stop fighting for something. So, you cannot tell me even why we should speak, [or] about what… Or talk about [stopping] fighting. Why?

Talk to stop fighting, to stop the death and the misery, the destruction, the pain.

The misery, the destruction, the pain and the death of whom?

Of Palestinians, of Israelis, of Arabs.

Of the Palestinian people, who are uprooted, thrown in the camps, living in starvation, killed for 20 years and forbidden to use even the name "Palestinians"?

Better that way than dead though.

Maybe to you, but to us, it is not. To us, to liberate our country, to have dignity, to have respect, to have our mere human rights is something as essential as life itself.

You called King Hussain a fascist. Who else among the Arab leaders are you totally opposed to?

We consider the Arab governments two kinds: something we call the reactionaries, who are completely connected with the imperialists, like King Hussain's government, like the Saudi Arabian government, Moroccan government, Tunisian government... And then we have some other Arab governments which we call the military petit bourgeois governments like, Syria, Iraq, Egypt, Algeria and so on.

Just to end with, let me get back to the hijacking of the aircraft.[3] On reflection, do you think that was now a mistake?

We did not make a mistake in hijacking them. On the [contrary], we did one of the most correct things we have ever done.

---

3 From 6 to 12 September 1970, PFLP *fida'iyyin* carried out a series of plane hijackings, with three of these planes forced to land at Dawson's Field – renamed the Revolutionary Airport during the operation – near Zarqa, Jordan. Earlier in June, the PFLP had forced the hand of the Jordanian regime with the holding of Western hostages at the Intercontinental and Philadelphia hotels in Amman, where, in response, the government fired two hated Jordanian army commanders guilty of crimes against the Palestinian refugees. On 12 June, George Habash had explained to the hostages: "Yesterday, I was only in one hospital, where the doctor told me that there are 280 wounded and 60 dead [Palestinians]... The day before yesterday, al-Wihdat camp was shelled for more than half an hour"; see George Habash, "Our Code of Morals is Our Revolution" (Amsterdam: International Center for Palestine Studies, 2022), 15–16. No civilians were killed in the PFLP hostage-taking or hijacking operations.

Ghassan Kanafani meets Scandinavian activists in Lebanon and examines the Swedish *Free Palestine* newspaper. Public domain.

12

Denmark: A Study in
Media Experience (1971)

Introduction by *Ibrahim Aoude*

The Denmark case study written by the martyr Ghassan Kanafani in 1971 provides rich lessons for Palestinian and Arab intellectuals as they continue to confront Zionist propaganda. Zionists have concocted a false history about the establishment of their entity in Palestine on 15 May 1948. Their success in "legitimising" their narrative resides in the colonial nature of Western societies and the organic link of Zionism to the Western colonial project. Despite great odds, the Palestinian people have made significant inroads over past decades in narrating the realities of Palestinian life and struggle against settler colonialism.

As one reads this study in the original Arabic or English translation, the extent to which Zionist propaganda and political and social influence are rooted in Western societies is clear. This multifaceted Zionist influence is still evident in the confluence between criticising the settler-colonial entity in Palestine and anti-Semitism, along with the legal repercussions that such accusations might engender for those daring to criticise the Zionist entity in the West.

It is interesting to note that Kanafani selected a rather mild case for his study to prove the depth of Zionist influence in falsifying history and erasing Palestine and the Palestinian people from the narrative of the so-called "Israeli war of independence". The controversy arose from a book titled *Children in Israel*, which was part of a series of 12 books written about children in respective "underdeveloped" countries. The "Israeli" writer falsified history to justify the existence of the Zionist entity in Palestine and presented "Arab" children (in "Israel") as filthy and ignorant, while depicting "Israeli" children in a positive light. The book was a manifest expression of Orientalism: racism, settler colonialism and arrogance. The way in which the Occident has represented the Orient has usually been with the imperialist speaking for the indigenous and narrating its "civilizing mission" in "saving" the Other,[1] as Edward Said saw it.

Kanafani's intent was "to draw media laws and rules for our complex battle against...'world public opinion'". Highlighting the exchange of letters that the PFLP had with the publisher of children's books, *Lærerforeningernes materialeudvalg* (LM), Kanafani was able to deconstruct what he (and the PFLP) understood by "world public opinion" and showed the difference between public opinion in "developed" and "underdeveloped" countries, which in current parlance are referred to as the "Global North" and "Global South" respectively. Kanafani also pointed out the difference in public opinion between classes in both parts of the globe. This point was crucial for the PFLP, even at the beginning of the modern struggle of the Palestinian people to reclaim their national rights.

Kanafani showed the significance of confronting Zionist propaganda in the "heart of the beast", as Che Guevara labelled the USA.[2] The Denmark case showed that the Palestinian resistance had scored several points in favour of the Palestinian narrative and stirred dormant waters in the swamp of Zionist propaganda. The exchange of letters between the PFLP and LM had put the publisher on the defensive, as evidenced by its delaying tactics and confused responses to the PFLP. More critically, the exchange of letters threw the LM front into disarray and exposed the divisions among the LM committee charged with coming up with recommendations as to how to proceed. The initial committee's recommendation was to withdraw the entire series of 12 books, as they all had serious problems regarding their views of other children in respective "underdeveloped" countries.

While the publisher wanted to keep the matter under wraps, its strategy and tactics opened the floodgates for an open debate in the country about educational methods and materials that Denmark uses to educate its children. That outcome was a victory for the strategy of confrontation with Zionism in the "Global North".

---

1   Edward Said, *Culture and Imperialism* (New York: Vintage, 1994), 131.

2   Teishan A. Latner, *Cuban Revolution in America: Havana and the Making of the United. States Left, 1968–1992* (Chapel Hill, NC: University of North Carolina Press, 2018), 27.

The stakes for Palestinian liberation in the current period are just as high, if not higher. Palestinian liberation faces social media platforms (Facebook, Instagram, X (Twitter), etc.) that are heavily influenced by the Zionist enemy. The owners of those media platforms decide what is permissible to appear and what will not appear on their platforms. They control the narrative in its variety of forms (text, pictures and videos). In addition, traditional media (television, radio, etc.) block narratives and individuals who express the ideas and aspirations of the Palestinian people as they struggle for liberation. Traditional media rarely allow even compromised voices to appear on their screens. The internet, however, has "allowed" for niches in its colonial/imperial cobweb, where bloggers and alternative voices could significantly counter the media of ruling classes in the West. Voices of Palestinian liberation have been utilising, to a significant extent, the contradictions that the internet by its nature makes available.

Palestinian narratives of liberation are also expanding to many areas of confrontation with the Zionist enemy. A case in point is boycott campaigns, including the Palestinian Boycott, Divestment and Sanctions (BDS) initiative. These have a foothold in the West and are becoming even more pervasive and effective. The Palestinian Campaign for the Academic and Cultural Boycott of Israel (PACBI) has also been able to score successes in multiple academic associations. By confronting Zionist organisations such as Canary Mission or Campus Watch, the Western public is being educated about Palestinian national rights and the appropriation of Palestinian land, the apartheid "Israeli" state, and the ongoing ethnic cleansing of the Palestinian people. These necessary confrontations have exposed the hypocrisy of claims about the human face of Zionism in Palestine.

More work still needs to be done in this matter. It is critical to continue to engage in such struggles and show the commonalities of the struggle among the peoples of the world against injustice, colonialism, imperialism and US capitalist class domination of the globe. Only then would Palestinian liberation triumph in step with the triumphs of the peoples of the world against settler colonialism in Palestine and Western global hegemony. We owe it to the genius and hard work of Ghassan Kanafani, who pointed the compass of liberation early on to include the struggle of the Palestinian narrative.

* * *

DENMARK: A STUDY IN MEDIA EXPERIENCE[3]

The following media example is presented as a case to study to draw out rules and regulations for communication in our complex battle against what is described, briefly (and sometimes in a blatant distortion), as "world public opinion". Perhaps there is no need to reiterate that our understanding of "world public opinion", and of the media role that the Palestinian resistance needs to play, stems from a written and declared political vision of the nature of our ongoing struggle, its perception locally and internationally, and the nature of the hostile forces facing us. Hence, it is crucial to divide what is simplistically termed "world public opinion" into developed and underdeveloped countries, and into different class interests within and in relation to each other. As a result, we turn our media towards the powers that have an interest in the success of the revolution. The importance of the following example lies in the way it closely deals with details of these generalisations and attempts to explore them empirically. It therefore sets a standard by which to answer questions such as: To what extent can the "persuasive dialogue" be successful within liberal milieu and on what basis does its development depend? And what are the possibilities of its partial success, at least, in clarifying the minor contradictions regarding "the Middle East question", which prevail among middle-class intellectuals in Western Europe?

The example below is a simple "story" and was chosen specifically because of its simplicity: an independent Danish publishing house released a book on Israeli children as part of a series dedicated to the children of the world. Since this book constitutes a model for indirect Zionist indoctrination, as a result of an unquestioned belief in the dominating culture, the Central Media Committee[4] of the Popular Front for the Liberation of Palestine (PFLP) attempted

---

3 Originally published in *Shu'un Filastiniyya*, Issue 9 (May 1972). Translation by Hiyem Cheurfa.
4 Kanafani was a member of this committee and represented *al-Hadaf* newspaper in its meetings.

to convince the publishing house to withdraw the book from the markets. The story told here is merely the details of this attempt as it clearly reflects the media laws, rules and regulations that govern such a case, and the crucial [importance] of knowing such rules and regulations, as well as how they function, and their strengths and weaknesses.

We have chosen this Danish publishing house and the afore-mentioned book due to their representing an "ordinary case". That is, this publishing house is not Zionist and is not assumedly under any direct Zionist pressure. Additionally, the complex of anti-Semitism (which constitutes an immense pressure upon the media) is felt to a lesser degree by Denmark's intellectuals and middle classes than in any other European country. The activity of this publishing house is directed, moreover, from a liberal milieu towards schools where taught subjects are supposedly examined by "public opinion", ensuring an "independent and appropriate educational system". We are, therefore, dealing with an exemplary case, which represents, on the one hand, the minimum threshold of obstacles that the Palestinian media is expected to face when directed towards average European public opinion. On the other hand, this case represents the ultimate level of results that the Palestinian media must expect on this level from a logical "persuasive dialogue" with European public opinion. So, what is the outcome? The publishing house, *Lærerforeningernes materialeudvalg* (LM), specialises in children's books distributed specifically to primary school libraries and used as educational materials. LM published the book *Children in Israel*,[5] aimed at Danish children (and Scandinavian children in general) aged from eight to ten years old. After the Central Media Committee of the PFLP had reviewed the book, it sent the following letter to LM, on 1 February 1971:

We have come across a copy of your book *Children in Israel* by Inger and Clyde Franklin, published in 1964, and again in 1967. We understand that it has recently been distributed widely in Danish primary schools and in other Scandinavian countries. We were prompted to write to you by our reading of this book,

---

5   Inger and Clyde Franklin, *Børn i Israel*, Volume 12 (Denmark: LM, 1964).

which incites racism and hatred, [constituting] another facet of racist fascism being fed into the minds of innocent children in your country, against Arab children. We are asking you to withdraw and abandon the book, and to cease participation in this horrendous brainwashing process aimed at your children, which incites hatred towards our children and our people as a whole.

The "glories" that the authors of your book have attributed to Israel are based in their entirety on an incredible contempt for Arabs. The pictures of Arab children that you have published could only be described as a biased, ill-minded selection, fit only for punishment or medical attention, for they consist not only of forgeries but represent the contemporary and ugly face of anti-Semitism, by which we mean the incitement of hatred against Arabs.

From a political, educational and ethical point of view, your book is a disgrace, and we ask you to halt its influence on the minds of the children of your country. And since we are accusing you of taking part in such a hate campaign against the masses of our people, we are not only asking you to stop this campaign by merely withdrawing and abandoning the book, but also by publicly apologising for it.

Israel, as an aggressor state established through armed repression and terrorism and built upon the dead bodies of thousands of our men, as well as our children, needs such a misinformation campaign to cover its crimes. There is no doubt that such a fact is worth drawing your attention to, the role that you are playing in this campaign: an opportunistic and decadent role of brainwashing, directed, most horrendously, at Danish children.

It is of paramount importance to us, before disseminating this letter more widely, to know your perspective, and your decision regarding this shameful book.

We had then to wait until mid-March to receive the following letter from LM publishing house:

We have received your letter dated 1 February 1971 and transferred it to our leadership board due to its harsh and major criticism against one of our published books; we have asked the committee to discuss the issue. We are, of course, aware of the tense situation between Israelis and Arabs in the Middle East, but we do not think that this should prevent us from publishing books describing conditions in that region.

The book you criticise is part of a series of 12 books, all of which describe the lives of two children, usually siblings, in a foreign country. Therefore, when we publish a book about the *Children in Israel*, it is not possible to avoid the fact that two Israeli children are the main subject. Nevertheless, the authors did show a demonstrable interest in describing the conditions of Arab children in the country, by referring to them in the book on numerous occasions.

We have studied the book very carefully and have found that it does not include any directly false information. However, in case there are mistakes, we would be glad if you would identify these for us.

In order for us to arrive at more complete picture of the situation in the region, we welcome any suggestion of an author who is able to write a new book for the series about Arab children in refugee camps. Such a book would be beneficial, [particularly as] we would be keen to publish a book on refugee children for World Refugee Year.[6] Since we do not know a competent author, we would like to hear your recommendations, or perhaps you could suggest a translated book. Either way, we ask that the subject of such a book should be treated as objectively as possible. In addition, and in response to your request, the committee has decided to make a critical review of the 12 books in order to, on the one hand, omit outdated topics and,

---

6   World Refugee Year (WRY) had been initiated by British participants in the UN (it had last been marked in 1959–1960) and was politically focused on what the imperialist countries saw as "victims of communism", the problems of Jews in Egypt and a scattering of other issues, including the Palestinians. Soviet opposition to WRY expressed the view that Western Europe had the capacity to resolve the forced movement of peoples, if it had the political will. Britain, for one, claimed to have taken in all of the refugees it could absorb and promised only a financial contribution; "World Refugee Year, 1959–60", *Social Service Review* 33, no. 3 (September 1959): 300.

on the other, to delete any false information. A subcommittee has been chosen to review the books carefully and repeatedly. It will then be decided whether these books should be re-edited or withdrawn from circulation once all of the copies are sold.

And in this regard, we would be happy if you could refer to the specific passages, and photos, that you claim contain false information in the book *Children in Israel*.

This letter was not unexpected, as this is the traditional way of avoiding direct dialogue. But what this response did not mention is that the PFLP letter, read during the aforementioned board meeting, had prompted concerns among several of its members that the racist approach was not limited to *Children in Israel*, but rather could be found in other books in the series. This tackled the roots of the subject, raising questions over the competence of the authors, as well as their integrity and adeptness as teachers. Despite this, the PFLP Central Media Committee moved the dialogue a step forward, accepting the challenge posed by the letter from the publishing house. [The PFLP] responded in the following, comprehensive letter:

We have received your correspondence dated 1 March 1971, responding to a letter that we had previously sent you on 1 February, on your publication of the book *Children in Israel*. While we thank you for your letter, in which you have shown an interest in the subject, we would like to answer the concerns that you have raised by reference to the following points:

1. You stated that you do not think the critical situation in the Middle East should prevent the publication of a book describing conditions in the region. We were very surprised by this observation because it is completely irrelevant to the topic in question. In our letter, there is no indication that this should be understood. On the contrary, we believe that the critical nature of the situation urges for the publication of books that detail the situation. What we object to is the *subjectivity* of these books and the extent that they serve peace, truth and justice. Your book does the opposite.

2. It seems from your letter that you were expecting us to find contentment in the fact that the authors of *Children in Israel* mention Arab children and their conditions several times. In fact, our objection lies at this precise point, for [Arab children] are referred to only through an outlook filled with racism and condescension, and which aims at distorting reality and highlighting the *superiority* of the Israeli child when compared with the Arab. Undoubtedly, you do realise that this kind of representation is a remnant of a colonialist culture, which you, as a publishing house targeting innocent children as an audience, should be seeking to eliminate.

3. You claim to have looked *carefully* through the book but found that it does not include any *directly* false information: does this mean that you admit to *indirectly* false information? The latter is more dangerous as it leads to unconscious misinformation. You have asked us to point out such errors. We would be pleased to do so, although we find it unfortunate that you have not noticed such errors – having studied the book so "carefully" – because such mistakes, as conspicuous as they are, do not require careful attention to be detected, as you will notice below:

- First, we present the following examples:

  a) "Only 16 years ago did Israel become a nation for the Jews. Before that time, the land was uncultivated and the people who came to settle there faced many threats" (pp. 4–5);
  b) "When the Jews were far from *their country*,[7] they heard their language only in the synagogue" (p. 10);
  c) "All this time we had been dreaming of fertile land, fields of wheat and orchards of oranges, but there was nothing but dust and sand" (p. 14).

These excerpts and many others (which we hope you notice) avoid – in what is assumed to be outstanding proficiency – any mention of Palestine and Palestinians. While we see this

---

7   Emphasis added by Ghassan Kanafani.

negligence as failing to serve the "objectivity" to which you refer in your letter, we may also note that the colonialist discourse on which the Zionist movement is based is not only tirelessly repeated but also deliberate. This discourse challenges historical reality [to assert] that Palestine (to which you refer to as "Israel", even before it was named as such in 1948!) was an uncultivated land, full of sand and danger. This, as you will know, is a discourse used by colonialists to justify their control over and persecution of other nations. It is repeated in pages 15, 16, 19 and 22, and constitutes a false basis upon which condescending, colonialist thought is instilled into the minds of the young, since your use of the words "progress" and "backwardness" are meant to signify subjugation and servitude.

• Second, we find examples of another type:

"Arabs do not like us. It is because they believe that the land we inhabited is theirs" (p. 15).

"These are the Arabs who said they will take the land from us... They said that if we reclaimed our land, they would attack us. The next day, they crossed the new borders... but, luckily, we forced the Arabs out..." (p. 17).

"Why are there Arabs in our country?... A lot of them lived in Israel(?) and they escaped when the war broke out" (p. 17).

These are other examples of misinformation which distort historical facts. When the rights of Palestinians are mentioned, phrases like "they believe" and "crossed the borders" are used. When Israelis speak about [Palestinians], the words used are "our land", "we drove them out of the border" and "escaped." One must be completely absent from our time to not notice the bias and misleading content of these phrases, or at least be completely ignorant of the topic being addressed. You introduce our people, who lived on the land of Palestine for

thousands of years, rooted in its history, and established civil-
isations and cultures, as a group of gangs invading the land
from outside. Your account is based on a fantasy far removed
from historical accuracy!

- Third, the book's view of Arabs (the name Palestinians
  is omitted from a children's textbook that fundamentally
  looks at the case of Palestine) is purely racist. It is not only
  based on the traditional colonialist viewpoint that looks at
  the traditional native population as second-class humans;
  it also questions their very ability to evolve. It endows
  settler-colonialism, the vilest form of oppression and
  exploitation, with a missionary character:

> "We must try to help the Arabs who live here, because
> they have not learned as much as we have, and so if they
> are going to help us cultivate the land, we must first teach
> them how to do it" (p. 17).

Based on exploitation, this condescension then becomes
insolent, questioning the human value of Arabs:

> "Many Jews are impatient with Arabs and say: 'it is useless
> to teach Arabs anything, they cannot and do not want to
> learn', but Musa's father does not agree…" (p. 37).

Oppression, persecution and societal racism, would then of
course find humorous explanations:

> "Some Jews and Arabs in Israel do not like each other.
> Jewish children and Arab children do not go to the same
> schools" (p. 17).

While it is labelled differently, this is the same reality existing
in South Africa. How else could the following phrases be
meant?:

"Arab children are always running... and they are very dirty" (p. 37);

"In an Arab household, you do not see the wife because she stays in the kitchen" (p. 37);

and, of course, when a Jewish girl passes through the village,

"an Arab girl approaches her and touches her beautiful, clean dress" (p. 39).

- Fourth, if the two authors had good intentions, they would not have deliberately chosen specific pictures of Arabs on pages 20, 23, 24, 26 and 38 as the only photos of them in the book. These pictures have been selected carefully (and not by chance, we believe) to instil that condescending outlook, as they are not only old pictures, but were all taken in the desert. They have nothing to do with the Palestinian cause but were selected to present an image that is antithetical to the pictures published about Israel, which – as it is the case with colonisers – represent cleanliness, health, innocence, purity and civilisation, surrounded by barbarians and the dangers of their backlash!

We do not comprehend how, with the abundance of images representing all aspects of life in the Arab region, the authors had to select on page 38 pictures from Wilfred Thesiger's books on the Arabian Peninsula, of two children from South Yemen – taken at an unknown time, in an unfamiliar and striking setting – to suggest that they are two Arab children from Palestine!

Do you not notice, even here, the meaning of the bias to which we have been referring?

4. There is a recent tradition in your country allowing the authorities to withdraw books that are described as anti-Semitic. While we believe that this tradition is one of the few lessons learned by the West from the tragedies of the past half century, we very much regret that it does not until now acknowledge that "hatred

of Arabs" is a new form of anti-Semitism. This is why, if successful, a brave initiative from individuals and organisations in this regard would have the value of a vanguard, deserving of admiration.

If it is not clear enough by now, our aim from this letter is not to discuss everything included in the book. Our interest in this particular book is primarily because it targets the minds of innocent children who are unable to defend themselves, nor to test the information that is being fed to them in order to prepare them to be habitually anti-Arab and distant from objectivity.

We accuse the authors of this book of deliberately distorting the image of Arabs and Palestinians, and of glorifying a colonialist wave that came on a sea of blood, built upon the skulls of our people, which has survived until now on oppression, subjugation and exploitation, and which resulted in hundreds of thousands of refugees who were expelled under Zionist terrorism, and about whom your book does not mention a single word. If the book was supposed to explain the reason leading Jews to immigrate to Palestine to the children of your country, you have ignored it. Such reasoning would draw the attention of your children to [understand] the gist of the problem early on. It would, therefore, condemn a mode of colonial thinking that is based on racism and oppression, that led Europe to a series of massacres against Jews, and that is still used with extreme audacity in a campaign of hatred, this time against Arabs.

What is happening here is that you are contributing to the brainwashing of your innocent children, with the same kind of culture that has caused all kinds of human tragedies throughout history, whether for Jews, Christians or Muslims. The truth is that, in this book, you are serving the first steps in a cycle of intellectual dominance practised by the reactionary mentality (al-'aqliyya al-raya 'iyya –العقلية الرجعية) of the Zionist movement. This occurs not only through distorting historical facts (which is one of the pillars of Israeli media hegemony) but also by promoting a colonial ideology, which – despite its brutality, fascism and oppressiveness – ascribes to itself a missionary character, promoting the logic of contempt against the people of the Third World.

This logic characterises your book from beginning to end. And if this book were given to someone with minimal knowledge on the Palestinian case and Zionist propaganda, and they were objective in a scientific sense, they would simply point out the four pillars on which your book is based: 1) Misinformation and historical distortion, 2) Emphasis on Israeli superiority, 3) Planting the idea of Arabs as being "second-class humans", 4) Presenting the military structure of an invasive Israeli society as a matter of "defence", resulting from the clash between "progress" and "barbarism"! To achieve this end, the book utilises not only a skilful method to deceive the minds of children, but also resorts to pictures.

We reiterate our demand that you withdraw the book from circulation among your children, since the indirect pains caused by such a book upon the children of our people, upon our people as a whole, and upon the cause of peace and justice in the world must persuade you to do so.

5. Of course, we have suggestions of Arab institutions that you may contact to inquire about whether they would like to contribute to your project, by writing or nominating someone to write a book about Palestinian children. We guarantee the objectivity of these sources (a condition that you required without actually applying to your book *Children in Israel*). You may also seek advice form the Palestinian Research Centre, the Fifth of June League, or from the Arab Women's Media Committee in Beirut.

6. In addition, we suggest that you consider the possibilities of publishing an objective book on Arab *Children in Israel*. Or, next time, your choice might be two Sephardic *Children in Israel* for a more objective depiction.

7. There are many names that you may contact for advice regarding books of this kind. And, since it seems important to you, many of these names are Jewish, and are familiar with Jews, Zionism,

Israel and the crimes committed against the Palestinian people. You may ask Moshe Menuhin or read his publications, or Elmer Berger. On the other hand, you could ask Maxime Rodinson or Ania Francos. If you prefer a further left perspective, we suggest Meir Vilner, Moshé Machover and Akiva Or. We assure you that "objectivity" has no particular religion, nor a specific passport, but is realised when there is a daring scientific mind behind it.

We trust your ability to maintain the educational and objective character of your institution and look forward to your reply.

This time, the reply of LM arrived as late as 12 October 1971! At first, it was said that our letter was not received and so another was hand-delivered to them. After a long wait, we received the following reply:

We thank you a lot on your undated letter (?) which we have received through (…).[8] It seems that the original letter was lost, since it had never reached us.

Aftcr receiving your first letter, the publishing committee associated with the teachers' union set up a working committee to study all 12 books of our series, including *Children in Israel*. This committee has carefully studied your letters and discussed all the points that you raise. On 28 September, the findings of the committee were presented to the main publications office, which has also received a copy of your letter. After a thorough discussion, the office has decided that the book *Children in Israel* must be reviewed and re-edited upon completion of sales of the printed copies. Now we shall inform the authors, who are of course aware of your objections, of their need to proceed with the reviewing process. In addition, we would still like to publish another book on Arab children. We thank you for your suggestions.

That is all!

---

8   Deleted by Kanafani, likely to protect the identity of the carrier.

The book would not be withdrawn but would be sold and then reviewed by the same authors for republication. The letter sent by the publishing house did not respond to any of the points that were raised by the Front's critical letter and nor was there any mention of the viewpoint [we] opposed.

So, was all of this a mere waste of time? Not completely, because the reactions and consequences of all this were moving forward on another level. It seems that the late reply of LM publishers was not due to the claimed loss of the Front's letter. It was because of a partial deadlock within the committee that was assigned to review the book. It was an impossible situation to contain, so it reached newspapers and magazines specialised in education in Denmark, and then, even if partially, other newspapers!

LM is a publishing house which undertakes the printing of educational materials and disseminates them across institutions, schools and educational centres in Denmark. Its main committee is composed of the representatives of 17 educational organisations in the country, in addition to 15 independent members selected for their educational competencies. Its funding is provided by the representative educational organisations and the Ministry of Culture. The main committee, composed of the aforementioned 32 members, elects 4 members who represent its management board.

When the PFLP letter reached the management board, a so-called working committee was elected, during a meeting attended by a number of members from the main committee, in order to follow up the study of the case. This working committee took a number of decisions that closely align with the Front's demands and are based on the same issues raised in the Front's letter. However, when these decisions reached the main committee, they were completely ignored and a fragmented decision (al-qarar al-mujtaza' – القرار المجتزأ), expressed in the letter sent by the president of LM publishing house to the PFLP, was made instead. Yet, the development of events was taking a different context. Let us follow it:

On 7 May 1971, Politiken[9] newspaper published a short article by a woman named Mary Gilstrap, in which she questions the accuracy of information found in Children in Israel. The author

---

9 Politiken is a liberal Danish daily.

focused her criticism on the pictures and biased information included in the book. Perhaps, as a children's book critic in *Politiken*, she considered this particular book to be an exception in the series published by LM. Two days later, two teachers were encouraged by this article to address LM in a letter harshly criticising the book. This letter pointed out that the article written by Gilstrap was not nearly critical enough. This was only the beginning. In *Folkeskolen* ('popular schools'), a magazine specialising in educational issues, an open letter was published by Elsa Hamrick and Chris Maisel, two members of the working committee created by LM publishing house and of its main committee. This letter, published on 15 October 1971, exposes the truth of what happened behind the scenes. It states the following:

> In February 1971, the LM administration created a working committee to review its series of books on the children of foreign countries in order to decide whether these books should be revised or withdrawn. This committee was created following discussions raised by a letter received by LM from the Popular Front for the Liberation of Palestine on the role of these books and specifically on the book *Children in Israel*.
>
> After reviewing all the books in the series, the working committee recommended that all of them should be immediately withdrawn from the market. The reasons for withdrawing these books were to be explained in the pages of educational magazines in order to open a dialogue on educational materials related to international relations.
>
> There was a suggestion, which only received a minority vote, proposing to continue selling the books *Children in Iceland* and *Children in Greenland*, while a special discussion on *Children in Israel* took place. The majority recommendation was to withdraw all of the aforementioned books from the market based on the following:
>
> 1. The books' attitude towards other nations is not adequate, with the following points confirmed: the books are based on old materials; there are direct comparisons that stem from a viewpoint that minimises the value of other traditions and

considers our lifestyle as exemplary; on many occasions, it has been asserted that poor countries cannot survive without the aid of rich countries through programmes viewed with absolute optimism; there are superficial and misleading explanations of underdevelopment in poor countries; there is an absolute neglect of the reality of class differences within the underdeveloped world; "modern life" has often been presented as positive in itself and has always meant the European way of life.

2. In addition, the working committee has seen, from a basic educational perspective, many negative aspects in these books: the pictures and the accompanying captions are inadequate as they impose information on readers without giving them the opportunity to decide on their stance. These books are not scientifically based and are unreliable sources of information. There are many books in the series that contain old information that do not rely on any sources of statistical data. In cases where the books mention statistics, they do not specify the time during which these numbers were accurate.

During the meeting held with representatives of LM publishing house on 28 September 1971, it was decided that "books 1–7 of the series must be withdrawn from circulation immediately". The reason given was that the information in these books is now outdated. Books 9–12 of the series (on Greenland, Alaska, Iceland and Israel) would continue to be sold until they were out of stock. Only then would they be revised or re-edited. We, as members of the working committee, feel that we must protest the fact that the committee's decision to withdraw all the books has been ignored. We regret that the representatives of LM insisted on basing their decision merely on whether the information included in the books is up-to-date or outdated rather than on their educational and humanistic approach, which we consider as more important. This is because we realise that this approach may hinder the students' international understanding. In addition, we feel that LM's refusal to withdraw the books and to take our reasons into consideration has prevented a wide debate on the issue of international relations, towards which we should guide our students according to educational methods. We were both elected as members of LM and are unaffiliated to any specific group or organisation, and so we are acting independently. We believe that since we cannot defend LM's decision, we hereby announce our wish to withdraw from the main committee of the publishing house.

In the same magazine [*Folkeskolen*], Issue 24 in December 1971, an article commenting on Hamrick and Maisel's open letter was published. It suggested considering this specific letter as an occasion to begin a public dialogue on culturally misleading educational approaches in Denmark, [namely] approaches that present racist information and stances towards foreign people and countries. The article raised the case of *Children in Israel*, and its author asserted that the book must be withdrawn immediately from the market because it is insulting and racist. The article also wondered what would have happened if the PFLP had not sent a letter to LM about its educational approach. This letter led to the creation of the working committee and hence to the discovery of the gross errors in teaching children racism and misinformation. The article pointed out that the working committee's report on *Children in Israel* mentioned almost all the points that were raised and insisted upon by the PFLP's letter. It also pondered the aim of LM in creating the working committee when the intention was to not adopt its decision. The article stated that in a 14 September 1971 discussion as part of Education is our Mission – an educational programme on Danish radio – a representative of LM responded to a question on whether *Children in Israel* would be withdrawn if the committee considered [the book] to be inappropriate. He answered that the committee's decision will be legitimate and that the book would be withdrawn if this is democratically approved. According to the article, one of the participants in this radio discussion stated:

It has been eight months since LM received the letter from the PFLP and the decision has not been made. We wonder if it would have taken the same time to respond to a letter from the Zionist side.

Later on, the [same] woman was dismissed from her position at the radio station under pretence that she had attacked the European Common Market in one of her children's programmes.

In its October 1971 issue, the magazine *Unge Pædagoger* (young pedagogues) published an article stating that *Children in Israel* is a biased book, especially the chapter on the war, which is based entirely on misinformation. [The article] states:

> It is possible to find in this book many words that are racially biased. This becomes a dangerous fact when such words are directed towards innocent and vulnerable minds.

The article concludes that: "LM must immediately withdraw the book from the market and burn its unsold copies."

However, as we have seen, LM did not reach the same conclusion and instead took a different decision. In its second issue (December 1971), the magazine raised the topic again. It attacked LM for its position in this case and wrote:

> The main committee of LM met on 22 February 1971 and at the top of its agenda was the letter received from the PFLP on the book *Children in Israel*, which was described as racist against Arabs inside and outside of Israel. A working committee was created to discuss this accusation.

The magazine noted that the decision of the working committee was to withdraw all of the books published by LM from circulation immediately. It then stated the reasons on which the committee's decision was based, stressing the importance of constructive public dialogue in educational and pedagogic magazines, as a way to learn from this incident and to prevent the publication of other similar books. The magazine also reported that, during the committee's meeting in September, only 19 of its 32 members attended, 7 of them voted for and 2 against the aforementioned decision, while the remaining members abstained from voting. The magazine continued:

On 10 October, the two members who were against the decision withdrew [from the committee], and on 7 November, it became clear that all of the books published by LM publishing house were still being sold and have not been withdrawn from the markets.

The magazine seized the opportunity to criticise harshly the working system of LM publishing house; it proposed a new approach of working and asked educators to adopt it as an alternative to the flawed existing system which facilitates such mistakes. The magazine reached the decision that there was no need for representatives from *Unge Pædagoger* to remain within the main committee of LM and, hence, they declared their immediate withdrawal from it.

The same magazine began to publish a series of articles critical of some of the books published by LM. A quick reading of these articles shows that Arab children were not the only subject of racism in the publisher's series, but all the children of the underdeveloped world. On 6 January 1972, an article titled "LM House Publishes Racist Books" was unexpectedly published in *Ekstra Bladet*, one of Denmark's biggest tabloids. At its onset, the article indicated that "young teachers in Denmark are protesting vehemently against the racist brainwashing that targets the minds of vulnerable children". The article stressed that teachers are demanding the immediate withdrawal of the book on Israeli children from bookstores, and that the LM administration had ignored these demands.

To the author of the article, a teacher said that: "I was trying to teach the children something on Jewish children when I noticed in the book a blatant form of racism and a campaign of hatred against Arabs." The teacher added that she thinks that LM's refusal to withdraw the book is for two main reasons: first economic, and second that events in the book occur in a distant country that, according to the publishing house, does not concern public opinion and is therefore unimportant. Another teacher said that the racist crusade against Arabs in the book is only one example of the mentality with which the issues of the developing world are perceived and handled. Both teachers mentioned examples of books on Arab and Israeli children taught in Danish schools which contain racist campaigns against Arabs. The first teacher referred to here said that "it is my duty as an educator to refuse and resist the attempts to instil the idea that Arabs are second-class humans".

Despite LM's long silence on the matter, their first [public] response appeared suddenly in an article titled "Who Decides What Danish Textbooks Should Contain?" in *Det fri Aktuelt* newspaper, the mouthpiece of the Social Democrats. The author of this article says that "the Popular Front demanded that LM withdraw the book *Children in Israel* from Danish schools because it is racist". The author continues that the parliamentary education committee asked the Danish minister of education a question concerning the position of the Danish [Social Democrat] government on such demands and asked what should be done. The parliamentary committee inquired about the possibilities of putting an end to all forms of pressure exercised on LM from groups or organisations.

Det fri Aktuelt published the words of an official in LM, saying that "16 educational organisations have reviewed the aforementioned book and informed LM of their opinions and suggestions, in light of which the book shall be re-edited". However, the official insisted that the book is not racist. The newspaper stated that, "it is very dangerous to succumb to the opinions of foreign organisations on what should be included in Danish textbooks".

On 27 January 1972, another article appeared in *Børn & Unge* ("children and youth") magazine issued by the Danish Boys Organisation, one of the state's social organisations. The article was written by a Danish teacher Minnie Johansson and titled "Palestinians Oppressed in Danish Textbooks". The article re-raised the issue, and its author pointed to the unusually large number of available books and magazines which not only aim to justify Zionist domination of Palestine but also to erase the word "Palestinians" from history. The article also criticised the methods of teaching used for topics that touch upon the Palestinian issue, speaking at length about "making the desert bloom" and other myths that aim at constructing false and devious values in children. The author revealed other books on Israel that are addressed to children in Danish schools. All of these books revolve around the same themes dealt with in *Children in Israel* and share the same level of misinformation and falsification which cannot be ignored.

The case is evolving, and it seems that the publishing house has now been backed into in a corner. Even its attempts to raise the issue at the level of parliament were not successful because members of the parliamentary education committee discovered beforehand that they could not openly defend such a book. We are aware, of course, that a miracle will not happen, and that biased pedagogies that reflect the interest of the ruling class will not be changed through persuasion. However, an experience such as this helps gain an unlimited number of lessons and rules that serve to lay down plans for future work.

We will not attempt to summarise these lessons in this study. We are rather interested in pointing out that when a battle becomes a media subject, it immediately takes the form of a confrontation between the society's left and right, and tasks and positions become immediately divided according to the interest of the parties involved. This means that a media battle cannot be won unless it is originally planned to involve left-wing parties in the country concerned and to allow them to completely navigate through the totality of existing contradictions in that society, not above or in isolation from them.

We immediately see that any Arab media case (as with all cases of resistance) can gradually become well established and urgent in the European society in which they are raised. Such cases can become central and closely related to society's everyday issues for which an ethical position must be taken, away from any personal interests. We have seen how the case of the book *Children in Israel* not only concerns a stance against Zionism or Arabs but is a part of a battle against the domination of reactionary forces, their cultural and educational structures within Denmark, and between it and other countries of the developing world.

A battle of this kind, therefore, needs exposure in the first place. It then requires following and linking its interests to the interests, opinions and positions of far-left forces of the society in which it is raised, with the best of its values. This is perhaps not only the mission of committees that support Arab causes but is also at the core of the tasks of progressive forces that are interested in issues of political struggles in their own societies.

The media model that we have presented in detail here may seem, at first glance, as unimportant and marginal. However, in our opinion, it constitutes an example that enables us to draw a number of indispensable communicative rules and regulations.

13

Concerning the Case of Abu Hamidu and Issues of Media "Exchange" with the Enemy (1972)

Introduction by *Asma Hussein*

Reading the final piece written by Ghassan Kanafani allows for a retrospective insight into his previous works, including his two-volume study of Palestinian resistance literature. Therein, not only was Kanafani a forerunner in using and applying the term "resistance literature", but also a pacesetter in bringing the literary output of pre- and post-Nakba writers into visibility and highlighting their avant-garde character. The latter emphasis starkly contrasts the undertaking he took upon himself in a different form of resistance literature, for his last journal entry, published in August 1972, a month after his assassination. In retrospect "The Case of Abu Hamidu" was not Kanafani's first critique of the flaws of the Palestinian revolutionary and resistance movements. It was preceded, for example, by a *Shu'un Falastiniyya* (*Palestinian Matters*) entry in January, "The 1936–1939 Revolution in Palestine: Backgrounds, Details and Analysis", later published as a PFLP pamphlet.

Compared to this earlier text, "The Case of Abu Hamidu" provides additional, contemporary dimensions regarding the cultural, social and media ramifications of the resistance movement and its flaws. The piece is a pioneering work in the sense of tackling the issue of normalisation long before it became a controversial issue in the aftermath of signing the Camp David Accords in 1987. In particular, Kanafani examined the question of cultural normalisation. In this piece, he juxtaposed three contemporaneous incidents: the Abu Hamidu case, concerning an alleged sexual abuse; the participation of Palestinian students in a BBC debate on the Palestinian question with two Israeli counterparts; and the so-called Finley case, involving a professor at Beirut Girls' College utilising a written passage justifying the Israeli occupation of Palestine. These ostensibly disconnected incidents are incisively melded into a statement on the unresolved dilemmas of political training in the Palestinian resistance movement and the bankruptcy of intellectual training in Palestinian (and Arab) schools and higher education institutions.

The first of these incidents involved a Fatah *fida'i* nicknamed Abu Hamidu, who was falsely accused of raping two sisters. The two girls were killed by their brothers to cleanse the "disgrace", while Abu Hamidu was sentenced to death in a "revolutionary court", upon the orders of Yasser Arafat.[1] The hanging never took place as the villagers at Hasbia, South Lebanon, refused the order and the *fida'i* purportedly died in an Israeli attack that targeted the prison where he was kept. Palpably, this is a prototypical episode of honour killing. Through Kanafani's insightful critical abilities, the alleged rape and subsequent results were anatomised into a versatile case, indexing at once phenomena of social, political and organisational backwardness on which Israel cashed in.

The television debate and the Finley case are interconnected under the category of normalisation. Yet, they are carefully contradistinguished. On the one hand, Kanafani perceived the media and cultural exchange with Israel as uncalled for and undermining rather than advancing the Palestinian cause. On the other, scientific and intellectual exchange is held as a "duty". The "scientific" aspect is foregrounded, linking the Finley case with another contemporaneous debate triggered by a medical reference on the library shelves of the American University of Beirut. Where he elsewhere studied Zionist texts to understand the founding logic of colonialist, enemy ideology, here Kanafani calls for all materials furthering the advance of the national cause to be made readily available.

---

1 George Hajjar adds: "[The] whole affair provoked a widespread dispute in Lebanon and in the ranks of the resistance. The facts were easy to ascertain had Fateh investigated them seriously. Two young women befriended Abu Hamidu and desired to join the commandos. Their brother shot and killed both of them, thinking that they had been molested by Abu Hamidu and his fellow commandos. Medical evidence demonstrated clearly that neither woman was violated..."; George Hajjar, *Kanafani: Symbol of Palestine* (Lebanon: Karoun, 1974), 164.

In summary, Kanafani's last journal entry could be seen as his codicil. Routed through a reflection on seemingly common-place everyday occurrences, the substrata of revolutionary and resistance work are profoundly examined and criticised by way of raising an alarm for the glitches which must be tackled in the movement.

* * *

CONCERNING THE CASE OF ABU HAMIDU AND ISSUES OF MEDIA "EXCHANGE" WITH THE ENEMY[2]

In the recent period, some peripheral events have erupted and deflected people's attention away from issues relating to the resistance in particular. Though such events were relatively unim-portant, they offered the opportunity to look at their roots. Such a look, however, has so far not been taken, not least because the debating parties have become bogged down in the superficial details of these events, but also because developments surround-ing the resistance movement were continuously accelerating; one would hardly find the chance to thoroughly examine an event in all of its facets before a new event would take over and eclipse all others, and so on.

Perhaps the most prominent event from the period in question, and one which falls in the aforementioned category, is the case of Abu Hamidu. A furore was excited by the allegations hurled at him concerning the rape of two girls, sisters from the town of Hasbia (حاصبيا), which spurred their brother to shoot them dead; the reaction of the locals who rose up to cleanse the shame that befell them; and the revolutionary court's death sentence against the *fida'i* Abu Hamidu, in order to "set a warning example to others", making sure that the sentence be executed in the town square. The rest is history. The locals decided against the execution of Abu Hamidu and pushed for the withdrawal of the *fida'iyyin* from the town and its immediate vicinity; the *fida'iyyin* did so and were shelled by Israeli bombers at noon the next day, before they

2   Original: *Shu'un Falastiniyya* 12 (August 1972). Translation by Asma Hussein.

barricaded and camouflaged their new strongholds. The Israeli bombers also shelled the town's streets indiscriminately. It was said later said that Abu Hamidu was injured during the bombardment and may have been one of the inmates of the prison which was deliberately attacked by the Israeli bombers.

While the Abu Hamidu case and its sequels occupied the largest part of the heated debates of the period, another case triggered a less acute reaction. A case which, in a nutshell, concerned the parameters that define media and cultural relationships with the Israeli enemy. Around the period in question, two students took it upon themselves to participate in a British television show broadcasting from Cyprus and debate the Palestinian question face to face with two Israeli students. Concurrently, the "Finley" case at the Beirut College for Girls – that is, the case of the teacher who turned a blind eye to a textbook passage justifying the Zionist land usurpation – was growing, finding its way to the dailies and arriving as far as calling for the teacher's dismissal. A [third] case regarding the existence of an Israeli medical reference in the library of the American University [of Beirut] received less attention, yet raised the main issue within these parameters. These three cases do not involve something fundamentally new; similar cases have occurred multiple times over the past years and, indeed, the logic that substantiates their emergence and the raging debate over them, time after time, remains undetectable. Far and above, this may happen while the weekly issue of the French *L'Express* [magazine] circulates all over Beirut and devotes several pages to racial and religious slurs against Arabs without anyone banning, countering or even reproaching its correspondent in Beirut! This actually happened, during the period when Professor Finley was the target of mass criticism in the Beirut press!

However, what counts in such cases and the various incarnations they assume from time to time is that, over the past period, agreeing on a set of standards and rules to define the parameters of the media and cultural relationships with the enemy in general terms remain unsettled. Hence, these issues remained subject to individual estimates and subjective, mostly temperamental, rulings.

Let us try, in what follows, to look at two cases: a) the case of Abu Hamidu; and b) the case of the media and cultural activities of the enemy, and our relation to them at all levels.

The Case of Abu Hamidu

This case cannot be understood unless deconstructed into its constituting elements. Otherwise, it will remain an unfathomable mass of mystery and emotions that cannot be solved. To fully grasp this issue (above all, its significance and roots), I think we have to break it down into three parts: the position of the revolution (any revolution) on the transgressions of its members; rape and honour killings; and the relationship between the resistance and the locals.

A. The Position of the Revolution on its Members' Transgression

It is indisputable that revolutionary movements demand a high level of disciplined conduct, principally towards the customs of the masses during intervals of mingling with them in times of armed struggle. This discipline extends to such far reaches that thinkers and revolutionary historians have been prompted to believe that one of the gravest threats facing revolutionary armies is its potential transformation into a conservative force due to its puritanical discipline. [Edgar Snow],[3] for example, says that the instructions given to the [Chinese] Red Army upon their incursions into Islamic provinces exacted unbelievably rigorous conduct, so much that Chairman Mao banned uttering the words "dog", "pig", or "liquor" in front of Muslims.

It is by no means an exceptional occurrence for a revolutionary army to execute one of its members over the rape of a girl – it has recurred innumerably. Indeed, when civil wars have reached fever pitch, revolutionary armies have issued death sentences against their members over trifling circumstances, in comparison to rape.

---

3   Edgar Snow, *Red Star over China* (New York: Modern Library, 1944), 353. An error on Kanafani's part attributes these observations not to Snow but to John Reed, chronicler of the Russian Revolution.

Hence, the death sentence against a *fida'i* who raped a villager cannot, in principle, be described as uncommon or out of the ordinary. Yet, issuing a sentence of this kind should be linked to two main considerations, among others. First: investigating the case according to scientific procedures, since sexual assault is one of the most complicated criminal cases, particularly if approached from a revolutionary viewpoint, rather than a conformist viewpoint that mechanically reproduces customary codes (more details follow under the rubric of rape and honour killings). Second: the necessity of examining a case of this kind in light of the rules according to which the revolutionary army members were edified: degrees of discipline and politicisation, approved codes of conduct, etc. Unless such rules exist at the heart of the political and military training of the armed forces, it makes no sense to enforce them exclusively in cases of punishment.

If we return to examining the Abu Hamidu case through these two considerations, we will conclude that what happened approximates a farce, and we will see later why.

Conspicuously, Abu Hamidu violated neither of the two girls; the harassment case that took place, gullible as it was, was not so simplistic, with Abu Hamidu not wholly to blame. The issue took the utmost form of naivety and simplicity and the brother's reactionary and gratuitous sororicides were the only verification, whereby his reaction is taken for proof of his sisters' indiscretion and Abu Hamidu's crime. The latter is not normally a valid conjecture, particularly when it is taken into consideration by a revolution sentencing one of its members to death.

Yet, the other consideration is no less significant and can be summed up in the following question: did Abu Hamidu receive, within the revolutionary forces, proper political and militant training, and puritanical organisational discipline to match its logic and rigidity the gravity of the punishment that followed his violation?

As mentioned above, in times of war – and more so when the armed conflict against the enemy rages among the masses – revolutionary armies set harsh limits on the conduct of their members, most often tolerating only a considerable measure of compliance with customary practices, as far as they pose no discrepancies with the high priority of the current agenda. But these armies do not impose these limits in the fashion of the state military penal code and nor do they impose them through the logic of intimidation and retribution, or through terrorisation; rather, they build [these limits] gradually through consciousness, whereby their observation becomes inseparable from revolutionary obligations, neither imposed nor sanctioned, but grounded in revolutionary consciousness, based on organisational discipline and deriving from deeply internal [moral] convictions.

Only then does breaking these rules become a grave crime, deserving of a grave punishment. This, indeed, explains the revolution's logic that sets the death penalty as retribution for the crime of rape, whereas conventional civil laws do not view this offense as deserving a punishment that exceeds a five-year prison sentence. That is to say, the revolution views the crime of rape as a political crime too.

Therefore, even if Abu Hamidu did rape a local girl, revolutionary conditions compel us to consider this crime – if we were to also view it as a political crime – consciously. And, if we consider it through the consciousness of Abu Hamidu, it is imperative to bear in mind the political training methods implemented in the organisation to which he belongs. If the given political training in that organisation is advanced and based on sensitisation, discipline, revolutionary codes of conduct and a good rapport with the masses, this [crime] would demand a different punishment to that imposed by an organisation that is loose, lacking in political training and disciplinary conduct, and an apathetic or disregarding attitude towards the masses.

In general terms, the work of a "revolutionary court" in a given revolution should be premised on laws. These laws usually emanate from the by-laws of an organisation, a party or front and the regulations annexed thereto. It goes without saying that the by-law of a party, movement or front is a reflection of its guiding ideology, which shows, in a few words, the underlying drives of the revolution's punishment logic – a punishment that derives from an outlook on humankind and the world different from the outlook adopted by a regime or a state under the sovereignty of the bourgeoisie, feudalism or colonialism. The revolution must link

punishment to consciousness. It is self-evident that consciousness for an organisation's member is closely associated with the
organisational question; hence, the logic of punishment should be
considered accordingly.

B. Rape and Honour Killings

Evidently, in a society like ours, rape is a complex crime, and
almost every case has more distinctive circumstances than any
other. It is redundant to emphasise that in a backward society
(*al-mujtama' al-mutakhallif* – المجتمع المتخلف) – which sets firm
barriers between the sexes and falls short of logically addressing
the problem of sexual repression (particularly after curbing the
practice of early marriage) while tolerating nude pictures, pornog-
raphy and the propagation of sexual "liberation" and its ethos at all
levels, and promoting it as a cherished ideal – sex crimes including rape cannot be considered in simplistic terms. We must be
cognisant that these "crimes", at their various levels, are compos-
ite and complex acts governed by unique circumstances, and we
cannot but scrutinise them if we seek accurate and unprejudiced
judgements.

The problem is that, despite the increasing complexity of the
nature, motives and outcomes of sex crimes, honour killings –
being the conventional response to sex crimes – retain their old,
self-same logic, with backward laws as well as the backward logic
of bourgeois regimes backing them with immunity and ensuring
their perpetuation. Despite the role of these regimes, directly and
indirectly, in creating the sex crime scene, they rush to back the
perpetrators of the honour killings (sororicides, mariticides, fili-
cides, parricides) via formalistic punishment – but fail to protect
and safeguard the lives of sisters, wives and mothers.

The Abu Hamidu case is paradigmatic of the inconsistent logic
that has dominated the general atmosphere throughout the crisis:

- The sororicide was unwarranted, even within the conventional context of honour killings, yet it was granted protection
  at all levels of state and society.

- Harbouring resentment against Abu Hamidu, without proof or investigation, and despite the faint outcries of forensic physicians, meant going to extremes in protecting the murderer and expending innocent blood.
- The Palestinian revolution's drift in this stream made matters worse! Facing a problem of this kind and in view of the complex reality of sex crimes and honour killings, the revolution was required to offer a serious and profound position, even at the (momentary) cost of a hard aftershock. For rape, as already said, is not merely a word. Rather, it is an act governed by specific circumstances and complex conditions: what the brother took for rape was not so and what the society took for gang rape was not so. The revolution ordained a death penalty that concurred with this misunderstanding instead of embracing the opportunity to address this subject objectively, to confront this misconception head-on, and to summon the national and progressive forces to have their say.

C. The Relationship between the Resistance and the Locals

In the previous sections, this article touched upon points that seem, at first glance, to have no immediate bearing on our topic, such as: the role of political consciousness mediated through the organisational process in imposing a punishment logic; the sexual predicament and honour killings in our countries; the role of the backward forces in creating the sex crime-scene and rushing to back the perpetrators afterward; the revolutionary organisation's mission to shock a society drifting in the current of delusion and misconception; the role of the revolution in examining the relationship between men and women through a scientific approach that meets the challenges through which we are living and not succumbing to verbal terrorism (*al-irhab al-lafthi* – الإرهاب اللفظي) marked by words like rape, violation, dignity and honour, so far as they are devoid of humane signification – complying with customs occasionally, without drifting in their current; and then the role of the national and progressive forces in Lebanon, towards the incident in Hasbia in particular. Nevertheless, these points are, indeed, at the heart of our subject, and constitute its form and its essence, and, if we are seeking a genuine understanding of the Hasbia case and the Abu Hamidu story, it is, in the first place, the total sum of these points. Had it been otherwise, the incident would not have developed with this reach. Evidently, what went wrong in each of these points is what transformed this "ordinary incident" into one with a resounding political tone.

This said, dozens of similar incidents occur daily in every corner of our Arab world and those who concern themselves with the life of resistance and it is known – it is no secret – that what was misconceived by some in Hasbia, has, in fact, happened in multiple regions in Arab countries, where organisations had considered each case in accordance with their regulations and internal relationships and implemented the appropriate measurements, and that, in most cases, matters are resolved before becoming aggravated.[4]

It would be of utmost gullibility to believe, even for one moment, that the thousands of young men constituting the living body of the resistance movement – affiliating with movements and forces with negative perceptions of the principles of political education and organisational training – are an army of godly and righteous saints, of whom misdemeanour or delinquency is unforeseeable, but such acts have been relatively few and below average in the past years.

Still, organisations have generally not hesitated in taking robust measures against the perpetrators of such delinquencies and transgressions. There is no doubt that these measures have sometimes been subject to far too harsh or far too lenient discretions, usually lacking basis in clear by-laws, while the resistance retained a certain degree of discipline and reasoning in its rapport with people at dif-

---

4 An opposite picture is given by the actions of colonialist forces. During the French imperialist war in Algeria, rape was used systematically as a means of punishing female national liberation fighters. Zionist paramilitaries raped Palestinian women during the 1948 Nakba in massacres at Dayr Yassin, Safsaf, Tantura and other locations. See Sabrina Kooistra, "Playing Out French Colonial Fantasies: Algerian Women's Bodies and the Algerian War of Independence, 1954–62", *The Mirror – Undergraduate History Journal* 42, no. 1 (2022): 149–64, https://ojs.lib.uwo.ca/index.php/westernumirror/article/view/15165; Ruba Salih, "Scars of the Mind", in Diana Allan (ed.), *Voices of the Nakba: A Living History of Palestine* (London: Pluto, 2022); and Alon Schwarz (dir.), *Tantura* [film], (Israel, 2022).

ferent levels. Why, then, did the situation in Hasbia erupt in this way?

This question brings us back to the roots of the issue, which undoubtedly lie further afield from the Abu Hamidu case and the revolutionary court's verdict. We should, from the beginning, put the issue in concise and precise terms: the Hasbia incident indexed an alarming flaw in the relationship between the resistance and the masses in the South [Lebanon], and expressed an eruption of snowballing distress. It exposed and brought to the surface a series of misconceptions in the approach [of the resistance] to its relationship with the masses in South Lebanon...

Limiting our focus on the Hasbia incident to Abu Hamidu, therefore, means dancing around the real issue!

Going straight to the root cause of the issue would explain why the Hasbia incident was unduly magnified, whereas similar incidents occurred in other regions and were settled, at times, on the initiatives of the resistance, and at others, by the locals' representatives.

Issues have accumulated over a stretch of time before reaching their culmination in Hasbia and one can see that, rather than a simplistically summative aggregation of everyday occurrences, the matter is a complex combination of consequences resulting from the following practices:

1. The weak relationship between the Palestinian resistance and the national and democratic forces in Lebanon; a weakness that was camouflaged by various mechanical "support" formulae or the cultivation of ties with the chieftains and dignitaries. But, in essence, the resistance has self-identified as an accidental and excrescent existence in the South, not [identifying itself as] an inseparable part of a larger national, democratic movement that correlates on a daily basis with and organised by national and progressive movements.

2. The resistance military brass insisted on introducing itself merely through its military character and practices which, in effect, propagated a flawed understanding of the concepts of the "military base" and of "developing combat capabilities" in the South, and transformed these concepts into practices that

correlate to the fringes of the masses' lives, without fathoming their inner workings and becoming part of their consciousness or daily movement.

3. This military character of the resistance's existence in the South, the dwindling combative operations, and the lately decreasing magnitude, quantity and effectiveness thereof have led to eliminating the *raison d'être* of its existence – from the perspective of a large sector of the Southern masses – to maximising negative attitudes, and having zero "tolerance", "understanding" or "rationality" in addressing the resultant mistakes emanating from an existence losing much of its *raison d'être*.

4. To this must be added that our enemy (which, for its part, is a synthesis of various components and quantities) lives off of mobile initiatives that could infiltrate through these circumstances and set the wind of its psychological warfare, moral-targeting strikes, and political and military pressures. The enemy has been largely successful in terrorising the Southerners and putting up a barrier of fear between them and the resistance, fuelled by apprehension at the thought of an Israeli "punishment" executed by the powerful and omnipresent intelligence bodies in the South. Before and after the Hasbia case, for instance, two organisations hanged a pair of spies who were successfully recruited by the Israelis; one of the hangings took place in the Siddiqin village square. During the Hasbia crisis, many of the angry locals firmly believed a rumour that 25 *fida 'iyyin* had taken turns in raping the two sisters, a rumour that was not detached from the enemy's intelligence activities.

We should not, at any rate, overplay the latter item as a priority, since it is evident that the enemy's capabilities would not have achieved easy success had the shortcomings in the resistance's relationship with the Lebanese masses and its perceptions of the nature of its existence and mission in the South been less severe.

The consequences that gradually built up as daily outcomes of these four paths or channels transformed into qualitative energy that has found, in the Abu Hamidu case, the first venue of self-expression; had it never occurred to that young man to harass two girls who happened to stroll near the camp that afternoon, the eruption in Hasbia, or in any other Southern village, would have happened all the same, perhaps a day or more afterward, occasioned by the self-same [circumstances] or any other incident.

Viewed from all of these angles, this incident signals, on its bright side, the urgency to stand boldly, review and rectify the experience through unifying the stance of the resistance on the plan and goal of working in the South, the form and extent of the relationship with the Southern masses, and the central role of the national and democratic forces in Lebanon in these missions.

It is ridiculous to ascribe wrongfulness to Abu Hamidu and leave it there, while it is equally ridiculous to blame the Hasbia villagers and take the dilemma merely as a fabricated fit of unwarranted anger. In the same vein, it should be said that neither the innocent blood of the sisters, nor the blood of Abu Hamidu, nor all of the moral judgements in the world could solve a problem of this kind.

It is almost impossible to avoid taking an instantaneous or tactical measure on being confronted with a real-life case of this kind. This is true, yet it is a terrible mistake if this instantaneous or tactical measure is emotional and detached from a proper grasp of the problem, which precipitates another fall to a similar problem.

The Case of Media Exchange

The case of "media exchange" differs entirely in its nature and dimensions from what transpired with the "Abu Hamidu problem".

As we have said, the Arab stance on the issues of media, educational and other cultural relationships with the enemy or with its affiliated institutions is, until now, still informed by personal judgements and subjective evaluations. Even though this kind of relationship is more complex and tangled than the relationships that fall within the purview of the laws and regulations of the Israel Boycott Office,[5] one can generally note that the common stance

---

5 Initially headquartered in Damascus, the Central Boycott Office was established by the Arab League Council on 19 May 1951, taking the place of the Permanent Boycott Committee founded after the Nakba. Various resolutions were passed and, from the mid-1950s, the boycott was joined by the Soviet Union. Of the Arab states today, only Syria and Lebanon have state policies of boycotting Israel, while Palestinian-initiated boycotts, including BDS, have taken

adopted by the overwhelming majority of Arabs who are asked to engage in a media "dialogue" with an Israeli is refusal. The boycott offices themselves get into complicated problems when asked to adjudicate a film star, a musician or a writer – these decisions would mostly be compromised by one or the other Arab country at one time or another – notwithstanding, the boycott offices' laws and decisions are – on the whole – observed in all member states in the [Arab] League.

These observations are essential to indicate how difficult – or even impossible – it is to claim the feasibility of crafting a model, or formulate a decision applicable in all cases, observable always, everywhere and at all levels. But, in any case, we must quickly say that this reservation does not mean that matters should remain loose, that standards should remain individual and temperamental – quite the contrary. The difficulty of formulating a decision suitable to all cases necessitates finding a body that is authorised to assess these situations on a case-by-case basis and to decide accordingly.

We are aware that such a body – obviously, it would be the unified media leadership of the PLO – will make miscalculations now and then, yet these miscalculations fall within the realm of the reasonable and are better than the laxity that occurs when a free rein is given.

This procedure emanates from the fact that we are in a state of war with Israel, that martyrs fall almost every day in this fierce war, that over half our people are exiled, while the other half is under the direct oppression of occupation and thousands are detained in prisons. Had the degree of contradiction with the enemy not reached such a fierce, confrontational level – epitomised in the armed struggle – a call for finding such a central body would be unwarranted.

Yet, to approximate the bigger picture, let us take miscellaneous events separately.

---

a lead internationally. Other international states boycotting the Zionist state have notably included revolutionary and progressive governments of Latin America, including Cuba and Venezuela.

1. *The Debate between Israeli and Palestinian Students on BBC London*

The Palestinian university students (a male and a female) who went to Cyprus to challenge two Israeli students on the Palestinian question succeeded in, from the perspective of many viewers, getting the better of the Israeli students who presented a case of helpless shallowness. Yet viewers also noted that the debate was framed in a manner that encouraged support for Israel. The majority of cases in which such debates have taken place, on various radio or television shows in Europe and America, concluded to the advantage of the Arab party. This result is not peculiar and those who know something about the Israeli viewpoint and its media techniques must know that they usually fail to stand the test of argument.

However, what compels us to call for refusing this luxury is not fearing the outcome of the verbal duel or fearing the "solidity" of Israeli acuteness that proves flimsy upon facing the minimum level of objectivity. The first reason [for rejection] is that we are in a state of war with the enemy and our boycott does not derive from a sentimental attitude, but rather from the nature of the confrontation that we experience against the enemy; hence, the boycott *per se* is a viewpoint and a position. We are aware that winning the world's public opinion – at this stage, at least – makes little or no difference to such verbal duels. Quite the contrary, the bourgeois media employ such duels to, eventually, carry its game far beyond, to achieve a stronger hold on the minds of its audience.

BBC London – whose "tolerance" went as far as offering the chance for two Arab students to win a verbal duel over two Israeli students just 24 hours before the [30 May 1972] attack on Lydd Airport – has deliberately refused to present any statement to the advantage of Palestinians in all of its newscasts, to the extent of resorting to falsifying Palestinian pronouncements and statements and decontextualising them in order to win recruits to its racist campaign. We have every right to believe that the verbal duel has served this biased approach in an unparalleled manner. This is certainly not the result of some diabolical conspiracy or clandestine plot, but a logical outcome of the political and ideological structures that drive media of this order.

Overall, and in spite of our experiences, we have not yet realised the extent of the bourgeois media's bias towards Zionism, which they perceive as a vital component of their logic and aspirations. The well-disposition of many of us towards the free democratic façades and their utility in these media, and the "parliamentary" and "dialogic" character that they assume, result, indeed, from the deep influence of these media on some minds.

Out of practical and realistic experience, I dare say that wasting hundreds of hours with thousands of foreign press and radio journalists over the past years has yielded next to nothing. The only thing that works is the magnitude of the armed and political work on the battlefield itself. This remark is not far removed from our topic, where every interview with a press or radio journalist is, indeed, an episode of fierce debate, which is – if we like – a form of verbal duelling. Media professionals could just as well open the stage to a charade involving Arab and Israeli students. Such a scene is not only worthless but is moreover harmful to us.

Boycotting the enemy and refusing the dialogue of persuasion via verbal duels is in itself a position. It is a standpoint. It is a form of confrontation. Nevertheless, this media form (verbal dialogue with the enemy) remains only one among many others that we may use in the West, provided that this use remains oriented to the following fundamental truth: shifting the balance of media power in the West will only take place on the battlefield.

Once we understand this fact deeply, we will be able to determine the most correct course to pursue vis-à-vis the various media forms: no television network would readily give a Palestinian a minute to express his opinion in the case of a dormant revolution, but would be obliged to open its network to the voice of the resistance when the combative and political magnitude of this resistance is considerable enough to enter or touch the daily lives of people in the West. Then we would no longer need to present the amusing scene of a verbal duel with our enemy, who is busy killing our people, to an American, Swiss or German eating a hotdog for dinner and watching television, and for whom it is all the same whether Arabs go to the desert or to hell, no matter how pedantic the Arab debater is.

Our media work in the West should be oriented to our friends, to the revolutionary movements in the Western bourgeois [states] and to that section of world public opinion that stands by us. It would then develop with the effort and adoption of these leftist forces; our friends could then decide, in light of the lived reality of a given place at a given time, on the best form of the media war.

Media is a battlefield – so says Lenin[6] – and, for us, our media war will not bring about a triumph if it is waged via a verbal duel with the enemy in front of a largely biased public opinion and on radio and television networks that stand fundamentally against our causes. Sitting with the enemy – even in a television studio – is a principal mistake in war and it would be a mistake to view this as a [merely] superficial issue. We are in a state of war which is, for Palestinians at least, a question of life and death, and the mass of Palestinian people must adhere to the conditions prescribed by a state of war of this order.

2. The Cases of the Professor and the Medical Reference

Perhaps the teacher in question was wronged in this campaign, since it has been maintained that [Professor Finley] was a long-time friend of Arabs, while the appearance of a "Zionist" passage in a book that he selected as a textbook for a class in the Beirut College for Girls was not intentional. Whatever the case may be, and if my impression was correct, I felt throughout the progress of this case that this affair was contrived – not because the American teacher in question is a friend or a non-friend of Arabs, but because the passage that raised all this furore is so ridiculous and is taught in the higher grades.

---

6 According to Lenin, in "capitalist usage, freedom of the press means freedom of the rich to bribe the press, freedom to use their wealth to shape and fabricate so-called public opinion. In this respect, too, the defenders of 'pure democracy' prove to be defenders of an utterly foul and venal system that gives the rich control over the mass media"; Lenin, "Speech at the Opening Session of the First Communist International", 4 March 1919, *Collected Works*, Vol. 28, 457.

I see no reason why high level [students] should not be familiar with the enemy's mindset; actually, I see no reason why this familiarity should not be obligatory. Had this passage or any Zionist reference been taught surreptitiously in a primary grade as a form of indoctrinating[7] (*ghazu al-'aqul* – غزو العقول) the innocent, defenceless minds of children who are unqualified to argue against that indoctrination, then the issue becomes a national crime. But I cannot understand how we might hesitate until now to have access, and to allow access, to the sources and forms of the enemy's thinking paradigms.

Was the professor smuggling a banned substance into defenceless minds? I do not think so and I was not convinced by the arguments insinuating it. The whole matter concerns a passage written by a half-blind, zealot historian, suffering from excessive intellectual naivety, meeting the eyes of students who are supposed to be advanced.

The same – almost – applies to the medical reference at the library of the American University [of Beirut] (indeed, AUB is full of books that reflect a Zionist and Israeli ideology in the fields of literature, sociology and economics).

Yet, all of this brings to light an important point that may be reached by posing the following question: Why do we fear these things? Should we do away with our right (and duty) in having access to – and utilising – the intellectual and scientific achievements of the enemy?

What lies behind this question is our conviction that the educational curricula in our countries remain fundamentally unqualified in tackling this issue. Had we the conviction that the national upbringing in our schools is based on scientific, solid, healthy and modern bases, the ridiculous passage in [Finley's] module would not have alarmed us, and seeing a medical reference produced by an Israeli scientist at the university's library would not have shaken our confidence in our own university students' ability to mark the difference between this reference and the continuation of the battle of national liberation against the Israeli enemy.

---

7 Literally "invading the minds".

A national programme of upbringing (*tanshi'a* – تنشئة) founded on scientific research, historical facts and sound analyses, that puts our primary and secondary [school] pupils at the heart of their nation's battles and interests, will make our treatment of such topics proper. Following a national foundation of this kind, it will become our duty to make available for our students in higher education everything generated in Israel: journals, books and achievements.

Of course, a national upbringing [programme] of this order would not avert the presence of a biased foreign professor insisting on wiping his hands, stained with the blood of anti-Semitic[8] (*al-la-samiyya* – اللاسامية) sin, upon Arabs' skins; or a religious fanatic filled with political myths – I doubt that there is a method capable of removing these kinds of people – but surely, then, the harm that such a professor, Arab or foreigner, may cause to students will be confined, limited and insignificant.

The ambivalence that requires no explanation, and which we experience every day concerning this issue, shows the superficial manner adopted by most Arab regimes to treat an important problem of this order. At a time when almost all Western press is packed with praising Israel and insulting Arabs, and finds its way, unchecked, into the majority of Arab markets, posing a continual, daily, racist media invasion, one finds that the campaign against books in the hands of university students merely stirs the controversy.

It must be underlined that, while we reject the nullification of our right (and duty) to have access to the enemy's achievement and ideology, we are not – once more – calling for laxity in the name of fake freedom, for opening the doors ajar to the media invasion of the enemy, for leaving it unbound in its psychological warfare

---

8   Kanafani is talking here about the possible negative influence of chauvinistic individuals remaining within the educational system after its nationalisation, or revolutionisation: a "wiping of hands" on Arab skins denoting contagion by such ideas. His use of the term anti-Semitism is interesting in that it here defines the hatred of Arabs – in the contemporaneous "Denmark: A Study in Media Experience (1972)" (Chapter 12), he and the PFLP term anti-Arab hatred a new form of anti-Semitism. In another published version of this text, the word *al-lasamiyya* is replaced with *al-Islamiyya* (الإسلامية), or Islamic. This appears to be a mistake.

against our people, and allowing the daily injections of surrender and incapability culture to go deep into the minds of our people without reservations... No, we must be cognisant of the state of war that we are in, of the enemy's methods at all levels, and respond according to the laws that grant us the right of self-defence – and, above all, rights – to prevent the infiltration of the enemy's toxins into the minds of our people. [We must] use all means, not only to construct a filter in this regard, but also to deter all of the malicious attempts that tirelessly employ talk about "freedoms", to open the door for the enemy's campaigns.

The essence of the positive solution is to "radicalise" the masses – to popularise a scientific, national culture – in other words, to press ahead with the revolution in the first place.

PART V

Intifadas of Thought:
Looking to the Future

"The Saudi Oil Flowing through Israel", *al-Hadaf* 1, no. 50 (11 July 1970).
The anti-normalisation position of the PFLP finds roots in articles written by
Ghassan Kanafani after 1967. Source: *al-Hadaf*, Gaza.

14

The Secret Alliance between Saudi Arabia and Israel (1970)

Introduction: "Sounding an Alarm Bell"
by *Nafez Ghneim*

It was significant and useful that, on the 47th anniversary of his assassination, the Popular Front for the Liberation of Palestine (PFLP) and *al-Hadaf* journal republished this article by leader and fighter, comrade Ghassan Kanafani. The article contained dangerous information that exposed the features of the direction in which Israel, Britain and the USA were seeking to push the Arab region: towards increased control and hegemony and the subjugation of a number of Arab regimes to their policies and interests. The article reveals the involvement of the Saudi regime in its economic and security relationship with Israel. As the article indicates, this strategy consists of an unofficial, secret alliance concentrated in the strategy of imperialist colonialism. During the 1960s, this plan was labelled the East of Suez strategy[1] and, as Kanafani argued, Israel and Saudi Arabia would play the roles of two jaws in a pincer movement against oppositional currents in the region.

The article adds that Saudi Arabia, as it continued to play its part in this great conspiracy, armed itself not only with a deceptive formality, with alleged support for Arab liberation fronts and guerrilla action, but it also armed itself with the influence enabled by official Arab silence, to apply pressure within the Arab League, with the aim of isolating the People's Democratic Republic of Yemen (PDRY). Kanafani responds to their mechanisations at the

---

1   The phrase "East of Suez" seems to originate in the Orientalist poetry of Kipling: "Ship me somewheres east of Suez, where the best is like the worst, Where there aren't no Ten Commandments an' a man can raise a thirst" (*Mandalay*, 1890).

September 1969 Islamic Conference and the Fifth Arab Summit Conference in Rabat. During this period, the reactionary Arab states were led by Saudi Arabia in playing a conspiratorial role against rising national and social liberation movements. This was clearly demonstrated in the face of the socialist orientation of the PDRY and its government. This revolutionary trend struck terror into the forces of reaction and backwardness in the region and greatly worried global imperialism, which, led by the USA, mobilised all of its capacities to destroy and kill off this experiment. Then, as now, the aim of the imperialists and their allies in the Middle East was to prevent the emergence of socialist, anti-colonial and anti-capitalist systems.

This article clarifies and confirms that Saudi Arabia has played and continues to play a reactionary role in the Arab region, not only in its secret alliances with Israel, but also with the imperialist countries, dominating and plotting against the interests of the Arab peoples. Its role has also extended to spreading Wahhabi ideology, which constitutes a cause of escalating Islamist extremism in the Arab region.

Comrade Ghassan realised the dangers into which the Arab region was heading, sounding an alarm bell to reveal the size of the conspiracy and its parties. Rereading and discussing this and other articles he wrote during the same period, we must reaffirm the necessity of popular revolution for the Arab region, with the aim of correcting the Arab path and destination. This must be a revolution that empowers our peoples to realise their dignity and status, respects their national sovereignty, and mobilises their capabilities in order to confront economic and social problems facing them. As Ghassan Kanafani knew, this must mean an end to the state of humiliating dependence on the countries of global imperialist domination and colonialism.

*　*　*

THE SECRET ALLIANCE BETWEEN SAUDI ARABIA AND ISRAEL[2]

*Prince Fahd and the Shah of Iran agree in Washington
to divide the Arabian Gulf
What is the truth behind the British–US military presence
in the peninsula?*

Unofficial collusion between Saudi Arabia and Israel is reflected not only in the Arab oil pumped from Saudi Arabia into European pipes under Israeli protection;[3] for this, the Saudi regime is paying for in cash to make sure Israel can better protect the interests of imperialism through its occupation of Syrian territory. It is also reflected in the news that Aramco,[4] in agreement with the Saudi rulers, of course, has secretly agreed to grant Israel $20 million in revenues from the passage of Saudi oil through the occupied territories. However, the two matters are merely the results of a deeper and more complex reality. It would be short-sighted to believe that such phenomena are separable from the objective connections arising from the totality of events, which are, in the short and long term, expressive of an unwritten but objective and secret alliance between the Saudi regime and Israel.

In short, we may summarise that this unofficial, secret alliance is centred upon the colonialist and imperialist agenda known as the East of Suez strategy. In this strategy, Israel has played the role

---

2   Originally published in *al-Hadaf* 1, no. 24 (10 January 1970). Translated by Lena Haddadin.

3   From June 1967 until 1982, the Trans-Arabian Pipeline, or "Tapline", sent Saudi oil from the Dhahran fields through the Zionist-occupied Golan, with the consent of Egypt and other Arab states. Through this pipeline, oil would eventually reach Washington DC and Western European capitals. See Asher Kaufman, "Between Permeable and Sealed Borders: The Trans-Arabian Pipeline and the Arab–Israeli Conflict", *International Journal of Middle East Studies* 46, no. 1 (February 2014): 96, https://doi.org/10.1017/S002074381300130X.

4   Aramco had roots in the growing competition between British, European and US imperialists in the period after the First Word War and, at the time of writing, remained a US multinational. From 1973, the Saudi government dramatically increased its shares in the company and, since 1980, has enjoyed outright ownership.

of one set of jaws in a pincer, while Saudi Arabia plays the role of its other jaw. This embodiment precludes a detailed look at many details pertaining to events, which cannot be truly understood if they are not placed in context: from the issue of the Islamic alliance, which ended in the shape of a deformed body in Rabat; through the issue of the expected British withdrawal from the Arabian Gulf; the bogus claims of Saudi support for Arab steadfastness and the *fida 'iyyin*; the aggression against the People's Democratic Republic of [South] Yemen (PDRY); to the well-known position taken at the recent summit; and finally, Saudi plans for the future of the peninsula, which do not seem achievable without current Israeli plans.

The confidential external report distributed on a limited scale by the British *Economist* magazine stated in its 18 December [1969] bulletin that the battles which broke out in the al-Wadiah region between Saudi Arabia and the PDRY were more violent than the world imagined. It also revealed that the Saudi forces used [British-supplied] Lightning aircraft in a wide range of its operations; Britain has provided Saudi Arabia with these aircraft since the signing of an agreement between Riyadh and London four years ago.[5]

In fact, the problem of military clashes in the al-Wadiah region is completely different from other border clashes that have erupted between several Arab states. The struggle here is not primarily a disagreement over borders, or over establishing direct control of a specific economic or strategic value but is related to the confrontational nature of the conflict between the reactionary Saudi regime and the effective and influential revolutionary focal point represented by the (PDRY).

The array of developments that have taken place and are taking place in the region have made the situation much clearer:

- The defeat of the Arab national governments in the June 1967 war and the extremely difficult prevailing conditions which will restrict their movement and besiege them in the long term, constitute for the Saudi regime – which immediately nominated itself to lead the counter-attack on the various national and progressive movements in the region – an appropriate opportunity to pounce and "settle its scores", supported by the strategic and economic interests of the USA.

- Scheduled for 1971, the British withdrawal from the Arabian Gulf has led Saudi Arabia to take advantage of such exigent circumstances to extend its power and influence on the eastern coast of the Arab Peninsula in unprecedented ways.

- Amid all of this comes the arms deal concluded by Saudi Arabia with the United States and Britain, at a value of £500 million. As the first batches and supplies of these weapons arrive, so will the Saudi role escalate rapidly, not only in the Arabian Peninsula but also in surrounding areas.

What preoccupies Saudi Arabia above all of this, as expressed in the *Economist*'s confidential report, is as follows:

Soviet and Chinese influence in the PDRY is evident, while there is clear Soviet and Egyptian influence in the Republic of Yemen. The Ba'athist government which has violently opposed the monarchy is in power in Iraq. And even in the Gulf itself, the so-called "Popular Front for the Liberation of the Occupied Arabian Gulf" has its command centre in Iraq and has – it is said – active cells in Bahrain.[6]

Regardless of the *Economist*'s approach to describing the dangers surrounding Saudi Arabia, and its linguistic bias towards it, when addressing these dangers, the truth is Saudi Arabia cannot expand in the Arabian Peninsula atop the comfort of its reactionary regime. This is especially true when revolutionary social and political changes are raging in the south of Yemen, and since the armed revolution led by the Popular Front for the Liberation of Dhofar[7] is steadily rising.

---

6 *Economist*, 18 December 1969.
7 The Popular Front for the Liberation of Dhofar also emerged from the Arab Nationalist Movement and shared the Marxist–Leninist and Arab liberationist

The confidential *Economist* report clarifies this fact in the following way:

> Saudi Arabia does not want to witness a country on its eastern border in the emirates of the Omani coast stirring trouble, especially when it has enough of these troubles in the north and south. A union of Gulf states not only constitutes a regional competitor in terms of political power but also provides a proper climate for the possible growth of anti-monarchy organisations in several places in the Arabian Peninsula.[8]

Axis of Saudi Blueprints

Either way, all of this brings to light one of the most complex and heated issues in the contemporary Arab world, parallel in any case with the pivotal conflict between Arabs and Israel. Of course, it would be foolish to consider that these two issues are not related to each other.

The facts of the Saudi strategy – if we can describe it as such, since this strategy is in fact the strategy of imperialism in the East of Suez region – are the same as those reflected in the armed clashes between Saudi Arabia and the PDRY in the al-Wadiah and Sharurah regions. They are the same [facts] reflected in the Saudi–Iranian role, "consistent but as yet not entirely coordinated", in developments towards a Federation of Arabian Gulf States. In fact, they are the same [facts] that were most clearly reflected in the Saudi position at the Khartoum Conference (September 1967), and their repercussions extend further than that:

- To an Iranian–Saudi deal, which was concluded between Prince Fahd and the Shah of Iran in Washington, with the blessing of the White House, during their recent visits to the United States.

---

politics of the PFLP; the organisation's proper name was the Popular Front for the Liberation of Oman and the Arabian Gulf. Based in Aden, the group led a social revolution and armed struggle in the region until 1974, when it divided into Omani and Bahraini branches.

8 *Economist*, 18 December 1969.

- To an increasing influence towards "embroiling" (*tawrit* – توريط) Iraq in the Kurdish issue.
- To steadily escalating attempts to "liquidate" the revolutionary presence of the PDRY, not only by conspiratorial action but also by direct military force.
- To a Saudi compulsion towards practically evading its – direct or indirect – responsibility to the raging battle against Israeli aggression, because avoiding the resolution of this battle constitutes, for Saudi Arabia, a submission to imperialist schemes, which have become an inseparable part of its own. In addition, "fastening" the Arab national movement in its current impasse represents a valuable opportunity for Saudi Arabia to fulfil its traditional aims.

What is the East of Suez Strategy?

Before proceeding to analyse all of this, however, we must take an objective look at what is conventionally termed as the imperialist strategy planned for the East of Suez, in order to discern the Saudi role within it, and therefore its current and potential role in the development of events in the region at large.

It is well known that in late 1965, Britain and the United States agreed to strategically unify their colonial policy in Asia and Africa, especially in the oil-rich Arab countries, to cooperate and share in the burdens of defending Anglo-American interests, in what has come to be labelled the new East of Suez strategy. To realise this unified strategy, US and British military bases were mobilised to play the role of an imperialist "belt":

A new set of British and US bases have been built on CocoCay, Diego Garcia, Aldabra and the Seychelles islands in the Indian Ocean. These bases are located approximately halfway between the British and US bases in Sumatra, Malaysia, the Philippines and Singapore, in Asia, and between US and British bases in Ethiopia and Kenya, East Africa. These bases are linked to other important British and US military bases, extending from the Gulf of Aden and the entrance of the Red Sea, then along the coast of Oman on the Indian Ocean and up the shores of the Arabian Gulf to Bahrain and Dhahran in Saudi Arabia.

On the one hand, this "subsidiary belt" (*al-hizam al-fir'ai* – الحزام الفرعي) of bases clearly aims primarily to encircle the Arabian Peninsula. On the other hand, it links it to the main "belt" which extends from East Asia to East Africa.

The new East of Suez strategy relies on two main key points, in addition to the traditional British centres in Africa (Rhodesia, the Union of South Africa and most of [Britain's] former colonies):

- First, the former Federation of Malaya (i.e. Malaysia, Singapore and the British colonies on the island of Sarawak and Kalimantan Sabah), areas rich in rubber and minerals.
- Second, and more importantly for imperialist interests, the region surrounding the Arabian Gulf, supported largely in the past by the British base at Aden, followed by the anchor points annexed to it in Qatar, Bahrain, Abu Dhabi, Dubai and Sharjah.

This region represents a major location for absorbing British industrial production, whose income exceeds £200 million each year and produces three-fifths of Britain's total oil imports.

Military Colonial Presence in the Peninsula

Considering these broad lines of the new colonial East of Suez strategy, we must look at the military embodiment of this strategy in the Arabian Peninsula, in which – since 1965 – it was decided that Britain would assume the role of the "colonial police", from Suez to Singapore.

Britain has the following [three] military bases in this region:

In Dhofar: the British Jalala air base is equipped with a striking force of jet planes, missiles, artillery units, infantry, a network of radars, weapons stores, ammunition, nuclear bombs and a powerful wireless station linking it to other bases in other regions. This base has committed itself to suppress the current Dhofar revolution.

In Oman: Britain holds Masirah Air and Naval Base, which contains ammunition and supply stores for the British fleet;

Muscat Naval and Air Base, Buraimi Air Base, Sharjah Air Base and other bases in neighbouring countries and regions: Ras al-Jed, Sohar, Ibri, Nizwa, Fujairah, Ras Al-Khaimah, Umm Al-Quwain, Oman, Abu Dhabi and others.

In Bahrain: The British Juffair Air Base, where three aircraft carriers, five destroyers, six minesweepers, a fleet infantry unit, troop carriers and a wireless station are continuously stationed. The intelligence headquarters of the British military in the Arabian Gulf are located there as well. The strategic Muharraq Air Base located on the island of the same name, which includes two squadrons of combat aircraft (Hawker Hunter) and a squadron of transport aircraft (Beverly) and a force of 3,000 paratroopers, a radar unit, a radio station, and a guard squad for the base, equipped with trained sniffer dogs. Hamala Land Base, located west of Manama, includes military units of infantry, artillery, tanks and engineers, a radio station, and weapons and ammunition depots. Britain used this base during its aggression against Egypt in 1956, in Oman in 1957 against North Yemen, against the revolution in South Yemen, and in suppressing the national movement in Bahrain in 1965.

It is worth noting that in 1967, Britain expanded these three bases and prepared them primarily for the ability to receive units of the US fleet and air forces active in the region.

The Saudi Role in the East of Suez

The two military belts, whose value increased after the consolidation of the British and US East of Suez strategy, namely, the "Singapore–Kenya belt" and the "Bahrain–Asmara belt", are in fact, incomplete if they do not meet at a fixed and pivotal point. This "key-point" is Saudi Arabia.

After its [1967] defeat in Aden, Britain chose the islands of Bahrain as an alternative to its famous Aden base. This choice was not only the result of "better conditions" provided by Britain's agreements with Bahrain, which were unequal, since they guaranteed British influence over Bahrain for long and unlimited periods of time, but was also the result of other equally important factors:

- Bahrain's strategic location in the frontline of the "Middle East" region.
- Its location in the heart of the oil region.
- Its political status, due to Iranian claims over it and Saudi attempts to pull it in its direction, which makes Bahrain more prone to "adapting" and bargaining.

However, Bahrain cannot present all of its strategic "talents" if it is not interrelated – as a direct colonial sphere of influence – to the central sphere in Saudi Arabia. Hence, the idea of an "Islamic alliance" came before 5 June, emanating from Saudi Arabia and coupled with the shipment of huge quantities of British and US weapons to Riyadh.

While Britain was expanding its three main bases in Bahrain, it proceeded – in partnership with the USA – to build large US bases in Saudi Arabia of stronger military value. Saudi Arabia agreed to hire 900 British officers to establish a new air defence network, which it installed, not on the shores of the Gulf of Aqaba, but near the borders of Yemen. Saudi Arabia received military transport equipment from the United States, including Hawk missiles, jet aircraft and radar equipment. London and Washington facilitated [Saudi] use of an army of foreign mercenaries; it is no longer a secret that Saudi Arabia is the only country to surpass the Congo[9] in using European mercenaries. And how was this aid reflected? It was reflected in the fact that Saudi Arabia established, in a relatively short period of time, 37 military bases, stationed less than 120 kilometres from Yemen.

Imperialist Perception of the Saudi Belt

To place all of this within a unified context, we must remember the assessment British Prime Minister Harold Wilson gave of this map:

Britain must remain strong in the East of Suez, as it cannot abandon its global role in that region, nor its obligations overseas, nor the legitimate rights of traditional interests.

---

9   Present day Democratic Republic of the Congo.

Wilson's talk about Britain's "global role", "obligations" and "legitimate rights" derives its meaning and context from these words in a document issued by the British Institute for Strategic Studies in 1966:

> Britain is officially committed to defending the Federation of South Arabia and the protectorates outside the aforementioned union, just as it is officially committed in the Persian Gulf to defending Bahrain, Qatar and Fujairah[10] against any attack or aggression. Besides these formal commitments, Britain considers itself – and is considered by many – to be morally committed to defending the remaining Gulf states that are still responsible for their foreign relations... All of this is important in confirming Britain's military presence in South-East Asia and the Indian Ocean regions.

The document continues, highlighting the main point:

> The military bases in the Arabian Peninsula and the Persian Gulf support Western influence in the Middle East and intervene against any local aggression, in addition to helping open a strategic route for the British military bases located in the Indian Ocean and South-East Asia, to limit communist expansion in the region. Likewise, the main purpose of their presence is to ensure the continuation of Middle Eastern oil shipments, to prevent any conflict in the neighbouring region, and to assist British military intervention.

The Agreement between Prince Fahd and the Shah

In rhythm with all of this, the Saudi regime entered the phase following the June [1967] defeat, making its position clear at the Khartoum Conference, the Islamic Conference and the Fifth Arab Summit Conference in Rabat. Saudi fingers thus began to play their own melody in discordant phrases alongside those played by other rulers of the Gulf emirates during last Ramadan. To the same

---

10   Fujairah is now one of the seven emirates of the United Arab Emirates.

beat, Saudi Arabia sent its forces to its al-Wadiah region to provoke armed clashes with the PDRY.

Following this rhythm, Prince Fahd, the brother of King Faisal, shook hands with the Shah of Iran.[11] These actions were guided by the shadow of Nixon during the Shah's recent visit to Washington, and their discussion – as the *Economist* report states, conservatively – was as follows:

Last November, reports stated that Prince Fahd, the Saudi interior minister, held a meeting with the Shah of Iran in the US, and stated that the two parties have reached an agreement to be put into effect following the British withdrawal from the Arabian Gulf. In this agreement, the Shah confirms Iran's claims to Bahrain and Faisal affirms Saudi claims to the al-Buraimi oasis [in Oman]. Qatar and Dubai will fall under Iranian protection and support [Iranian] claims to Bahrain.

In this agreement, Saudi Arabia and Iran will make efforts to maintain peace in the Gulf, by realising their spheres of influence there. It was mentioned that the Shah assured Prince Fahd that Iraq would not pose a threat to regional stability. The Shah informed Prince Fahd that 16,000 Iraqi soldiers are in Jordan as part of the Arab military force against Israel and that 30,000 are busily fighting against the Kurdish revolution in the north. The Shah of Iran is currently supplying the Kurds with weapons to form a Kurdish state [in Iraq], which creates issues and conflicts between Iran and its Kurdish minorities.[12]

Whatever the *Economist*'s particular understanding of the issues raised in its aforementioned confidential report, what concerns us is this joint Saudi–Iranian role, the dimensions of which have become clear in light of what we have said about the new East of Suez strategy, and the wave that developments are taking, regard-

11 Signalling the continuing alliance of Saudi Arabia and the Shah, Fahd visited Tehran in July 1974, three months after Khaled's succession of Faisal, and Fahd's own appointment as crown prince. The alliance was disrupted by the Iranian Revolution of 1979, with the roots of a broader crisis in this earlier period where Israel, Saudi Arabia and Iran formed a pro-imperialist triumvirate in the region.
12 *Economist*, 18 December 1969.

less of these plans, not only for the coast of Oman and its emirates, but also for escalating Saudi mobilisations against Yemen.

The totality of these facts indicates, in an increasingly clear manner, an unofficial, secret alliance between Israel and Saudi Arabia: these Saudi plans – which form an inseparable link from the imperialist strategy in the Middle East – are in essence complementary to Israeli plans, which in turn, form an inextricable link to the strategy of imperialism in the Middle East.

While it continues to play its part in the grand conspiracy, Saudi Arabia does not only arm itself with a deceptive formal appearance, such as alleged support for the Arab fronts and *fida'i* action, but it is arming itself with the influence afforded to it by official Arab silence, to exert pressure within the Arab League to isolate the PDRY, making plans for its liquidation. It aims to gag the Arabs behind the curtains of the Islamic Summit Conference, about the conspiratorial role it plays alongside Iran, in the interests of the imperialist East of Suez strategy for the region.

15

Towards a Constructive Dialogue on Palestinian National Unity (1969)

Introduction by *Tahrir Hamdi*

In his "Resistance literature in occupied Palestine", Ghassan Kanafani writes, "[t]he literature of resistance in occupied Palestine is thus linked to a social aspect, pledging allegiance to the toiling class on whose shoulders hang the guns and fate of resistance".[1] Of course, for Kanafani, armed resistance inevitably springs from the great suffering of the masses, the toiling or working classes. It is these masses that form the very essence of *fida'i* action, writes Kanafani in this August 1969 article, "Towards a Constructive Dialogue on Palestinian National Unity". All forms of resistance writing and cultural production, insists Kanafani, must pledge allegiance to the masses. At the present moment, the revolutionary masses upon whose shoulders the "guns and fate of resistance" hang are the people of the refugee camps inside and outside occupied Palestine. These are the masses of whom Kanafani spoke decades ago and who now live in a semi-permanent temporariness in 75–76-year-old refugee camps and who, after several generations, like Naji al-Ali's character Handala, await their return to the homeland. The Jenin refugee camp has now become one centre of the armed resistance inside occupied Palestine.

In this article, Kanafani underscores the absolute necessity of constructing an open dialogue on Palestinian national unity in order to ensure the successful use of armed resistance that would inevitably lead to liberation. One is struck by Kanafani's emphasis

---

1   Ghassan Kanafany, "Resistance Literature in Occupied Palestine", *Lotus Journal* 1, nos. 1–2 (1968): 78.

on the inclusivity of ideas and ideologies and warns against exclusion and hostile debate. This unity, argues Kanafani, cannot be imposed in a tense atmosphere or through pressure, but through constructive, democratic dialogue with the aim of achieving Palestinian national unity, an aim which for Kanafani was of the utmost importance, especially after the disastrous Naksa of 1967. After the Naksa, Palestinian factions started looking inwards, with their main concern being strengthening Palestinian national unity, and Kanafani was the strongest advocate for this unity; the urgency with which Kanafani writes here for *al-Hadaf* is driven by the sensitivity and danger of the moment – all efforts of Palestinian and Arab liberation movements must be directed at fighting the Zionist entity, which is a creation of world imperialism.

Kanafani's emphasis on national unity and a united front before the mounting of a successful armed struggle for liberation were ideas later echoed by other thinkers from the Global South, such as Amilcar Cabral:

[I]n order to face colonial violence, the liberation movement must mobilize and organize the people, under the direction of a strong and disciplined political organization, in order to resort to violence in the cause of freedom – the armed struggle for national liberation.[2]

Cabral's "strong and disciplined political organization" is in line with Kanafani's insistent emphasis on a strong national unity in order to form a united national front for *fida'i* action. This unity must be constructed upon solid foundations with a clear, revolutionary and liberationist vision that can withstand any petty disputes between different factions. As Kanafani explains, any weakness or crack in Fatah is also a weakness in the Popular Front: the parts weaken the whole. The ultimate goal, Kanafani explains in this essay, is liberation, not allegiance or loyalty to any organisation or particular faction.

These words and ideas ring even more true today. The phrase *wihdat al-sahaat* is often heard within the context of the Palestinian armed resistance in recent years, especially in Gaza, the Jenin refugee camp and other areas of occupied Palestine, which

2 Amilcar Cabral, *Return to the Source* (New York: Monthly Review Press, 2023), 93–94.

have seen the rise of a new generation of armed factions. These include the Lions' Den, the Jaba' Brigade and the Tulkarem Brigade. *Wihdat al-sahaat* translates into the "unity of the fronts", a unity that has the effect of producing a fighting people, a fighting culture. It is indeed this unity that creates a successful armed struggle for national liberation.

* * *

TOWARDS A CONSTRUCTIVE DIALOGUE ON PALESTINIAN NATIONAL UNITY[3]

The subject of Palestinian national unity is currently the dominating discourse and central concern of *fida'i* action, as well as being the concern of the masses, who ultimately form the foundation and the essence of this action.[4] This self-evident fact immediately assumes that *fida'i* organisations of all sizes and ideological orientations prioritise the urgent task of finding a real and solid formula to unify the front of the Palestinian armed struggle.

Within this scope are a series of facts, which must be recognised with equal responsibility by all parties:

First: Any setback to any active *fida'i* organisation, whether militarily or fundamentally, cannot be limited to that organisation, but rather is immediately reflected on all other organisations. Stated more clearly: any wave of weakness that befalls Fatah will bear its costs on the Popular Front's very existence, and vice versa; any conspiracy that faintly targets the Popular Front will reflect itself on Fatah.

Second: The ideological differences among the operating *fida'i* organisations and the resultant ongoing partial disputes between them can and must be adapted to serve the central confrontation between the Palestinian and Arab liberation movements on the

3 Originally published in *al-Hadaf* 1, no. 4 (16 August 1969). Translation by Lena Haddadin and Ourooba Shetewi.
4 The literal translation of this section evokes a "spear and shield", with the masses forming both the foundation and the sense of direction for armed action.

one hand, and the Zionist usurper movement, as an authentic representative of world imperialism, on the other.

Third: The dangers and challenges surrounding Palestinian national action are so great that it is doubly urgent to find a formula to unify guerrilla action at this stage, or at least to consolidate it into an effective united front.

Fourth: The various *fida'i* organisations put at the heart of their strategy and at the basis of justifying their existence the issue of liberation through armed struggle. The fighters who sacrifice their lives and offer their blood do so only for the sake of liberation, and not for the glory of their chosen organisation. However, a fighter's choice of a specific organisation through which they may perform their role and achieve their national aspirations is, in turn, a matter of conviction that must be given due respect.[5] The "mistake" does not lie here, but in turning their choice into a fabricated justification to exchange accusations, increase tensions, and create a kind of "dialogue" that aims to negate the other, when this very choice must be the subject of healthy debate, understanding dialogue, and mutual recognition that push the cause of unity miles forward.

Achieving National Unity

In light of these facts, which together constitute extensive grounds ripe for constructive dialogue, the discussion of national unity must take its course. If it does so in such a climate, it will cultivate positive formulas that serve the revolution, amplify its effectiveness and accelerate its pace.

However, the crucial issue of national unity cannot be imposed in a charged and tense atmosphere, nor can it be achieved through

---

5 Kanafani alludes here to the situation in the Palestinian National Council, whose fifth session in February 1969 had been boycotted by the PFLP over the group's greatly reduced share of seats in comparison to its mass base and influence. Fatah domination of this session had seen Yasser Arafat elected as its chairman, a position he occupied until his death in 2004.

pressure, accusations or siege. And even if it were to be accomplished in such circumstances, it would then be in danger of exploding at any moment, since it bears the seeds of its own destruction from the beginning. Recognising this fact calls for changing much of our approach to the issue of national unity. Such unity is not a temporary "tactic", employed by one organisation to compete with another, to incite a third party, to achieve media gains, or be rid of a state of siege. It is rather a more serious and critical issue in the long run, especially if the decision to head towards it stems from a deep conviction of its historical necessity, its revolutionary value and its fateful meaning. If the issue of national unity was merely the issue of a temporary tactical manoeuvre imposed by and ending with specific circumstances, the decision towards this unity would be effortless. But it is not, and hence requires a specific type of effort and a healthy atmosphere of constructive dialogue based on mutual recognition of existing disagreements that are a natural result of different ideological positions, and which cannot be dissolved in a unifying or frontal programme through "exclusion", cancellations and accusations.

Two Perspectives Regarding the Question of Unity

Different points of view are present in the efforts currently being made to achieve national unity. This is normal, otherwise there would be no justification for the existence of different organisations, with great political and combative sizes. What is abnormal, however, is to consider these different views as hostile stances, or as fabricated justifications for unilateralism, and to consider that the only means to encourage a party to abandon their point of view would be through pressure, accusations or devaluing those views.

We are so far familiar with two views in the Palestinian arena on the issue of national unity:

The first view considers that the PFLP decision to enter the leadership of the Palestinian armed struggle is a primary and central issue, under which it is possible to arrive at a resolution to other issues.

The second view is that of the PFLP, which believes that its decision to lead the Palestinian armed struggle can only be the result of an agreed-upon programme, which clarifies a number of primary issues that the Front views as crucial to the tasks of *fida'i* action at this stage.

These two viewpoints naturally bring to light other related issues in the context of the dialogue: Does the leadership of the armed struggle constitute a real formula for national unity? Will PFLP leadership of the armed struggle initiate an immediate solution to the conflicting issues, especially when a clear agreement has not been previously made? Does the PLO, in its current organisational, legislative, executive, political and military circumstances, constitute a framework capable of accommodating a unitary action with advanced revolutionary missions? Can a national unity be achieved by bargaining over the number of representative chairs in this or that body? Does an agreement of this type constitute a solid national unity that is not prone to fracture? Is the issue of this or that organisation's representational ratios of real importance, especially when an agreement on a clear and conclusive programme constitutes the basis for the meeting?

How Can We Reach an Agreement?

These issues and the questions stemming from them are not a matter of luxury, nor do they fall under the category of what is necessary or unnecessary. However, they constitute a fundamental and substantial issue in the pursuit of any national unity.

It is unwise to believe that the various parties in the Palestinian liberation movement will reach, at least in this period, a comprehensive formula that constitutes a complete agreement on all of the issues and positions raised. Therefore, the five points proposed by the PFLP are not necessarily the inevitable programme for Palestinian national unity, with its finalised texts written by the Front, but they present a clear view of what the Front considers to be a strategic issue. Moreover, the Front does not unrealistically ask for the *fida'i* organisations' "signatures". Rather, it presents the Front's stance on the issues which it regards as a priority in any talks of true national unity. As for the issue of agreement on the programme and the arguments that surround it, this can only be the result of a healthy and serious dialogue.

Only such dialogue can reveal the true level of agreement. This is a very serious issue when entering a discussion on the nature, extent and size of the possible unitary or frontal action, which will set a strong and solid base for the future. National unity cannot be built from above, nor achieved by a higher decision separated from the tasks that this unity will face. Moreover, [this unity] is not [merely] a transient, tactical decision that may be improvised and abandoned later.

To achieve different results that avoid the fate of previous attempts at Palestinian unity over the past five years,[6] parties should establish a dialogue in a positive atmosphere and stop insisting that the proposed viewpoints negate each other and constitute an impossible diametric.

---

6   The Palestinian National Council (PNC) had been founded in Jordanian-administered Jerusalem on 24 May–4 June 1964, at which the PLO was formed. Supported by Egypt, its leader Ahmed Shukeiri resigned following the June 1967 defeat and was replaced on 24 December by Yahya Hamoudeh. The intervening years had seen clashes over the roles of Jordan and other Arab states, who effectively dominated the organisation, while the post-1967 period saw Fatah take the reins of the PLO leadership.

"Unity of the Armed Struggle: A New Path", *al-Hadaf* spotlights Palestinian youth in the coming battles; *al-Hadaf* 1, no. 19 (29 November 1969). Source: *al-Hadaf*, Gaza.

16

The Armed Action Unit: In Light of Recent Developments (1969)

Introduction by *Tahrir Hamdi*

The burning of al-Aqsa is a political deed whose aim is not the building of temples – for Zionism [has] rarely concerned itself with spiritual affairs – but the completion of the process of Judaisation of Palestine and the elimination of its Arab history.

Ghassan Kanafani
September 1969[1]

In this article, Ghassan Kanafani addresses the Palestinian armed resistance in the aftermath of the 21 August 1969 arson attack on al-Aqsa mosque by an Australian Zionist in occupied Jerusalem. Kanafani makes his views crystal clear: armed action must target the Zionist state and all imperialist and capitalist interests that collude or align themselves with it. The progressive element of the Palestinian resistance is underscored by Kanafani in contrast to the racist, exclusivist character of Zionism, following another crime in a long line of criminal behaviour.

Kanafani's emphasis on a progressive vision that shuns all nativist and religiously and ethnically exclusivist ideologies precedes a similar argument by Edward Said in his seminal book *Culture and Imperialism*:

To leave the historical world for the metaphysics of essences like negritude, Irishness, Islam, or Catholicism is to abandon history for essentializations that have the power to turn human beings against each other; often this abandonment of the secular world has led to a sort of millenarianism if the movement has had a

---

1 *Al-Hadaf* 1, no. 10 (27 September 1969), in George Hajjar, Kanafani: Symbol of Palestine (Lebanon: Karoun, 1974), 147.

mass base, or it has degenerated into small-scale private crazi-
ness, or into an unthinking acceptance of stereotypes, myths,
animosities, and traditions encouraged by imperialism. Such
programs are hardly what great resistance movements had
imagined as their goals.[2]

Almost two decades before Said, Kanafani was able to see the
dangers involved in such essentialisations and their connection
to imperialist aims. As he emphasises in this article, such objectives were resisted by the struggle for Palestinian liberation, which
refused to serve the interests of imperialism by turning the confrontation "into a religious or racial one".

Kanafani's call for the unity of armed action units, then, is based
on an inclusivity of Palestinian resistance groups. This unity would
be based on a solid formula, a governing principle that rejects
the "powerless territorial sovereignty" logic we now see in the
defeatist Palestinian Authority (PA), set up after the Oslo Accords,
in favour of a revolutionary and popular war of liberation. What
Kanafani theorised in his political writings, he also represented in
his literary writings, specifically in *Returning to Haifa*, where his
character Said sees that the only way to truly return to Haifa is
by means of a full-scale, popular war of liberation: "Palestine is
something worthy of a man bearing arms for, dying for... Didn't I
tell you from the beginning that we shouldn't come – because that
was something requiring a war?"[3] No halfway measures or powerless territorial sovereignty are acceptable to Kanafani. Thus, the
national unity of the Palestinian armed resistance is to be based
first and foremost on a "shared foundation of mutual and firm
convictions", and these convictions must at the core involve revolutionary action – this Kanafani does not compromise.

Notwithstanding the above points, Kanafani is not under any
delusion that disagreements between the armed factions do not
exist; however, as Kanafani explains, these disagreements must
be negotiated in open, equal and democratic dialogue that
would guarantee a united front based on a strong foundation of
Palestinian national unity. In this article, Kanafani offers practical

---

2   Edward Said, *Culture and Imperialism* (London: Vintage, 1994), 228–29.
3   Ghassan Kanafani, *Palestine's Children: Returning to Haifa and Other Stories*,
translated by Barbara Harlow and Karen E. Riley (London: Lynne Rienner, 2000),
187.

solutions – three scenarios that the armed factions may take in their progress towards this sought after unity.

* * *

THE ARMED ACTION UNIT: IN LIGHT OF RECENT DEVELOPMENTS[4]

The events that have unfolded in the Arab region during the last week may not seem significant when viewed individually. However, when examined collectively and placed in relation to each other, they tell a different story:

- While Arab foreign ministers were convening a conference to determine the appropriate response to the burning of al-Aqsa Mosque, the Palestinian resistance was firing missiles into the skies of occupied Jerusalem.
- And while reactionary Arab regimes were taking advantage of the emotional response to al-Aqsa's burning to liquidate the progressive aspects of the Palestinian armed struggle,[5] the armed resistance was extending its confrontation with the enemy to encompass the imperialist and capitalist interests that collude with Israel.[6]

And while, by burning al-Aqsa mosque, the enemy revealed its racist, reactionary and fanatic essence, the responses of the Palestin-

---

4 Translated by Lena Haddadin. This article was originally published in *al-Hadaf* 1, no. 6 (30 August 1969).

5 It was indicative of Kanafani's comments that the regional monarchies rushed to build a committee, including ministers from Saudi Arabia, Iran, Somalia, Pakistan, Morocco and Malaysia. The overriding narrative among this group was that the attack represented a war on Islam, rather than being an act of political terror grounded in Zionist colonisation. The Jordanian UN ambassador Muhammad al-Farah saw the arson attack as primarily adding "to the fears and worries of the Muslims about their holy shrines". See Hana Hussain, "Remembering the Arson Attack on Al-Aqsa Mosque", *Middle East Monitor*, 21 August 2017.

6 These capitalist interests included the British business Marks & Spencer, targeted in PFLP operations and exposed as having Zionist roots in the pages of *al-Hadaf*.

ian resistance reflected a continuation of its progressive objectives – the refusal to turn the struggle with imperialism and its international apparatus, Israel, into a racial, religious confrontation.

And while it was evident, in official Arab meetings, that some Arab countries were shirking their responsibilities towards Palestine and using the "Arab consensus" to mask their regressive agendas, safeguard their regional interests, and pursue the narrow goal of powerless territorial sovereignty, the Arab masses in various capitals throughout the region rushed to bear Palestinian martyrs on their shoulders, revealing the interconnected fate between the Arab masses and the vanguards of the revolution, and their rejection of the logic of territorial sovereignty.

And while, last week, Israeli officials repeated their threats to Arab countries and publicly declared their desire to annex the occupied lands, armed resistance operations at home escalated to a new level, while Israeli newspapers reported that Gaza, for example, "resembles a region ruled by saboteurs".

Dangers and Missions

This news campaign, when each news [item] is compared to another, brings new and clear features to the rising movement of armed struggle and reaffirms the revolutionary choice, which those at the vanguard of the Palestinian people have baptised with their blood, as the choice most capable of confrontation, the most correct in combating the dangers surrounding the Arab nation and the surest in achieving victory through protracted and deepening operations.

Undoubtedly, this type of confrontation gains self-confidence and the confidence of the masses through its continuous escalation, expansion and tireless perseverance in transforming itself into a comprehensive popular war of liberation. The fact that [this movement] finds itself, sooner or later, facing increasing dangers and multi-party conspiracies constitutes daily proof that it poses a real threat to the interests and prospects of the imperialist establishment and its various affiliates in the region.

This reality raises, like never before, the utmost necessity of uniting the ranks of the fighting organisations and reaching an effective and solid formula for Palestinian national unity, which not only shields the revolution but also presents the greatest opportunity for its steady progress.

National Unity and its Horizon

The dangers facing the Palestinian resistance, as evidenced by the contradictions arising in the events of the past week, highlight the immediate need for any effort towards Palestinian national unity to be based on a joint and agreed-upon understanding of the tasks of the Palestinian revolution and the pivotal issues that form the core challenges that it faces.

As such, any discussion of Palestinian national unity that ignores the meaning and essence of these tasks and challenges constitutes, at best, no more than running with eyes blindfolded into a minefield. A formula for unity that lacks a shared foundation of mutual, firm convictions will only lead to blind enthusiasm and ultimately fail to meet the responsibilities placed on the shoulders of the revolutionaries. For any common ground to be truly solid and serve as a starting point, there must be an equal agreement on a clear and specific programme of action capable of addressing the challenges and tasks posed by the current battle and its foreseeable prospects.

Agreement and Disagreement

Expecting complete agreement between various *fida'i* organisations would amount to unwarranted optimism. But it is also overly pessimistic to believe that no common ground can be found that could serve as a foundation for joint action and be further developed through ongoing dialogue.

However, this common area of agreement on a clear programme of action cannot have a firm foundation unless it is reinforced by a shared understanding of the points of emerging disagreement, and by a formula of relations with regards to such occasions. It is wrong to formulate a programme for joint agreement while neglecting these points of contention – which may result from points of disagreement – and [not consider] how to resolve them.

The Map of Confrontation

All of the above means:

- That the leadership of the armed struggle is merely an executive tool for an action programme and cannot be considered a formula for national unity in and of itself.
- Any action programme suitable to be the basis for a joint agreement cannot be approved by vote as long as differences are not quantitative, but rather over political, intellectual and strategic points. The preferable route towards approving [this programme] is through an equal dialogue resulting in common principles.
- The nature of the recent dangers facing Palestinian armed action, as shown over the past week, requires that any joint agreement between the *fida'i* organisations be based on an objective examination of these dangers, a detailed discussion of them and the development of a clear programme of action to confront them. The response to [these dangers] should not be through uncalculated, emotional outbursts.
- In any unified programme of action, the emerging signs of contradiction – between the Palestinian revolution on the one hand and the reactionary method of Arab action on the other, and between the revolution and the imperialist forces allied with Israel – necessitates a detailed vision of the future of this contradiction, and the means of confronting it, now and in the future.
- The emotional reactions in the Arab world over the al-Aqsa Mosque fire, which were aimed at diverting the revolution, and the confrontation with the enemy from their progressive goals to ineffective, retrogressive bids, highlights the importance of a unified stance among revolutionary groups on the concept and nature of the revolution. This example emphasises the need for a dialogue on the ideological and political strategy of Palestinian revolutionary action, as it is essential for achieving any effective formula for Palestinian national unity.

- The sixth [meeting of the] Palestinian National Council, which will convene in Cairo this week, must develop specific formulas for a detailed practical programme that could be a guide to achieving national unity or a united front.[7] It cannot be satisfied with loose formulas that are qualified, by their indefinite nature, to gain the support of all parties.

It is only logical that a working guide of this kind cannot be achieved by voting or by shaming [tactics]. On the contrary, it can only be achieved through an equal dialogue culminating in agreed rules. It therefore becomes reasonable, within the framework of these agreed rules, to decide on daily steps, by voting or other means. However, voting – in the absence of an action programme – represents a form of exclusivity practised by the majority in the name of democracy, to force another party to deviate from the framework of its programme, which [for the organisation] consists of convictions and practices that cannot be abandoned.

Which of the Three Options is Being Considered?

Whatever the outcome of the ongoing talks on the eve of the National Assembly, the current situation indicates three possibilities:

1. That all armed factions participate, through equal dialogue, in exercising legislative authority that leads to the development of an action programme that is agreed upon by all parties and expressed – through appropriate means, numbers and dimensions – in the executive institutions emanating from this legislative authority.

---

7   Held from 1–9 September 1969, the summit now included the Democratic Front for the Liberation of Palestine (DPFLP, later DFLP) and the Popular Front for the Liberation of Palestine – General Command (PFLP–GC), both of whom had split from the Popular Front for the Liberation of Palestine (PFLP). Though calling to "escalate and develop the armed struggle", its focus was on the development of the Palestine Liberation Army, the military wing of the PLO, rather than on organising unified action. Its statement restated rejection of UN Resolution 242 and "all solutions leading to surrender". See *International Documents on Palestine*, 1969 (Beirut: Institute for Palestine Studies, 1972), 778–80.

2. That one or two factions of the fighting organisations unilaterally form an "opposition" within the National Council. In this case, a dialogue will be renewed about the representative size of this or that party, and the discussion about the number of seats will be raised again. The aim will be to guarantee the opposition's ability to have their voices heard and the ability of the other party to prevent the opposition from imposing its decisions.

3. If neither of these two possibilities can be reached, one or more factions of the armed Palestinian struggle may participate in the National Council with symbolic representatives. Their presence would indicate a commitment to continuing the dialogue to reach a mutually agreed-upon formula, rather than severing ties with this dialogue.

So far, on the eve of the [Palestinian National Council] Assembly, no specific formula has been reached. However, unconfirmed news indicates that the third possibility may be the most likely.

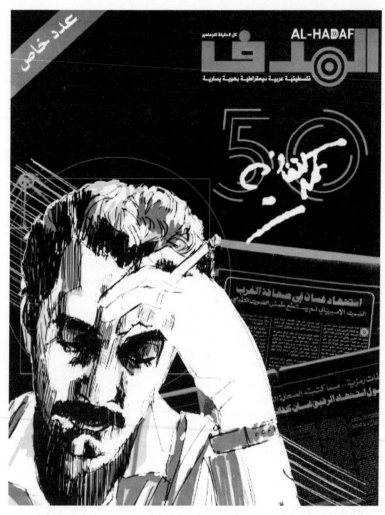

An *Al-Hadaf* special edition marking 50 years since the assassination of Ghassan Kanafani; *al-Hadaf* 40, no. 1514 (August 2022). Design by Guevara Abed Al Qader. Source: *al-Hadaf*, Gaza.

APPENDIX
Reflections on the Early Works of Ghassan Kanafani[1]

Amira Silmi, Romana Rubeo, Ramzy Baroud and Malek Abisaab

Introduction by *Louis Brehony*

Contributing to the special edition of *al-Hadaf* which marked the fiftieth anniversary of Ghassan Kanafani's assassination, Yusra al-Ghoul writes: "The cause refines writers and artists into relentless fighters."[2] Though this truth carries its burdens, she adds, glory awaits those who dedicate themselves to the struggle for liberation. In the first decades after the Nakba catastrophe, the process whereby Palestinian revolutionary thought was "refined" (*tusqulu* - تصقل) or positively altered was shaped by collective experiences, observations, alliances and events that made necessary an almost total rethinking of political strategy. In 1972, Kanafani saw, in political works he had written a decade earlier, an underdeveloped "analysis and understanding of society", compared to his earlier development as a novelist.[3] At the point of reflection, his commitment to Marxism–Leninism was well known, as a leading spokesperson for the Popular Front for the Liberation of Palestine (PFLP) and editor-in-chief of its weekly newspaper, *al-Hadaf*. The life-and-death nature of armed struggle, he said, meant that novelists now had other priorities.[4] This was *Ghassanuna*, "our

---

1 This chapter was published initially in an *Arab Studies Quarterly* special edition on Ghassan Kanafani, Summer 2024.
2 "*Ghassan Kanafani: al-Mushtabiku allathi la yamut*" ["The Undying Fighter"], *al-Hadaf* 40, no. 1514 (August 2022): 11.
3 See "On Childhood, Literature, Marxism, the Front and *al-Hadaf*", Chapter 1.
4 Interview with James Zogby, "Kanafani the Novelist", *Middle East International* 47 (May 1975): 27.

Ghassan", according to PFLP cultural figurehead and leader in Lebanon, Marwan ʿAbd al- ʿAl.[5]

Though marginally incomplete, publications and translations of Ghassan Kanafani's literary works – novels, short stories, play scripts, poetic studies – have often given the impression that his political writing was secondary. A note should be added here to state the obvious but frequently unrecognised fact: all of Kanafani's works were political, and his stories arguably constituted writings of resistance as much as any of the more "direct" materials he wrote as editor of *al-Hadaf*. But though these literary works are voluminous, they constitute a minority of Kanafani's writings: as editor, board member or contributing journalist, his work with Palestinian, Lebanese and pan-Arab publications spanned 17 years, brutally cut short by his assassination at the hands of Golda Meir's Mossad on 8 July 1972. These years included writing for daily publications, and generating whole indexes under at least six pen names, most notably Fares Fares. The prolificacy of his political writing was bound with the intense environment at *al-Hadaf*, the weekly newspaper for which he had left behind higher-paid positions at the Dar al-Sayyad publishing house. A leading member of the PFLP central media committee (he would be appointed to its political bureau posthumously), Kanafani was the organisation's de facto cultural and media ambassador, and built an unmistakably avant-garde, Marxist and revolutionary Arabist culture.

Following the publication of newly translated political works *The Revolution of 1936–39 in Palestine* (1804 Books, 2023) and *On Zionist Literature* (Ebb Books, 2022), our new volume of 16 writings, *Ghassan Kanafani: Selected Political Writings*, makes a further contribution to addressing an imbalance between published fields in the works of Ghassan Kanafani. But – being a *selected* works, with all that this entails – the publication contains its own imbalances. One of these is a focus (though not a complete one) on materials produced by Kanafani in the period around and after June 1967, itself a watershed and turning point in the Palestinian revolutionary struggle. This phase marked a coming of age for many and it is a firmly held view, including by contributors to

---

5 Interview with Louis Brehony in Mar Elias camp, Beirut, 17 July 2023.

our project – and by Kanafani himself – that his PFLP era saw the culmination and crystallisation of his political maturity. Consolidating his Marxist standpoint, which had developed profoundly during trips to socialist China in 1965 and 1966, and which (like Mao) he saw as a "guide to action", this period infused the works of Kanafani and other contributors to al-Hadaf with a concrete internationalism. And, following the strides taken by the Vietnamese people – a model of revolutionary organisational practice through which the seeds of victory may be planted in the region.

Though it intensified tangibly, Kanafani's tendency for prolificacy had always been there. Alongside his first half-decade in political journalism, he produced many other writings and notebooks, as significant in his output as Marx's *Economic and Philosophical Manuscripts*, or Che's Latin American diaries were to theirs. Though Kanafani chose not to publish these works – and looked back at what he saw in them as youthful underdevelopment – reading them with hindsight offers unparalleled insight into his thought processes and trajectory. Despite his best intentions, selections of these writings did make their way into publication, years after his death; some had even accessed them privately upon his martyrdom on 8 July 1972.[6] Edited by his brother Adnan Kanafani, *Ma'rij al-Ibda'* (*The Rise to Ingenuity*) contained articles, draft speeches, radio sketches and even poems from the period 1951–1960;[7] some of these works were unfinished and undated, raising question marks over the certainty of when they were drafted. For the majority of the period defined by Adnan, Ghassan was an Arab Nationalist Movement (ANM) activist and writer, and this selection of writings provide a window into his political development alongside George Habash and the radical Arabist milieu. The inspiration of Nasser is clear, while the fierce critique of many political trends had much in common with Kanafani's later writings as Fares Fares. We learn that, for all of his adult life, Kanafani considered himself a socialist. While this would later mean, like Che, the creation of "many Vietnams" – or,

---

6 George Hajjar, *Kanafani: Symbol of Palestine* (Lebanon: Karoun, 1974), 150.
7 Adnan Kanafani (ed.), *Ghassan Kanafani: Ma'rij al-Ibda'* [*The Rise to Ingenuity*] (Jordan: Dar Mu'assasat Filastin lil-Thaqafa, 2009), 181.

for Kanafani and the PFLP, "Arab Hanois", – his earlier conceptualisation of socialism meant many Cairos, or at least accepting
Cairo's leadership. Though others in the Kanafani family were
rather nonplussed by Adnan's selection and publication of these
earlier materials,[8] the writings made available through *Ma'rij
al-Ibda'* present a window into Kanafani's revolutionary morality
at an important historical moment.

Two of Kanafani's longer notebooks from his early twenties were
published in Arabic as chapters in *al-Dirasat al-Siyasiyya: al-Majallad al-Khamis (Political Works: Volume 5)*[9] in 2015, namely,
"Marxism in Theory and Practice: A Discussion" and "The Arab
Cause during the Era of the United Arab Republic". Presented
alongside a selection of published works from Kanafani's PFLP
period, and his epic journalistic work on China and India, *Thumma
Ashraqat Asiya...* (Then shone Asia...) from 1965, the contents
and positions of the two private notebooks date their composition
to the same period covered in *Ma'rij al-Ibda'*. But, like the latter
collection, there were issues with how Kanafani's unpublished
works were presented. The *Volume 5* introduction, for example,
dated the critical notebook on Marxism as being written in 1970,[10]
forming the basis of a series of articles based on this assumption,
which skewed a real understanding of Kanafani's development.
This false assumption has also led to a number of miscompre-
hensions on Kanafani's later role – it would have meant that his
private notebooks were written in opposition to his publicly stated
position and role as PFLP spokesperson and raised questions of
his loyalty to the "party line". We are now able to clarify for the first
time publicly that the notebook, "Marxism in Theory and Practice:
A Discussion", had actually been written in the mid to late 1950s.[11]

A further issue complicates the translation, publication and even
the republication of existing texts. According to Kanafani family
members, both "Marxism" and "The Arab cause" should never

8   Private conversations, 2023.
9   *Al-Dirasat al-Siyasiyya: al-Majallad al-Khamis* (Cyprus: Rimal, 2015).
Volumes 1–4 had included literary works and studies.
10   Fadle al-Nakib, "Ghassan Kanafani: 'Atifat al-Muqawama" ["Passion of the
Resistance"], in Kanafani, *Al-Dirasat al-Siyasiyya*, 47.
11   Conversations with Leila and Anni Kanafani, Beirut, July 2023.

have been published in Arabic, since Ghassan Kanafani had chosen not to publish these texts himself and may not be included in subsequent printings of the 2015 Arabic volume. As we will see below, and as these notebooks suggest, Kanafani's interest in Marxism pre-dated the official transformation of the ANM, showing particular concern for how socialism was applied or understood by socialists internationally, with some focus on socialist construction in the Soviet Union.

As objects of study, Kanafani's early writings offer many opportunities for understanding the origins and course of his revolutionary politics, and show the beginnings of a transformation, in comradeship with George Habash, Basil Kubeisi, Wadi' Haddad and many others. The reflections in this chapter are based on our translations of three early essays Kanafani wrote as a member of the ANM, roughly from 1957 to 1961, and which he chose not to publish during his lifetime. It should be underlined that Ghassan Kanafani was martyred at the age of 36. He was still the "young Kanafani" – learning and growing with the pulsations of repression and resistance – at the time of his assassination. The prolificacy and breakneck speed of his development, therefore, should be seen in this context.

1. A Methodology for Implementing Arab Socialism

Kanafani on the Use and Abuse of Socialism

by *Amira Silmi*

For two centuries, the word socialism has represented the solitary bread for the dreams of hungry workers and one column of people after another have fallen in devotion for higher, socialist ideals. Today, when we find ourselves facing the problem of building socialism in the United Arab Republic (UAR), we feel, in an astonishing manner, how far removed all the books released by twentieth century publishers have been from us. And we feel, in a similarly astonishing way, that socialism requires – before we fully comprehend the machine – a prior comprehension of life, for any civilised work that is without human roots will be spontaneously rejected by humanity.[1]

In the short and incomplete essay, "A Methodology for Implementing Arab Socialism", Kanafani displaces any mechanisation or technicalisation of the term socialism, attempting to retrieve its deeper meaning as a philosophy of life, a mode of being, one that is concerned first and foremost with life, and with the human being as life, rather than a machine or a force of production and/or consumption. For Kanafani, socialism means that people live their lives enjoying their basic rights, but such a meaning can be used and abused by different and disparate actors to further their interests. Socialism, thus, becomes a site for manipulation and a property over which different parties with contradictory agendas fight.

---

1   Ghassan Kanafani, "*al-Manhaj al-Tatbiqi lil-Ishtirakiyya al-ʿArabiyya*" [circa 1958–1960]. Original publication: Adnan Kanafani (ed.), *Ghassan Kanafani: Maʾrij al-Ibdaʾ* [*The Rise to Ingenuity*] (Jordan: Dar Muʾassasat Filastin lil-Thaqafa, 2009), 181–88. Quotations from the translation by Amira Silmi.

While recognising that socialism at one point in history could have been the dream of the hungry worker, it is still associated with the machine and this association with that which is mechanic, that is, that which is lifeless or lacking in life is among its weakest points. Socialism, thus, has to be reattached to life and measured according to its requirements, that is, it must be freed from the mode of being imposed on humans by the machine. Kanafani here seems to be seeking that other, not yet achieved socialism, that which has been defined with the fulfilment of human needs and capacities, rather than that which reduces the human into an economic machine, whose needs are as well reduced to that which reproduces them as productive forces, which translates moreover to humans turned into cogs in the productive machine, as Marx had it.[2]

Positioning the human being as the measure for socialism, Kanafani cannot be at ease with a socialism that takes experiment and error as its principle, for it is human beings and their lives that are and were subjected to experiment and were/are the ones who would and did pay the price for any errors that might or did occur.

Good intentions and noble goals are not justification enough for such an experimentation in the human: ends do not justify the means for Kanafani. But this then poses the question of the means – here the means is socialism – and the question becomes how we reach the truth or achieve that true socialism that fulfils the needs and capacities of the human, without degrading the human into an object of experimentation and at the same time reduce him to a machine, or part thereof, which is fuelled with basic needs.

The problem for Kanafani lies in becoming blinded by the goal, to the extent of becoming unable to distinguish errors when they take place. He, just like Marx writing against capitalist modes of production, is worried about another capitalist inversion in which errors themselves become the way, becoming something inherent to what socialism is. The idea (i.e. socialism), then, is no longer a positive force, but rather a blinding ideology that obstructs our

---

2   Karl Marx, "Draft of an Article on Friedrich List's Book: *Das Nationale System der Politischen Oekonomie*", Marx-Engles Archive, http://hiaw.org/defcon6/works/1845/03/list.html.

ability to change the path when it leads to more errors, while promising a truth from which it moves away. To keep on a path, which we blindly see as leading to truth, and in which human life is annihilated, is "to bury the voice of human consciousness under thundering ideas", writes Kanafani.

Kanafani does see socialism as the road to happiness, but again it is the human individual and their happiness that is at stake for him. It follows that, with Marx in the *Eighteenth Brumaire*, a revolutionary movement cannot march in a straight line without stopping to revise where that line is leading to; the path cannot be assumed from the beginning, for the march itself is a process and, as such, what was perceived as the end of the line at the beginning of the movement might not remain the same during the movement.[3] Moreover, the history created by that movement is the history of the human race as a whole. This means that other peoples do not start from scratch or a point zero, they rather join a process that has already started, but joining this process does not mean that they blindly add themselves to what is already there, or march in a parallel line, imitating an existing formula that repeats the same process with the same errors. Rather, their joining the process means that they create points from where the process can be revised, displaced, shifted and hopefully redirected towards the idea that is no longer a mere justification for a process that involved human debasement or annihilation. Joining the process, thus, cannot be a peaceful one, it is one that will be based on conflict and struggle, for it takes the force of revolutionary violence to redirect a path that justifies itself by the truth it claims as its end.

This revolutionary violence is not and cannot be an ideological construct. For it to have the power of creation (and not be a mere force of destruction), since life is its beginning and end, it has to stem not from a universal abstract idea, but has to be derived from the particular materiality of people's lives. This too cannot be reduced to an abstract formula. For Kanafani, the material is not only money, nor food or what are universally declared as basic needs but includes the deep forces of conviction and feeling that

3 Karl Marx, *The Eighteenth Brumaire of Louis Bonaparte* (Peking: Foreign Languages Press, 1978).

lie within people. These are unquantifiable, and any revolutionary movement seeking socialism should be able to recognise and mobilise feelings and convictions rather than dismiss them following a capitalist presumption of a *homo economicus*. Moreover, these forces should be mobilised on their own terms, that is, as forces of life and not those of a machine.

What mobilises belief in Kanafani cannot be a superficial, external motivation: people do not sacrifice their lives for basic needs that have been defined for them by external entities but are willing to fight and even sacrifice their lives for a cause that addresses the holes and gaps that make their lives less than what it should be. Religious belief had that power, for religious belief did address the limitation of their lives, it was able to fulfil their needs in their integrity rather than reduce them into mere parts of what they are. Of course, in Kanafani, it is not belief as a blinding weakening force that can be the force of mobilisation, but belief as a source of a deep energy that is an integral part of the being of the human, the belief with which comes a certainty that overcomes the feeling of lacking and helplessness rather than an ideological belief that feeds on and nourishes these feelings.

Kanafani is not calling for a regressive movement – in fact, he is writing against repetition – but, while he is indeed not calling for a return to the past, it is the endless repetition of a present moment that is of concern to him, a revision, or a look into the past or into that which is deep inside our lives; it is this that could allow us to see how we are trapped in an endless repetition of the same, as one main feature of a capitalist world. What Kanafani seeks here is a revolutionary mobilisation of people that would be able to overcome and move beyond that which is stagnant in the present.

Speaking about how the Soviets had to invoke Christian and Tsarist heroes of the past to mobilise the people to fight a Soviet war is not a call for a return to a chauvinist nationalism based on mythic heroes of the past, but rather it is to remind the people of their descent from a heroic past. This past cannot be repeated, for, as Marx wrote, it would only be a caricature of what it was.[4] But recalling the past, or some of its heroic moments, constitutes a

---

4 Marx, *The Eighteenth Brumaire of Louis Bonaparte*.

motivational force, a mobilisation of deep buried roots, that allow people to fight for a cause that is theirs, and which they perceive as one of life, rather than for an abstracted idea, or entity such as the state or the political party.

Kanafani is neither a liberal bourgeois intellectual searching for a transcendent free willing individual, who can transgress all obstacles, nor is he that socialist who perceives of the people as a herd or an aggregate of anonymous individuals to be lead and employed in a "revolutionary" machine, which is fuelled by the masses consumed by it.[5]

In the final part of this essay, Kanafani points to Gamal Abdel Nasser, as the "possible" influential hero, who embodies the "hero-principle" formula that Kanafani puts forward. Nevertheless, while the essay ends here posing a question that is left unanswered about Nasser, Kanafani, did find his "influential hero" among the people,[6] for his hero is of the people and within them: his hero is the *asheq* ("lover") in his story *al-Asheq*,[7] a peasant and a fighter

---

5 See for example, *al-Mithaq*, the document presented by Gamal Abdel Nasser, in 1962 to the National Conference of Popular Forces. In this document, which marks Nasser's shift towards socialism, or Arab socialism after the collapse of the unity with Syria, Nasser refers to the people, *al-sha'b*, as the main governor and decision and policy maker. The people, workers and peasants are not cogs in the machine according to Nasser but are the ones who control and operate the machine. Nevertheless, the term "people" throughout the document takes an abstracted form, and in most references, the people are referred to as a productive force. Kanafani's reservation, that life and the human should be the main measure does not appear to be something that a governing leader who seeks to build and run a state, even a socialist one, can be "practically" and "politically" concerned with. This also reminds us of George Habash's reservation about the compatibility of the state and a revolution of liberation, which remained a point of tension in his relationship with Nasser; see, for example, *Safahat min Massirati al-Nidaliyya: Muthakirat George Habash*, ed. Sief Da'na, (Beirut: Markaz Dirassat al-Wihda al-Arabiyya, 2019). Of course, other socialist examples, such as that of Cuba, show that people's lives and happiness were in fact the main measure.
6 See, for example, Mohammad Jamal Barut's summary of *Harakat al-Qawmiyeen al-Arab: al Nash'a, al Tatawur, al-Massa'er* [*The Arab Nationalist Movement: Emergence, Development, Destinies*], https://books-library.net/free-317272581-download (accessed April 2023).
7 Ghassan Kanafani, "al-Asheq" ["The Lover"], in *al-A'mal al-Kamila I: al-Riwayat* [*The Complete Works I: The Novels*], 4th edn (Beirut: Mu'assasat al-Abhath al-'Arabiyah and Mu'assasat Ghassan Kanafani al-Thaqafiyah, 1994).

with a gun, a horse and nothing else. This hero is also one found in his *Of Men and Guns*:[8] ordinary peasant men who will fight for the land, for their freedom, and for their lives with whatever means they have available. These are not men concerned with the abstract world of things – neither that of money or basic needs, defined as the limitation of the lives of human beings – these are men whose whole energies are mobilised in their fight for a life of integrity and freedom, in their most immediate and particular form, that is, in and through the people's being on the land and their relationship with it.

---

8   Ghassan Kanafani, "'An al-Rijal wal-Banadiq" ["Of Men and Guns"], in *al-A'mal al-Kamila II: al-Qisas* [*The Complete Works II: The Short Stories*], 3rd edn (Beirut: Mu'assasat al-Abhath al-'Arabiyah and Mu'assasat Ghassan Kanafani al-Thaqafiyah, 1987).

2. The Arab Cause during the Era of the United Arab Republic

Seismic Changes and Shifts

by *Ramzy Baroud and Romana Rubeo*

Colonialism and Israel constitute two enemies, of course, but so far share common plans based on mutual interests. The reactionaries, opportunists and regionalists constitute special types of enemy, who attempt to preserve their conditions through personal struggles, and who were forced to cooperate with colonialism in the face of the fierceness of the battle and the weakness of their influence within it.[1]

In some ways, Ghassan Kanafani's ideological evolution followed a similar path to that taken by many Palestinian and Arab socialists at the time. This essay is a testament to this assertion, as the young Kanafani emerges as an Arab nationalist. The political discourse articulated here is a reflection of the period in which Kanafani's intellectual formation took place, years before the radical intellectual fully embraced the PFLP's Marxist structure. Kanafani's socialism, at the time, was fully justifiable as part of rational historical dialectics, inspired, in no small part, by Nasser's pan-Arab vision – one that is situated within a socialist framework and guided by revolutionary ideals. Though Nasser's socialism was rationalised as part of historical materialism, the Egyptian, pan-Arab leader did not share the Soviets' view of internationalist socialism. At that time, many pan-Arab socialists agreed; Kanafani was one of them.

---

1   Ghassan Kanafani, "al-Qadiyya al-'Arabiyya Fi 'Ahd Jim 'Ayn Mim". Original publication: *al-Dirasat al-Siyasiyya: al-Majallad al-Khamis* [*Political Works: Volume 5*] (Cyprus: Rimal, 2015). Quotations from an unpublished translation by Ameen Nemer.

Like other Palestinian socialists, Kanafani's ideology was not a mere intellectual exercise, with no clear, definable goals. It was the direct outcome of his status as a refugee. His goal, from then until his assassination by the Israeli Mossad in July 1972, was the liberation of Palestine through an anti-imperialist, anti-colonial struggle against Israel and its imperialist benefactors, not only internationally but also regionally. These ideals were perfectly suited to George Habash's Arab Nationalist Movement (ANM) and its three core principles: anti-colonialism, anti-imperialism and Arab nationalism.

At the time of writing this essay, Kanafani's ideas of a pan-Arab nationalistic project directly clashed with those of the Arab communist parties, which considered the notion of nationalism as a "bourgeois product". In his critique of the communists of the time, Kanafani went as far as listing them among the "hostile camps", along with colonialism, Israel, reactionaries, opportunists and regional currents.

Though Kanafani intellectually morphed and ideologically shifted with time, the core of his ideals and values remained unchanged. Throughout his life, which was cut short at the age of 36, his struggle remained committed to fighting colonialism, Israel and Zionism, and the reactionary forces, which, in his view, served as de facto colonial agents. In his mind, there seemed to be total clarity regarding the mutual benefits that these "hostile camps" obtain as a result of the direct or indirect cooperation of colonialism and Zionism.

His criticism of the communists, however, was placed in a different context, and was considered to "occupy a specific position". They constituted "a new type of enemy which has recently entered the battlefield, in remarkable harmony with the plans of the right, attempting to make full use of the ingenuity of colonialism in blocking the great tide". The young Kanafani defined his rejection of communists as being based on their seemingly blind allegiance to the Soviet Union and also on what he saw as their rigid understanding of class division. Like many engaged Palestinian intellectuals, Kanafani was fully aware of the Soviets' early recognition of Israel, three days after its establishment, and their failure to appreciate the creation of Israel as a centre for global imperial-ism in Palestine.

Kanafani hints at the communists' "failure in the cause of Pales-tine in 1948", attributing that failure to their inability to "think with their own mentality, but with the mentality of Soviet strategy":

> First, this mentality absolutely rejects the idea of fighting on a national basis. Second, it is a source of pain for such a mental-ity that people may live in dignity by means other than through the class struggle; that is, by avoiding the division of society into classes.[2]

Only two years after the writing of this essay, the ANM inched closer to "Nasserism" and its view of the Arab national project. Kanafani strongly embraced the ideological shift and moved to Bei-rut to work as an editor for *al-Hurriyya*, the daily newspaper of the Movement. More dramatic changes followed, motivated partly by the seismic political shifts underway in Palestine, and the region as a whole. In 1967, Kanafani would become one of the leading mem-bers of the Popular Front for the Liberation of Palestine (PFLP), a wholly Marxist movement, established by Habash himself.

But Kanafani's intellectual roots in his principled fight for the liberation of Palestine remained unchanged. In 1972, around 14 years after the writing of this essay, and shortly before his death, he wrote *The Revolution of 1936–1939 in Palestine*, showing that his priorities remained the same: the liberation of Palestine through an anti-imperialist and anti-colonial struggle. More experienced and intellectually grounded, Kanafani, however, placed his analysis within a Marxist view of history. The enemies remained the same but was articulated in a less abstract way: "the local reactionary leadership; the regimes in the Arab states surrounding Palestine; and the imperialist-Zionist enemy".

Though some may rashly attribute Kanafani's ideological shifts to blind allegiances to Habash and the PFLP, to the lack of intel-lectual maturity at the time or to other things entirely, Kanafani

---

2 Kanafani, "On Childhood, Literature, Marxism, the Front and *al-Hadaf*", Chapter 1.

explained his position in full, weeks before his assassination. In a 1972 interview with a Swiss journalist, which appeared for the first time in July 1974 – two years after his death – Kanafani discussed his position:

> [I]n our society and in the ANM, we were very sensitive to Marxism–Leninism. This position was not the result of our hostility to socialism, but the result of the mistakes made by the communist parties in the Arab world. That is why it was very difficult for the ANM to adopt Marxism–Leninism before 1964.

Indeed, in the 1960s, relations between the Soviet Union and Israel started to deteriorate. The Soviets attributed this deterioration to "the anti-human, reactionary essence of Zionism" which, according to the *Great Soviet Encyclopaedia*, is an "overt and covert fight against freedom movements and against the USSR". US sources, however, explain the historical break-up based on something else entirely. According to a report issued by the Office of the Historian Bureau of Public Affairs of the United States Department of State in 1964, "Israel launched an intensive effort to obtain modern US tanks to counterbalance Soviet-equipped UAR forces". As Israel emerged as the closest Western ally in the Middle East, the ruling Communist Party of the Soviet Union listed the "main posits of modern Zionism" as "militant chauvinism, racism, anti-Communism and anti-Sovietism".

Whether the Soviets' anti-Israel rhetoric was mere political opportunism or an outcome of ideological conflict between Soviet socialism and Israeli Zionism, or both, the outcome was the same. This resulted in a change in the conversation among Palestinian intellectuals and political movements. Indeed, the intellectual migration to socialism, resulting largely from the internal discussions between the "right" and "left" within the movement itself, was seamless:

> In each round, the left came out on top because our position on anti-imperialism and reactionary standpoints was preferable

[to the position of the right]. This resulted in the adoption of Marxism–Leninism.[3]

Reading this essay by Kanafani furthers our understanding of a particular moment in history when seismic changes and shifts at a geopolitical level had a direct impact on the theoretical construct of the influential Palestinian intellectual. Kanafani demonstrated the famous maxim by Niccolò Machiavelli, showing a certain degree of flexibility when it came to the means, without compromising on the final end: the liberation of Palestine and the defeat of imperialism and colonialism anywhere in the world.

---

3   Kanafani, "On Childhood, Literature, Marxism, the Front and *al-Hadaf*".

3. Marxism in Theory and Practice: A Discussion

The Pivotal Issues of Class and Nation

by *Malek Abisaab*

Every human intellectual effort is a small victory for mankind over its crisis, and is a new brick in the grand building of humanity.[1]

A new class of people began to rise on the backs of the labour of the poor workers, a class that was later called the bourgeois class. Europe's affairs seemed extremely complicated and the Industrial Revolution, and its accompanying production, consumption and employment, seemed to be the cause of all this chaos. It was obvious that this situation took up space in the thinking of philosophers. It was also obvious that thought would arise as a tool to serve life, or rather, [as] a means to remove it from its crisis... People think to face the difficulties in their lives. It was natural for this thinking to take on the economic character that dominates Europe and subjects it to the chaos of industrial improvisation... History seemed to be preparing this plot to create misery and want in people... So, a group of partially philosophising theories emerged that were soon lost, faded, or merged into a new philosophy with a comprehensive view, later called the philosophy of Marxism.

Ghassan Kanafani left Palestine during the Nakba, when he was eleven years old. Born into a middle-class family, his father was

---

1   Ghassan Kanafani, "*al-Markssiyyah fi al-Majal al-Nazari, al-Majal al-Tatbiqi: Munaqasha*". Original publication: *al-Dirasat al-Siyasiyya: al-Majallad al-Khamis* [*Political Works: Volume 5*] (Cyprus: Rimal, 2015). Quotations from an unpublished translation of excerpts by Maha Saleh.

a lawyer and Ghassan studied at a French missionary school, but, like many Palestinians, the social standing of the family was devastated as they became refugees. Kanafani worked afterwards as a teacher in a local school to help his family and also to pay for his own secondary education. In Damascus, where the family sought refuge, he enrolled at the University of Damascus where he studied Arabic literature, but he was expelled for political reasons. He moved to Kuwait and remained there for six years, during which he continued reading and began to write. In 1953, when he was 14 years old, he became interested in politics and, in the same year, in Damascus, he met with George Habash (1926–2008), a founding member of the Arab Nationalist Movement (ANM) and later the Popular Front for the Liberation of Palestine (PFLP), which was established in 1967. Kanafani immediately joined the ANM after meeting Habash. In 1960, Kanafani moved to Beirut at the request of the ANM to work on the party newspaper; then, in 1967, he was asked to join the PFLP, working as the editor of its newspaper *al-Hadaf* from its founding in July 1969 until his assassination on 8 July 1972.

Initially, the ANM was a movement against colonialism, imperialism and reactionary governments, and did not adopt a specific ideological line, according to Kanafani.[2] Its move towards socialism, he said, was inevitable, as the anti-imperialist struggle would eventually radicalise the movement if it did not stop in the midst of the confrontation and continued the struggle until victory. Leading members of the ANM realised that they would not win the war against imperialism if they did not position the movement within the struggle of social classes fighting for dignity, bread and life. Their path would ultimately lead to socialism. In the 1950s and early 1960s, the ANM and Arab societies more broadly were acutely sensitive towards Marxism–Leninism. This did not come from an abhorrence of socialism but was largely a backlash against the missteps committed by Arab communist parties. Reflecting in 1972, Kanafani refers to perceptions held by these parties – and the

2 Information drawn from the 1972 interview, "On Childhood, Literature, Marxism, the Front and *al-Hadaf*", *Shu'un Falastiniyya* 36 (July 1974).

Soviet Union – on the 1947 UN decision to divide Palestine and the consequent creation of Israel in 1948.

Kanafani's own sensitivity to Marxism during this earlier phase could be easily be found in *al-Markssiyyah fi al-Majal al-Nazari, al-Majal al-Tatbiqi: Munaqasha* (*Marxism in Theory and Practice: A Discussion*), a notebook he wrote in the mid- to late 1950s, according to his family.[3] From the first pages of this notebook, one can read where he stood at this moment, as he states that the Soviet Union and other socialist countries, in spite of their socio-economic and political accomplishments, could not defeat nationalism, which remained strongly rooted in the political discourse of the communists themselves. For evidence of the latter, he uses China, Yugoslavia and the Soviet Union as examples. Further details, Kanafani asserts, would lead the reader to "undoubtedly decry Marxism".[4] This statement sets the tone of Kanafani's early perspective vis-à-vis Marxism.

In the first section of the text, Kanafani explains in an interactive and lucid style, possibly addressed to a cohort of adherents, the major theoretical premises of Marxism. His discussion in this section demonstrates a neutral approach, which leaves readers to decide their own response. In the brief section covering "Marxism in Practice", Kanafani chronologically outlines the major turning points in the development of Marxism, focusing on the Bolshevik Revolution. One central aspect of Marxism, Kanafani highlights, is its undogmatic nature, as Marx and Engels, and later Lenin emphasised that Marxism is not a dogma, but rather a guide to action. Marxism then is not a body of sacred texts and Marxists should incorporate in their visions what reality provides, and constantly verify their beliefs with experience. Kanafani concludes this section by raising a question: whether the economic achievements and progress in socialist Russia could be attributed to communism? The question implies, in my opinion, Kanafani's uncertainty of Marxism as a viable revolutionary force and whether it was being genuinely implemented.[5]

---

3   Louis Brehony discussion with Anni and Leila Kanafani, Beirut, July 2023.
4   Kanafani, *Al-Dirasat al-Siyasiyya*, 56.
5   Kanafani, *Al-Dirasat al-Siyasiyya*, 76.

In the final section of the notebook, dedicated to discussion of the themes of the first two sections, Kanafani points to what he then saw as the inappropriateness of the concept of class, a pivotal premise in Marxism, questioning in particular its methodological use in explaining societal realities in the colonised part of the world. Kanafani stated that anti-colonial sentiments, embedded in the consciousness of the colonised people, had been the driving force that galvanised colonised peoples into collective, revolutionary politics, rather than class struggle. Kanafani, thus, finds that Eastern societies are coherent and enjoy a "social peace" to an extent that possibilities for class contradictions and antagonism had no chance to emerge.[6] This statement, in my opinion, presents the limitations of Kanafani's early criticism of Marxism, on the one side, and his favouritism, on the other, of an analytical method based on nation, rather than class, as the engine of history in the Eastern world. While the question of class, in my view, should not be separated from the question of the national struggle, Kanafani perceives the two variables as sovereign entities.

It was not until 1967, Kanafani asserts, that the PFLP openly embraced Marxism–Leninism, being the only party within the ANM that took such as step when the ANM changed its name to the Arab Socialist Action Party and its Palestinian branch became the PFLP. Kanafani continues his 1972 account on how Marxism–Leninism found its way into the PFLP by pointing to another factor that facilitated the transformation of the ideological doctrine of the PFLP. There had been, Kanafani concedes, a constant ideological strife within the ranks of the ANM and later PFLP between the right wing and the left wing, and that the positions of the left had always won out, since it had displayed such a solid and uncompromising stand against imperialism and reactionary governments. Implying hesitancy towards adopting Marxism–Leninism, Kanafani discloses that he does not remember if he leaned towards the right or towards the left at that time, because the line of differentiation between them was tenuous or not as clear-cut as it is nowadays in developed political parties.

---

6   Kanafani, *Al-Dirasat al-Siyasiyya*, 90.

What he remembers though is that the ANM embraced young members, and he was among them; they ridiculed the senior members who were highly sensitive towards communism. Kanafani asserts, nonetheless, that the youth were not yet communists, but the extent of their sensitivity to communism was less than that of the senior comrades. Kanafani's own predilection to Marxism had double origins: first, was his overwhelming love and admiration of the Soviet literature; and second, was his communist brother-in-law, whom Kanafani looked up to as a role model. The first influence, Kanafani reveals, assisted the fading away of the *jabal al-jalid* (iceberg) which he, at the time, held towards communism. Moreover, he acknowledges that his early "animosity" towards socialism, and "our [ANM] sensitivity toward Marxism–Leninism", evolved as a reaction to the mistakes committed by the Arab communist parties.

Thus, he believes that the young generation played a major role in causing the shift towards Marxism–Leninism of the PFLP. More importantly, Kanafani attributes the shift of the new generation of the ANM towards Marxism to their social background, as most of them belonged to poor classes, which cemented their political commitments and loyalty to the principles of the ANM. Their political and ideological roles became influential to an extent that they became the "pressure force" within the ranks of the ANM. Reversing his earlier position on class, in 1970, he would write that:

[B]ecause of the specificity of the Palestinian issue, in that one section of the people lives under colonialism and the other remains uprooted from their land, the national dimension of the battle becomes a pivotal issue. And because of the specificity of the Palestinian issue, in that one section is tied to the limb of imperialism, while the other languishes under the chains of exploitative regimes tied more or less to the wheels of imperialism, the class dimension in the battle becomes a pivotal issue as well.[7]

---

7 Kanafani, "*Al-Muqawama wa-Ma'dilatuha*" ["The Resistance and its Challenges"], in *al-Dirasat al-Siyasiyya*, 196.

Notes on Contributors

Louis Brehony is an activist, musician and scholar of resistance cultures. He is the author of *Palestinian Music in Exile: Voices of Resistance* (2023) and director of the award-winning documentary *Kofia: A Revolution through Music*. Louis has published, edited and translated work in international journals and platforms including *Arab Studies Quarterly The Palestine Chronicle, Arab Media and Society* and *al-Hadaf*.

Tahrir Hamdi is Professor of Decolonial Studies and Rector of the Arab Open University, Jordan. She sits on the editorial board of several prestigious journals including *Arab Studies Quarterly, Journal of Holy Land and Palestine Studies* and *Janus Unbound*. She has published widely on resistance literature, including analyses of the writings of Ghassan Kanafani. Tahrir is the author of *Imagining Palestine: Cultures of Exile and National Identity* (2022).

Ourooba Shetewi has lectured in linguistics and sociophonetics at the UK universities of Edge Hill, Lancaster and Newcastle, and at Hama, Syria. She completed her PhD in sociolinguistics at Newcastle University, based on field research among Syria-based Palestinian refugees. Ourooba's published research has appeared in the book *Language and Identity in the Arab World* (2022) and *Languages* journal.

*   *   *

Rabab Abdulhadi is founder and senior scholar of Arab and Muslim Ethnicities and Diasporas studies at San Francisco State University. Founder of *Islamophobia Studies Journal*, she has published over 80 articles and chapters, and edited *Arab and Arab American Feminisms* (2015).

Malik Abisaab is a Lebanese scholar, activist and Associate Professor of History at McGill University, Montreal, Canada. He is author of the books *Militant Women of a Fragile Nation* (2009) and, with Rula Jurdi Abisaab, *The Shi'ites of Lebanon* (2014).

As'ad AbuKhalil is professor of political science at California State University, Stanislaus. He has authored innumerable articles, reviews and essays on many international platforms. As'ad's monographs include the *Historical Dictionary of Lebanon* (1998) and *The Battle for Saudi Arabia* (2004).

Max Ajl is an associated researcher with the Tunisian Observatory for Food Sovereignty and the Environment, and postdoctoral fellow at Ghent University. He authored *A People's Green New Deal* (2021) and has written for publications including *Monthly Review* and *Agrarian South*.

Ibrahim Aoude is Professor Emeritus in Ethnic Studies at the University of Hawai'i at Mānoa and Editor of the *Arab Studies Quarterly*. Author of dozens of articles, book chapters and essays, Ibrahim was a contributor to *Our Vision for Liberation* (2022).

Ahmad Baha'iddin Sha'ban is a widely published Egyptian writer, socialist and former political prisoner. He has written for many newspapers and journals, including *al-Safir*, *al-Mashhad* and *al-Hadaf*, and has written and contributed to many books, including *al-Qadiyya al-Falastiniyya fi Mu'ituha al-Thaniyya* (2017).

Khaled Barakat is an Executive Committee member of Masar Badil, the Palestinian Alternative Revolutionary Path and a leading international figure in the study of Ghassan Kanafani. He writes for *al-Akhbar* and *al-Adab*, and appears regularly on al-Mayadeen and other media outlets.

Ramzy Baroud is a Palestinian-US journalist, media consultant, author and founding editor of *The Palestine Chronicle*. His books include *The Last Earth* (2018), *These Chains Will Be Broken* (2019) and, as editor, *Our Vision for Liberation* (2022).

Hiyem Cheurfa is an assistant professor of post-colonial literature and comparative studies in the Department of English at Larbi Tebessi University, Algeria. She is author of *Contemporary Arab Women's Life Writing and the Politics of Resistance* (2023).

Nafiz Ghneim is a Gaza-based writer, activist and former political prisoner. A member of the political bureau of the Palestinian People's Party and PLO central committee, Nafiz represented Palestine at the 2002 International Meeting of Communist and Workers Parties in Havana.

Lena Haddadin is a writer, translator and journalist from Jordan, now residing in the Netherlands. She holds a bachelor's degree in journalism, supplemented by a master's degree in political science and international relations.

Barbara Harlow (1948–2017) was and remains a leading international scholar of resistance literatures and Third World studies. Defying academic boundaries, she translated and wrote many seminal studies on Ghassan Kanafani and other Palestinian literary figures.

Patrick Higgins is a doctoral candidate in history at the University of Houston. His research charts the history of US imperialism in West Asia and has been published in *Middle East Critique, Viewpoint* magazine and many other platforms.

Thomas Hofland is an activist, writer and board member of the International Center for Palestine Studies in the Netherlands. He edited the book *Our Code of Morals is our Revolution* by George Habash (2022) and organises with the Samidoun network.

Asma Hussein obtained her PhD at Masaryk University, Brno, Czechia. She has taught widely on literature, post-colonialism and philology at Georg August University Göttingen and at Ada und Theodor Lessing VHS Hannover, Germany. Currently, Asma is an assistant professor at Al-Ahliyya Amman University, Jordan.

Hania A.M. Nashef is professor at the Department of Media Communication, American University of Sharjah. Her publications include *Palestinian Culture and the Nakba: Bearing Witness* (2019) and *The Politics of Humiliation in the Novels of J.M. Coetzee* (2009).

Ameen Nemer is an Arabian activist and translator currently working in Scotland as a professional interpreter.

Wisam Rafeedie is a prolific writer and former political prisoner. He lectures in the Department of Social Sciences at Bethlehem University. Wisam wrote his recently translated novel *The Trinity of Fundamentals* during his imprisonment at Naqab prison camp in 1993.

Romana Rubeo is an Italian journalist, writer and managing editor of *The Palestine Chronicle*. She has a master's degree in translation and interpretation and has published many articles and book chapters, including *Las Nuevas Extremas Derechas en el Mundo* (2023).

Amira Silmi is Assistant Professor of Rhetoric at the Institute of Women's Studies, Birzeit University. An authority on Aimé Césaire and Ghassan Kanafani, she has published widely on colonial discourses and anti-colonial Arab women's writings, and contributed to *Voices of the Nakba* (2022).

Nejd Yaziji is a US-based lawyer, translator and essayist, and has published works on the politics of Palestinian literature, identity and exile, alongside seminal translations produced in partnership with Barbara Harlow.

Index